A Voice
for Now

Anne Dickson is a psychologist, writer and trainer specialising in communication skills, psychosexual counselling and the management of emotions. For the past two decades, Anne has trained women and men in a wide range of contexts: within management and commercial organisations, academic, medical and religious institutions, and the voluntary sector.

Her special commitment to women inspired her to establish in 1980 a unique nation-wide network of women trainers in Britain and Ireland. Her book *A Woman in Your Own Right*, first published in 1982, is the core text for assertiveness trainers all over the world. Translations of this book have given her the opportunity to work with women from many different countries ranging from Japan to Hungary, Soweto to Switzerland, and from Scandinavia to Uzbekistan.

This experience has widened her understanding of women's predicament and their concerns in the world. It has also deepened her commitment to help women find their voice and to enable them to be agents of their own change.

A Voice for Now

Changing the way
we see ourselves
as women

ANNE DICKSON

PIATKUS

Copyright © 2003 Anne Dickson

First published in 2003 by
Judy Piatkus (Publishers) Limited
5 Windmill Street
London W1T 2JA
e-mail: info@piatkus.co.uk

The moral right of the author has been asserted

A catalogue record for this book is available from the British Library

ISBN 0 7499 2398 9

Edited by Alice Wood
Text design by Paul Saunders

This book has been printed on paper manufactured with respect for the environment using wood from managed sustainable resources

Typeset by Action Publishing Technology Ltd, Gloucester
Printed and bound in Great Britain by
Butler & Tanner Ltd, Frome, Somerset

For Jenny
with love and recognition

Acknowledgements

The process of this book has been a very personal and private endeavour.

Among those few who have been involved and whose contribution I now wish to acknowledge are Arlene and Edmund Faris, who provided me with a home from home for several months last year in Northern Ireland so that I could write. Their respect for the demands of the creative process, combined with their easy warmth and support, were a wonderful gift at a critical time. Arlene, too, encouraged me in my initial decision to experiment with fiction.

In the early stages, David Elliott took the time to read a section of the manuscript and gave me some sound advice while Gill Bailey's shrewdness and sensitivity were a great help towards the end.

When Judy Moore offered to read the completed manuscript, she was the first person to do so. Her response was therefore crucial. Both from an intuitive and objective standpoint, she understood the book and, as it became part of her own life too, I felt less alone and immensely grateful for her sympathetic criticism.

I would like to thank those friends – especially Liz Clasen, Barbara Elliott, Patricia Hodgins, Agnete Munck – who through my times of misgiving and self-doubt have never failed in their encouragement. Thanks also to Myrtle Berman and Leigh Tooze for their steady dispatches of affirmation and support.

I also want to acknowledge the vital role Gus plays in my life: his daily routines keep me firmly grounded while his staunch devotion reminds me, always, of the possibility of joy.

Foreword

This book is about a gentle revolution.

No evangelising. No converting. No rejection or imposition. It starts small, and essentially from within. Not in the head alone. It doesn't even necessitate words. It is an attitude, an approach to yourself, to others, to the world around you.

This revolution is rooted in personal power, a quality that shines through the way you take responsibility for any other power you may be granted temporarily in this world. It shows in the way you meet others as equals, neither looking up to nor pitying them. It shows in the way you do not subjugate yourself to others, by giving your own power away.

It shows especially in the way you deal with your fear. You acknowledge it, you feel it, but you continue through it. Sometimes, you decide from this place that the danger is too great and you move away, you draw in your resources and you protect yourself.

This power is evident when you say no clearly, surprising others, perhaps, or disappointing them but never, never crushing them.

It shows when you protest, softly or loudly, to someone who, knowingly or unknowingly, has gone too far. You are not afraid to be angry when a boundary is transgressed and yet, from this place of power, you have no need to trade in the currency of blame and retribution.

When you compromise in negotiation it is present. When you are flexible while also maintaining consistent boundaries for those who need them even when they attack or resent them, this power is clear. It is apparent always in the way you are prepared to withstand being unpopular and disliked as the cost of being true to yourself.

You may surprise others with your forthrightness because you are not afraid to speak out, especially if someone invites you to. This power is clear in the way you respond honestly and emotionally to a situation but then move through it, like meeting a wave, allowing yourself to go through it to the other side.

The power of gentle is revealed in the way you do not blame or apologise automatically. Yet you will admit your mistakes and errors and are keen to listen to and learn from others' criticism.

You are willing to take due responsibility for the harm you have done to others through intent or neglect: you do not need to hide behind the sterility of guilt but can feel the sorrow that comes with true acknowledgement.

You do not compromise emotionally because you know that, if you do, you will deny something in you that is part of the beauty of who you are.

You can be alone. You may not enjoy loneliness but you do not avoid it. You know the circumference of yourself. You've tested your limits; you've felt your substance. This power enables you to experience happiness equally in either solitude or intimacy, savouring each in its own time.

You look upon yourself as you would look upon a very dear friend, knowing how to separate rubbish from raw material, being able to see and accept the presence of the whole. You can accept and acknowledge everything that is in you: attractive, unattractive, likeable, unlikeable, the magpie, the eagle, the mouse and the monster, the servant and the queen.

This power often cascades out in laughter. Laughter at the sheer mess and absurdity of it all. How hard we strive to look good, to be good, to please, to carry others, to make a success of things: we make such efforts to do the right thing and make the right impression. But the world is not balanced. This means we will experience moments of madness. This is the power of crazy. It is mad, this whole situation, and it is dangerous.

It is time for us to stand up and speak with a new voice. It is time for gentle anarchy.

The revolution of the power of gentle is a revolution of being.

1

Today promised the possibility of some change. As Clare turned her car off the main road into Butterwell Lane, this precise thought went through her mind and cheered her. She was due for a change, she told herself. She needed something new, a new direction, some movement, a new challenge, anything to get her out of what she increasingly felt was a stuck and sterile place in her life.

There was the large brick house on the right. She slowed down and glanced at her notepad on the passenger seat. Another half-mile to the sign to Harwell House. She continued slowly, seeing the car clock said only 10.33. She wasn't due until 11. She soon arrived at the sign and pulled off the road on to a grass verge. She stopped the car and turned off the ignition. She couldn't actually see the house from where she was parked as it was obscured by a hedge. She sat back and closed her eyes to compose herself.

2

'Helen?' Clare enquired as the door opened.

'Yes.' The two women stared at each other for an eager split second before looking away. 'You must be Clare. Come in.'

'I hope I'm not early.'

'No, you're absolutely on time. Shall I take your coat?'

'Thanks. Your directions were very clear.'

She followed Helen into a sitting room. It was bright and colourful and, even on this overcast day, the yellow walls threw off a lot of warmth.

'Do sit down. Would you like some coffee?' asked Helen.

'That would be lovely.'

Helen went out.

Helen looked younger than Clare had imagined from her voice on the phone. She guessed that, in fact, they were about the same age. That same age, neither young nor old, just a non-specific, invisible, in-between age. Helen wore a ring but not a wedding ring. Was she divorced? Separated?

Clare looked around the room. A striking triptych of the back view of a reclining woman occupied most of the space along one wall. Over the open fireplace hung a watercolour of a birch wood. Lots of photographs around, of family and friends, she assumed. She liked the room. Comfortable furniture but nothing matching. No theme or packaged look. She imagined that each item had an individual history. The windows all round looked out on to trees. Lots of different greens and a glimpse of a neighbouring house in the distance. It was quiet and peaceful and she felt herself relax.

'This must be a lovely place to live. Have you been here a long time?' she asked as Helen reappeared with a tray, followed by a small white dog. She wasn't over-keen on dogs. No particular reason, just a lack of familiarity.

'Mmm . . . it must be . . . seventeen years now. This is Rusper,' said Helen. 'Are you comfortable with dogs?'

'I'm not frightened of them − I just don't have much experience with them really,' replied Clare. She looked at the tray Helen had placed on the table. A pot of coffee, a jug of milk, two china mugs, a small sugar bowl and a plate of biscuits. Nothing actually matching, she noticed, but everything somehow belonging together.

'Do you take milk and sugar?'

'Just a little milk . . . that's fine. Thank you.'

'Biscuit?'

'Thanks.'

They both settled back. Rusper lay down at Helen's feet. His back legs were spread out behind him so that his whole body was completely flat to the ground. Clare observed this with curious amusement before Helen spoke.

'We need to talk, don't we? Shall I explain what I want? The ad wasn't very specific because I couldn't really write everything down on paper.'

'All it said was that you're an author and you wanted an assistant.'

'Yes.' Helen paused. 'Yes,' she repeated, gazing into the distance. 'I'll try to explain.'

3

As Clare drove home, her head was buzzing. She'd found Helen fascinating: very articulate and very passionate. She could see in Helen the potential to be rather manic in her intensity but this didn't particularly bother her. She'd always been intrigued by someone's real commitment to their convictions, especially when they weren't popular ones.

At times Clare had found something in Helen's gaze unnerving. Here was a woman who cared deeply. She hadn't mentioned her personal circumstances and had made no reference to family other than one allusion to both her parents having died.

In relation to practical matters, Helen had explained that she wanted an assistant to do mainly typing and possibly some research on two mornings a week, occasionally three. This suited Clare. It was enough to occupy and interest her and would give her a bit of extra money. It was even nearby. Furthermore, she sensed somewhere in her being that she was going to find whatever she did for Helen stimulating.

On the seat beside her were a couple of Helen's past books. Helen had insisted that Clare acquaint herself with what she was getting involved with before making a final decision. As she started making a mental list of the job's advantages – stimulation, being useful, involvement, challenge – she found herself approaching her own road. She felt quietly certain that, whatever these books contained, this job would suit her perfectly.

4

Clare read Helen's books over the next few days. She discovered that she recognised the earlier of the two from twenty years ago. A colleague at school had persuaded her to join an assertiveness training class which was how she'd come to read this particular book. She'd identified with its concepts and examples, like many other women of her generation. Disadvantages were obvious at the time: disparity of work in the home or inequality of pay in the workplace provided a visible goal towards which women could address their energy for change. It was the right book at the right time and the suggestions and ideas seemed to work.

Clare had never thought of herself as a feminist – to her the word implied something far more radical than she felt herself to be. Reading the book brought back memories of the class. It was at work – she'd been head of Business Studies in a large comprehensive – that the issues had seemed most relevant to her. She found it very hard to challenge junior staff or colleagues who were doing far less work than she was. She tended to avoid whatever might rock the boat. She was aware that inside the steady, stable Clare that other people saw, there lurked a coward, prone to laziness, who would do anything to avoid direct confrontation.

It also brought back memories of Len's illness. It hadn't been long after the class that Len had first been diagnosed. She wondered where the years after that had gone to.

Suddenly she heard the sound of the phone. It was Angie.

'Hi there. I thought I'd ring while I've got a free space. How are you doing?'

'I'm fine. I think I've found the perfect job.'

'With the author you went to see?'

'Yes.'

'So who is she? Tell me everything. Oh God . . .'

'What's the matter?'

'I've just seen a message on my desk to phone someone before three. Can I get it over with and ring you back in a few minutes?'

'Sure. I'm in all afternoon.'

'Great. Talk to you soon.'

Angie was Clare's closest friend – they'd attended the same secondary school together and had remained friends ever since. It was a friendship based on attraction of opposites as Angie represented to Clare everything she wasn't. Angie was as outrageous as Clare was conservative. She was now principal lecturer in counselling at the university, and also in charge of the student counselling service.

What Clare loved about Angie was her huge heart. This was also why her students liked her. Angie would always be there in a crisis for people she cared for and if she gave her word, she'd keep it.

She heard the phone ring again and went to continue their conversation. It turned out that Angie had heard of Helen and had also read some of her books, ages ago.

5

Opening her eyes, Helen saw the clock said 7.40. She lay quietly listening to the morning sounds. Suddenly, at the edge of her bed, appeared the face of her dog. An invisible tail wagged, giving his head an endearing gentle sideways movement as he watched her, intently waiting for the signal to join her for their morning ritual. She lifted the duvet slightly and patted the mattress; he jumped up and curled himself, nestling into the curve of her body under the covers. He leaned heavily against her, settled his head into the convenient bend of her knee and lay completely still.

Helen loved these moments, when the distinction between animal and human, fur against skin, became blurred by the warmth of mutual belonging. For her, it wasn't so much that it made up for the lack of a human body alongside. It was quite a different experience: neither better or worse, just different. And this daily wordless ritual became more special with each repetition.

Taking care not to disturb their peaceful arrangement, she

turned her head to look again at the clock. Another five minutes and she'd get up. Clare was due at 10. Helen wondered whether they would work well together.

6

Stretch your arms wide and breathe into your heart

Clare watched these blue words floating across the screen in front of her. She wondered how their first session would go. Helen had already explained that she wanted Clare to type as she dictated. Helen found the logistics of gathering words from the spread of different pages laid out in front of her – some handwritten in pencil or pen, some printed out, different versions, different vintages – quite enough to manage. She wanted to be free to sit with the unfolding process while someone else handled the mechanics at the keyboard.

Clare looked out through the windows to the layers of green beyond. Helen came in and carefully placed a cup of coffee for her on the desk, before settling on a cushion on the floor slightly behind Clare, out of her line of vision.

'I don't know if this is going to work,' she heard Helen mutter behind her. Then a silence. The computer hummed. The birds sang outside. The papers rustled. Rusper pushed open the door and Clare turned round to see him settle alongside Helen, completely covering one pile of papers. She watched as Helen patiently extricated the papers from underneath him.

'I'm not saying anything because I'm not sure where to start,' said Helen a moment or two later, slightly defensively, as if Clare had expressed impatience.

Clare remained silent. This was only her second meeting with Helen but she had some idea that 'artistic' people could be difficult so she was content to sit and look at the trees.

'Right!' declared Helen suddenly. Clare's gaze returned to the screen. '***Stretch your arms wide and breathe into your heart***' floated across, this time in orange. 'Vision,' said Helen.

Clare put her hands on the keys. 'Do we call this Chapter One?'

'No,' said Helen. 'Not yet. Just put "Vision".'

'Do you like your headings underlined?'

'No. I don't like anything underlined. Either bold for headings or italics for emphasis. Never underlined.'

'Fine.'

Clare typed 'Vision' in bold.

'"A vision lost",' said Helen. 'Make that the heading instead.'

'OK.'

Silence. Humming. A deep sigh behind her. Clare found herself tensing with some kind of anticipation. What on earth was coming? she wondered. She tried to breathe into her heart and wondered where in her body that actually meant.

7

A Vision Lost

To think differently, first of all, we need to *see* differently. Let's go back to the beginning of our lives. Back to birth. If a child is born with normal visual faculties intact, her eyes will function as a pair of binoculars. Each eye reflects a separate image on to the retinas. Here both images will coalesce to form a combination of the two: they merge into one single composite image when focused.

By the time we're around five years old, one eye will have become dominant. As that one eye overworks, the other eye correspondingly 'under' works and weakens. This interests me because of the existence of a similar process occurring in our psychological development.

All sorts of children's experiences describe their ability to pick up and 'see' things that adults cannot any more. They see things in the round, without the imposition of logic or reason or the need for scientific proof. Self-expression through paint or play convey a different awareness of what is going on around them. Imaginary friends, fairies, animals, objects with which they communicate strike adults as foolish or fascinating. In the same way that children can sense what they need to eat, without knowing what it is, and can detect tension without any conceptual capacity to understand, they see things differently. They see and love and need from a different place. One could say a child's place or a simpler place, an innocent and irrational place. One could say all sorts of things to justify why this place has to be superseded by what we call the concrete picture of reality, a reality agreed upon by mature adults.

However, the loss of emotional and psychological 'binocularism', the ability to merge two images, has a profound and devastating effect: for the rest of our adult lives, we will be encouraged to *monocular* vision. We stop seeing two possibilities and habituate our eyes and brains to receive *one* image only by suppressing the other. This single image is what we then use exclusively to define an appropriate reality for ourselves and for others.

To make this easier to understand, we can separate out the two ways of seeing the world around us, two distinct ways of defining our approach to everything that happens to us throughout our lives.

Looking through the right eye

What is the shape of the world seen through the lens of the right eye? We see life shaped like a ladder. Movement is linear – up or down. We are not sure what's at the top of the ladder because, like the end of the rainbow, it's only an illusion. When you're looking up you aim at the top rung, but once you've reached that particular rung you find that, from your new perspective, there is yet another top to the ladder. Each time you repeat the process upwards, the same thing occurs.

Looking in the opposite direction is unpleasant and perilous. It makes your stomach drop. You really don't want to look down or fall down. You're not exactly sure why not but instinctively you hold on tightly. As movement is confined to up or down, we aim upwards: we look towards goals, keeping them in our sight. There is a comfort in these goals because they give us structure and purpose and, above all, a clear direction. A straight path to follow. No room for sideways thinking or considerations, no room for distraction. Best to leave as little room as possible for error or doubt and ensure everything is in its due place with its due entitlement. We need to know how things and people are going to behave. We need to know where we are. For our own security of position on the ladder, we need to control.

Dualism

One way of controlling any situation is by division – separating or reducing everything to smaller pieces, making each piece more manageable than it would be as an unwieldy whole. Control is made easier by dividing everything into two. This is known as dualism. It means that everything – people, events, behaviour – are fitted into two categories: male or female, through right or wrong, through life or death.

Everything is defined by and set against its apparent opposite. This means that each pair or duality, in the vision of this right eye, exist as a fixed negative and a fixed positive, in relation to each other. Rational or emotional, for example, are two aspects of this positive/negative demarcation. So being rational (positive) stands on a higher rung of the ladder than being emotional (negative).

All of us absorb these negatives and positives without realising it. They become fixed, even permanent, once established in a culture, and are very, very slow to change. Think, for example, of the effect of the positive/thin and the negative/fat opposition on our attitudes to appearance.

How does this affect the way we perceive each other? We assess and compare ourselves according to whatever 'positive' or 'negative' attributes are prescribed at that time in that context.

External factors — appearance, age, gender, achievements, wealth — are used to make this assessment. More or less. Pretty or plain. Stronger or weaker. Richer or poorer.

We make professional, social and sexual assessments on an up/down scale of reference. We have to do this quickly, relying on audio-visual cues. The priority is to establish exactly where the relative positions are on the ladder so that we know how to behave in order to ensure survival. Survival can mean literal physical survival but usually describes less dramatic outcomes like saving face, clinching the deal, coming out on top, scoring, getting laid, avoiding sanctions, escaping exposure or making the right social impression.

Different ladders exist in different situations. Several ladders coexist concurrently in our lives. Some are only in our minds, some are real in life around us: what they have in common is the exclusively linear up/down movement. You may experience yourself on a different rung within your family from where you believe you are at work or at school. You may feel lower down in one relationship to one person and higher up in another. You may feel comfortably settled on a rung in a particular context and then find that the sudden appearance of another person or an arbitrary event like redundancy or the onset of an illness or a partner's affair dislodges you from your familiar position. You feel your status falling.

Perpendicular power

What motivates people to move up and what is it that we lose as we move down? The answer is power. The meaning and definition of power through each eye is different. Through the right eye, power comes from status, resources, expertise, or charisma.

Status
This describes official power conferred through the laws and social arrangements of the culture in which we live. It includes the power that comes through being a parent (over a child), a

teacher (over a class), a king (over his subjects), a chairman (over a committee), a manager (over a department), a boss (over an organisation), a government (over a nation), a religious leader (over their community).

Nearly all of us have this kind of power over others at times as part of our roles in life, both personal and professional. We experience, at the same time, others having this power over us.

Resources

Power is possessed by those who have access to important resources. Examples are money, water, land, information, weaponry, armies, a workforce, oil, diamonds, mineral deposits or a strategic geographical position. We all experience this kind of power in relation to money, finding ourselves over or under others, who have less or more than ourselves.

Resource power affects us in personal relationships. Which partner is earning more? Who holds the purse strings? Nobody can be truly independent without personal access to money. We may become aware of the lack of power when we are excluded from certain decisions in the workplace. More generally, we are affected in much wider contexts of national health versus private health, or the global distribution of wealth where nations higher up the ladder depend on the poverty of those further down.

Expertise

This power belongs to those who have the skills and knowledge that someone else doesn't have but needs. You can be a garage mechanic, medical consultant, lawyer, vet or computer technician and enjoy a degree of expertise power over others who don't have the know-how. Most of us will have a measure of this kind of power over others at times, depending on our particular range of expertise; similarly, we all require and have to acknowledge the power of experts when we need them. Traditionally, we acknowledge this (higher) power by payment of money.

Charisma

Some people have a magnetic appeal, others have a strong popular appeal. It's difficult to analyse exactly but charisma can be described as a powerful personal presence. Charm, graciousness or even holiness can sometimes be aspects of charisma, but certainly not always. Repeated exposure on television can imbue individuals with this kind of power, regardless of personal characteristics: the magnetic power of the screen itself can make someone 'famous'. Stars of pop, opera, film and sport illustrate this kind of power as do certain politicians, religious gurus, dictators or princesses.

Charisma exerts a strong influence over others. People are drawn to emulate charismatic individuals, to behave or dress like them, to give money, vote or fight for them. We hurry to buy the underwear or special ingredients, houseplants or cosmetics, whatever it is that helps us *copy* in the hope that this will confer the same kind of power on ourselves.

Hallmarks of power

What is common to these sources of power is that each is measured on an up/down, over/under basis. Just as we can identify ourselves with having power when someone else hasn't (now in the 'over' position), we can also recognise that there are as many occasions when others have this power over us (now we are in the 'under' position). Being powerful means having power over others: being *powerless* means being under others who have power over us.

A second factor in common is the temporary nature of this power. It may last a long time, sometimes a very long time, but it is not permanent. Since this power is conferred from *outside* us, it can be taken away. Even rights inherited as part of a longstanding tradition and assumed to be permanent are subject to the caprice of political climate changes.

Resources turn out not to be infinite but exhaustible. They are vulnerable to changes in market forces: as a resource diminishes, your power diminishes. Similarly, expertise only confers power when it is in demand. Changes and technological developments have made many kinds of manual expertise completely redundant. Redundancy and retirement can trigger a profound loss of status and identity. Even parental power wanes as children grow up and leave home.

Perhaps the most obviously ephemeral power is charismatic power. If we are easily swayed one way, we can be just as easily swayed in another direction. Physical beauty and prowess fade with age and celebrity status evaporates with passing moods and fashion.

All these aspects of power are easy to recognise. The world, through the right eye, is demarcated in a way that few of us question. We simply assume that power is always measured along the perpendicular, that these are 'the ways of the world', so much so that it is difficult even to *imagine* any alternative.

8

'Would you like a break?' asked Helen. 'It's a good point to stop if you do.'

'I wouldn't mind a stretch.'

'Me too.' Helen rose to her feet and left the room. 'I'll put the kettle on.'

'I'll come down when I've saved this,' Clare replied.

A few minutes later she found Helen in the kitchen.

'How are you finding it, working like this?' asked Helen.

'It's fine. How about you?'

'It's certainly quicker having you here.' Helen poured water on to the coffee and placed two mugs on the table. 'It's too chilly to sit outside but I'll open the doors to let in a little air.' She opened the doors to the garden and joined Clare at the table.

Neither spoke for a minute or so.

'It's so nice seeing your garden,' said Clare. 'I miss mine. I live in a flat now.'

'A modern one?'

'No, it's on the ground floor of a large converted Victorian house. Six flats altogether.'

'Is there no garden at all then?'

'There's a small bit at the back belonging to the basement flat. I used to look out on to a sweet little front garden but unfortunately that was paved over not so long ago.'

'What a shame. How long have you lived there?'

'Just over six years. When the children moved out, the house seemed far too big . . . and I really needed to make a break.'

'You said when we met that your husband had died. Was that long ago?'

'Fourteen years now. We had eighteen years together – we met at university – and then they diagnosed cancer, first in his pancreas and then in his bowel.'

'That must have been awful,' said Helen.

Clare's voice went very quiet. 'It was. A horrible, drawn-out dying.'

'And your children?'

'Daniel was fourteen and Sophie was twelve when Len died.'

'You must have had a hell of a lot to deal with.'

'Yes,' said Clare, nodding in agreement.

'How are they now?'

'Danny's now in the States – in California – he's got a good job in computer technology. He earns a fortune! He's fine, as far as I know. He's got a girlfriend called BJ who I haven't met yet. He's trying to persuade me to go over for a visit; he's even offered to pay my fare.'

'Why don't you go?'

'I don't know. Somehow I haven't quite found the energy. I'd love to see him though. Maybe I'll get there one day.'

'And your daughter?'

'Ah,' Clare sighed. 'She's a bit more of a worry really. There have been a few problems, you know, in the past. She's got a boyfriend who's pleasant enough and she works as assistant curator of a museum. She's always been passionate about the past but she doesn't make much money.' Clare paused. 'Sophie ... I don't know ... always seems less well adjusted than Danny. I worry about her more because she always seems slightly lost and at odds with the world.' She stopped and looked at Helen. 'What about you? Do you have any children?'

'No. I don't, sadly.'

A moment of unease hovered in the air.

'Shall we get back to work?' said Helen, clearly keen to pre-empt further conversation. 'I'm going up to sort my papers out. I'll see you when you're ready.'

Clare was curious about Helen's response but felt no great need to know everything. She didn't mind people being private. She sat for a while drinking her coffee and enjoying the garden, before getting up to join Helen upstairs.

9

A Vision of Balance

So by way of introduction, or reintroduction, let's see how the world looks through the left eye.

Looking through the left eye

A very different experience: like going from a neon-lit office into a sombre cave. A little adjustment is needed after the glare. We can make out shapes and patterns. Movement appears chaotic and random but, gradually, we can make out repeats or almost-repeats. When an outside object appears, it is accommodated or drawn in, subsumed into the existing shape, becoming part of the new and constantly changing pattern. Continuously changing forms, random fragments, splitting off, to rejoin and reform the whole. This vision thrives on paradox, with no clear or permanent division between this and that, between right and wrong. Endless possibilities, complex and simple, changing and the same.

This is a world of the interior, of dreams, of a reality not defined by an outside assessor. This is personal and impersonal. It contains difference and similarity together, perceiving connections, integration of mind and body, of heart with head. Weakness is considered not as the negative opposite of strength but as an intrinsic *aspect* of strength. This is an approach characterised by both, and not either/or. Nothing is split – you are apart and a part simultaneously.

There is a rhythm, not always predictable. You can be certain only that there is one inherent somewhere in the process. No linear direction is apparent, more a continuous process of evolution, shedding and accommodation. The up/down positions are missing because no position of power is fixed: hierarchy has no meaning here because the structure is ever-changing. There are many, many variations but here difference and equality coexist, side by side. Everything belongs equally to the whole.

The positioning of things, people, events, phenomena, real and abstract is different. Instead of an established system of upper and lower, we see everything, through this eye, on the level, along a continuum. The straight lines of the ladder are replaced by a spiral, integrally connected, and constantly in motion. The perpendicular becomes the horizontal: fixed order becomes cyclical.

Instead of a determination to control, there is an atmosphere of openness. A stranger, as assessed through the wary right eye, becomes, through the left eye, an unknown person with whom we can establish a connection. Similarities coexist with differences. We are different rather than inferior/superior.

In a vision that is not ladder-shaped, not perpendicular, where does the concept of power have a place? If nobody is higher up or lower down, how is importance ranked?

A different power

Power in the world as seen through the left eye is a different kind of power. It is not so easy to describe as assets, attractiveness or expertise but it is nevertheless quite tangible and we can tell when someone possesses it and when they don't. It is a power, first of all, that comes not from outside as the previous kinds of power. It isn't conferred by official title or status or rank. It is a force that emanates from within you.

If you think about someone you know or have met who impressed you because of some inner quality, you may have been struck by this kind of personal power. Maybe you called it peace or composure, maybe you defined it as radiance or compassion. Maybe you were struck by an ability to stay detached and withstand pressure. It may come across as strength of will or great courage and commitment, expressed without any undue noise or arrogance. Sometimes this kind of power comes across as joyousness or vitality. All of these are attributes related to personal power. So what are its defining characteristics?

Characteristics of personal power

At the heart of personal power is a fundamental care for others and in equal measure a care for oneself. The principle of equality at the core is much more than an ideological buzzword: it is deep, real and heartfelt. Power, through this line of vision, is more interested in connection with others and less concerned with competition and division.

The heart is central so personal power means being comfortable with the place of emotion − its language and expression − and being prepared to be vulnerable. It doesn't necessarily mean talking a lot about feelings, especially since the current practice of 'emotional speak' often acts as a defence against the very vulnerability that genuine emotional experience involves.

Balance is also a key quality. Balance between self and other, emotion and reason, between love (reaching out to others) and anger (saying no and setting limits). Another hallmark of personal power is a clear sense of boundary – knowing where you start and where you end – providing a balance between openness to others and a necessary self-protective layer.

Another characteristic is integrity, rare enough to be at risk of extinction in a culture preoccupied with image and impression. Being truthful with oneself is essential. Indulging in denial and pretence automatically corrodes personal power because they damage our ability to be true to ourselves.

Although self-esteem can be an aspect of inner power, we can easily be misled. Too often it becomes self-*delusion*, as with 'you can achieve anything you tell yourself to', self-*obsession*, 'put yourself first and ignore others' or self-*defence*, 'keep on your armour and avoid being vulnerable'. Real self-esteem entails honesty, equality and openness.

Personal power is both constant and changing. It is not a fixed commodity. Like a candle flame, it flickers and it glows. Although it can sputter quite alarmingly at times of chronic stress and is subject to periods of decline, it survives to be renewed and fanned into strength again.

Unlike external power, inner power isn't temporary because it doesn't depend on external events. As the wheel of fortune turns, as inevitably it does, inner power stays, abiding within. This is what outlasts all ups and downs, all dualities and every loss of outside power. This is what remains when everything and everyone else are no longer in the picture. For a while, it may be the only thing we have left, the only source of strength to keep us going, but it can be enough until circumstances change once again.

10

Clare stopped typing. They'd finished for the day. Scrolling the pages to check for errors she was aware of having only half listened to what Helen had been reading out to her.

As she tidied up the desk, she hesitated, then asked: 'Helen, would you mind if I took a copy to read at home? It's just that I can't take it in when I'm typing and I'd like to go over it . . . simply for my own interest. Could I do that?'

Helen looked surprised and smiled almost shyly. 'Course you can. Just print it out for yourself, if you really want to.'

11

It didn't take long for Clare to read through what she had typed for Helen. She found it interesting. She was familiar with left brain/right brain concepts but the idea of seeing differently through different eyes was new to her. And what Helen described as 'the ladder approach' made her think. Actually it all made her think even though it required some concentration. She associated this sort of writing more with studying than with a casual read.

Over the following days, the idea of being on a ladder and socially assessed stayed in her mind. The image seemed to describe something she'd been dimly aware of for the past few months. Without employment or the domestic status of being in a couple, she was, in fact, fairly low down on the social 'ladder'.

She no longer felt any status even as a mother now that her children had grown up. They loved her, of course, but they didn't need her any more. She felt she had become almost invisible to the outside world. More and more when going into shops, into the bank, into a café, or anywhere, she found that people looked through her as if she wasn't there. Classifiable neither as old nor young, she seemed to have reached an insignificant age in between, where she had to make a real effort to get any attention.

No label, no title, no function – a disturbing thought. She reminded herself she was a woman of some substance, a survivor. She wasn't lacking in ability; she had a lot of experience and expertise. That must be worth something, she thought, and yet she knew she was worth little in the linear scheme of things.

She thought about phoning Sophie. She hadn't talked to her for a while but, as usual, hesitated, hating the fact that she felt wary of telephoning her own daughter. Clare felt sad listening to Sophie's voice on the answering machine and put down the receiver, not knowing what to say.

What she *wanted* to say was, let's meet for lunch or spend an evening together, but the reality was, from past experience, that whenever they were together, there was always an awkwardness. If they'd been strangers, they could gradually have got to know each other. As it was, their mother/daughter relationship seemed to restrict their interaction, leaving both of them with a feeling of disappointment and frustration. Consequently, each was aware that the other was making an effort on her behalf: an awareness that stifled any real opportunity for spontaneity or closeness between them.

Clare took a deep breath and redialled the number. This time she managed a light-hearted enquiry about Sophie's welfare and asked her to get in touch when she could.

12

Helen suddenly realised she had speeded up without noticing it, so she stopped and looked through the woods behind her. No sign of Rusper. She waited until his white shape came into view in the distance and then continued along the path more slowly.

She was looking forward to their next session, excited to be at last bringing the strands of her book together. She wanted to inspire others as she herself had been inspired.

She checked to see Rusper had almost caught up and walked on, drifting back into her thoughts. She had been thinking about Mrs Sisulu. They'd met years ago now, when the state of emergency in South Africa was still in place. Nelson Mandela, Walter Sisulu and other leading ANC members had still been in jail.

Helen had been preparing a book, gathering interviews with

people 'on the ground', about the experience of South African women. She'd been shocked by the visibility of the system of apartheid. In parts of Johannesburg the demarcation was unmistakable. On one side of the road, she saw houses built of brick and furnished with electricity; on the other, rows of shacks squatted in smoky darkness.

Helen remembered the 'black/good–white/bad' perspective so beloved of the Western media at the time. In reality, it wasn't that simple. She interviewed middle-class white women who organised integrated educational or social events and risked social ostracism by letting their children play with black children. She talked to other white men and women who risked their own and their families' lives every single day through their political activity and determination to end apartheid.

She also heard first hand from the conservatives: that blacks were by nature less sensitive, less sophisticated, simpler people, a less developed species who could not govern themselves and needed to be held in check.

By the time Helen met Mrs Sisulu, she was overwhelmed by the whole situation. It seemed to her that she was experiencing both the best and the worst of humanity.

The heartbreak of one typical incident always remained with her. She'd talked with a leader of one black community which had put all its work and hope and energy into planning a community fair where people could come to display their trades and skills to try and get out of the cycle of poverty. For four months, they fought for a venue and facilities, encountering bureaucratic intransigence every inch of the way, only to arrive on the day itself to find that the electricity supply had 'inexplicably' been turned off.

It was impossible not to feel a kind of vicarious battle-weariness because she had heard so many times how hope had been broken, efforts had been crushed and constructive action undermined by dominant, stronger forces.

She remembered vividly interviewing Mrs Sisulu in a car, parked (for security reasons) in the middle of a large crowd of family picnickers. Throughout their meeting, there were regular interruptions as various people came to seek her opinion or counsel. Helen questioned her about hatred because she'd seen so little actual evidence of revenge in the eyes or voices of black South Africans. Mrs Sisulu had replied, with the patience of the wise talking to the foolish, that there was absolutely no time for aggression. It was a huge waste of energy, she'd insisted, and they had to use every ounce of their energy constructively. She talked about the futility of hating the individual. She truly hated the *system* and she had devoted her life, as thousands of others had done, to changing that system.

The idea of not displacing hatred or blame on to an individual but, instead, channelling that hatred against a system had been new to Helen at the time.

What Helen had witnessed in six weeks had increased her sense of despair. The force for change had so few resources compared to the force of the system that upheld it. She asked Mrs Sisulu what kept her going. How did she and her people find the strength to sustain hope in the face of what seemed to be impossible odds?

Her answer had been simple and profound. 'We have the truth on our side,' she'd replied, and then added, 'It may not happen in my lifetime, but I know it will happen – maybe in my grand-daughter's time – and that's what keeps me going, keeps us all going, because it is our truth.'

The importance of humility, commitment to truth, courage and gentleness made a lasting impression in Helen's mind. They constituted the seeds of a vision of a very different form of power, one that she had not been able to articulate before. As she hurried along, keen to be on time to start work with Clare, she was aware of how vigorously those seeds had taken root. It struck her, too, that those who were oppressed by a system were capable of a far more sophisticated form of thinking than those who maintained it.

13

Binocular or Monocular?

If two lines of vision – through the right eye and the left eye – exist, why is one much more familiar? Why is it so easy to identify perpendicular forms of power but difficult to grasp the less tangible aspects of power, even though we recognise them? The reason we don't find it as easy to articulate left-eye vision is that it goes *beyond* words. Left-eye vision enters the realm inhabited by those we label mute, mystical or mad.

We have an awareness of shadows, of the imaginary, of the luminous, the numinous and the dark. Of that which is almost formed. Of that which is real, yet undefined by intellectual concepts, so cannot be subjected to the scientific rigours of analysis. We are familiar with lateral and linear thinking. Science has established the difference between right-brain and left-brain function; we know which parts of the brain regulate our emotional, linguistic and artistic abilities. In some measure, we also acknowledge the existence of the paranormal.

Yet this whole field of vision remains shadowy, existing on the fringes, a poor relation to the real thing. It exists only as a reflection of the main vision, rather than as a vision of validity in its own right.

Through the left eye, we are encouraged to see that *both* images have validity. The right-eye approach is essential. We need to obey and to yield. We need to acknowledge superior forces and to allow others to have the right of way. We have to obey certain rules because a linear approach is helpful in ordering life. It makes for convenience and speed of transaction. We need boundaries, goals, reason and intellectual ability. We need structure, order and discipline. We need containment and stability. We need to assert ourselves individually, to think of ourselves, to fight our corner and go for what we want ... *sometimes*.

The left-eye approach permits us to see that there is no reason at all why a combination of inner, personal power and external, perpendicular power cannot work hand in hand. Through binocular vision, where both lines of vision coexist and merge, all the temporary trappings of external power simply exist within a wider context. Through the right eye we see what we want and need to see to ensure short-term physical and psychological survival in this uncertain world. Through the left eye, we see what is. In the middle of the spiral, the left eye is a central witness to the equality and connectedness of all beings, a constancy throughout the ever-changing dualities of good/bad, happy/sad, saint/sinner, under/over.

Binocular vision allows us to see beyond the ladders. They still exist but we see them for what they are: temporary demarcations established in the right eye of the beholder. Through the left eye, perpendicular and personal power can coexist. Through the right eye, however, perpendicular power is seen as the only kind that matters: everything and everyone has to be positioned in a higher/lower context. Any alternative to this fixed order appears as a potential threat. So instead of acceptance, left-eye vision is deemed by the right eye to be naive, childlike, simplistic or, most dangerously, unreal.

Whereas binocular vision allows for an amalgam of images through both eyes, monocular vision insists that we see through one eye only.

14

The Source of Aggression

Monocular vision gives rise to a monocular system: a man-made one into which we all fit somewhere along the perpendicular, where power is measured exclusively through the definition of the right eye and where the vision of the left eye is systematically occluded.

Monocular vision underpins the vertical systems we see in

every area of life: political, domestic, social, commercial, interpersonal and bureaucratic. We are born into them and die within them. Without us necessarily being aware of it, they have created a way of *seeing* (monocular) that we then apply to ourselves, arranging our thoughts, feelings, opinions and perceptions along the same lines.

It is difficult for us to imagine how automatically the perpendicular system affects our interactions. When we're in the under position, we look upwards to try to reach the 'over' position. However, even the over position is never ultimately secure: there is the ever-present threat that someone will overtake us when we are least expecting it. Life on the ladder is precarious as we're always on the lookout for signs that our position is falling; we need to remain alert and ready to retain our position if necessary. There are times when we have the luxury of getting off the ladder and relaxing but as soon as there is any possibility of conflict, real or imaginary, we are faced once again with the alternatives of up or down.

The push for power

Why do we want to keep moving up? Why is it so imperative? What is it that makes downward movement so undesirable? Clearly, we don't want to go down because we want to be on top: we want status, money, clout, beauty. We want to be the one in the more powerful position. And when we have that power, we want to hang on to it.

Why do we want so desperately to hang on to that power? Because we dread the alternative. We don't want to be down there. The one without the power. The dregs. The reject. The negativity of the 'loser' is strongly imprinted in our imaginations but, more importantly, at a deeper emotional level, we are all reminded of our individual experience of having been, at times, in the 'under' position. Living in a perpendicular system, this is inevitable. Even the more vivid experiences, for example being:

> bullied at school
> mocked by teachers
> unwanted at home
> treated like a dispensable commodity in an organisation
> battered by an abusive partner
> helpless in the hands of impassive officials
> rejected by one's peers
> intimidated at work
> ignored because of being inarticulate
> made a scapegoat
> ill and at the mercy of incompetent doctors

are not that unusual in ordinary lives.

Being powerless in a monocular system is understandably equated with painful and unpleasant experiences. We have learned the lesson over and over again that there are only two positions. In our determination to avoid powerlessness, we have to make sure we come out on top: this is the source of aggression.

We are all familiar with the tactics of aggression. Spreading from the playing field or battlefield, where aggression has always been sanctioned, it is now also applauded in commercial and corporate spheres. Aggression is so usual and widespread that it is central to the dynamic of most human interaction.

If we don't like what is happening to us, our responses tend automatically to the up/down position of aggression. We may react passively for a while in the 'down' position, obeying inner voices that tell us to keep quiet, take it, ignore it. We remain fearful (of losing): 'there's no point; there's no way to/I couldn't/can't win'. However, when feelings reach a certain pitch – at some point, at some time, with someone – we swap to the 'up' position. This can mean a direct attack or a more subtle form of hurtful behaviour that establishes us on top.

We witness aggression everywhere. We hear it, we read about it, we watch it on our screens, we cheer it, we encourage and reward it. Even if personally uncomfortable with it, we assume aggression is natural because it's all we've ever known. The dynamic of aggression has become the 'norm'.

15

Stirring stuff, Clare concluded. She had been sitting with her feet up along the length of her sofa and, putting down the papers, leaned back feeling tired.

She wasn't entirely sure that she knew the difference between aggression and anger; neither was she sure that aggression was as widespread as Helen was describing. Of course, there were all sorts of violence and abuse in the world but she couldn't relate that to herself.

She turned on the television to see if she could catch the news and sat down again. There were a few minutes to go and a chat show was still in progress. She watched somewhat half-heartedly. There was a simulated underwater scene, the sound of bubbles rising. The host's voice was heard over the picture saying, 'Well, ladies and gentlemen, we're in very deep down here . . .' (more bubbles) '. . . and I think what I'm looking at . . . is a very old wreck.' The camera immediately switched to a close-up of an elderly woman in the studio audience. There was hysterical laughter from the audience in response as the woman looked taken aback while she took in the implication before joining in and smiling along with everyone else.

A few minutes later the host was chatting to one of his star guests, and referred to this same woman as 'Doris'. The guest asked whether the host had ever interviewed Doris herself. The presenter replied, 'Yes, we interviewed her some weeks ago. She's had a make-over now.' Turning to the audience he added, 'Haven't you, Doris?' He then turned back to his guest, with the quip: 'You can imagine what she looked like before that!' The camera again switched to 'Doris' as howls of laughter and applause erupted from the audience.

Something in Doris's smiling face suddenly made Clare very uncomfortable. She switched the TV off and decided to have an early night.

Before she went to bed, she remembered the following day was Wednesday. She tied up the rubbish, went through her own door and, still in her dressing gown, opened the front door of the house. As she stepped out, she was surprised at the beauty of the night sky. She went round to the dustbins at the side of the house and deposited her bag, then stood still and gazed at the stars for a while before going back. As she reached the front door, she almost collided with Moira, who grinned at her beneath her crash helmet. Moira lived on the second floor, the same floor as Jackie and her two sons. 'Sorry! I'm late,' she said as she rushed by. As she reached her bike, she added, 'I was meant to meet a friend at the club at ten but I was babysitting the boys and Jackie was late back . . . ' She turned the key in the ignition, climbed on and revved up. ''Bye,' she yelled and Clare smiled as she zoomed off into the night.

Before she went into her own flat, she stopped to ask Ellen if she could take out her rubbish as well. Ellen, a retired head-mistress and quite elderly, lived on the ground floor opposite Clare.

'That's very kind of you, dear,' said Ellen as she gave Clare her bag. 'You know which bin mine is, don't you? It is the second one from the front.'

'Yes, I know,' Clare replied. 'Goodnight then.'

'Goodnight.'

16

Clare made herself some tea. She was glad there was still some evidence of neighbourliness in the house. When she'd first arrived, she'd been struck by the friendly atmosphere. The Hadleys – John and Jane – had invited her to have a drink soon after she moved in and the other residents had been invited to meet her. Moira and Ellen were on their own, like herself. Ellen had been there the longest, about twenty years, surviving her husband who had died a few years before. Jackie was a young single mother with two small boys, and then there were two couples: the Hadleys and the Jordans. They were all nice, ordinary people.

They had to meet officially once a year (Clare suddenly remembered that the next meeting was very soon) to sort out repairs and maintenance of the house. Clare had been impressed during these meetings by the genuine consideration everyone showed for each other. There was a sort of give and take which managed to accommodate and survive occasional irritation at Jackie's sons and their friends' skateboarding down the path at the side of the house or the inconvenient position in which Moira would sometimes park her motorbike outside the door. These meetings somehow balanced individual needs with the group as a whole.

Everyone was quite separate but there were lots of little informal kindnesses in evidence. Clare had even held a little party and invited everyone to come and celebrate her retirement. All the residents had turned up except for the Jordans.

Nobody saw much of the Jordans, who both worked away a lot, so when they heard, a little over a year ago, that the Jordans had moved, there wasn't any sense of loss. The new residents turned out to be the Allinsons – Mark and Danielle.

From her first meeting with them, Clare had, unaccountably, felt uncomfortable. Even when the Hadleys invited them to have a glass of wine, they appeared for ten minutes and then disappeared again. Whenever she encountered them near the entrance to the house (they lived in the basement), they smiled with courtesy but without warmth.

Then the trauma of the front garden! A few months after they moved in, she'd come back late one morning from shopping to find two men had dug out all the shrubs and plants from the small front garden and were in the process of laying down slabs of concrete paving. Poor Ellen was standing in the front doorway, completely distraught and dishevelled.

'What's happening?' Clare had asked.

'I don't know,' said Ellen. 'They say that they've been asked to lay paving all over the front area by the Allinsons. They've taken everything out, Clare, all those shrubs, everything. They can't do that without asking us. We're meant to be consulted.'

Clare was quite shocked – first, by the suddenness of the

removal and at the total transformation of a familiar, pleasant aspect into a complete mess; then, with a dawning realisation, by the Allinsons' nerve.

Later that evening, John Hadley had knocked on the basement front door. He didn't like confrontation but felt it his duty to represent everyone else and he also felt genuinely upset by the incident.

Mark Allinson had opened the door and looked at him with apparent surprise.

'We would like an explanation for the removal of our front garden,' John began.

Mark sighed. 'First, it wasn't your garden. The area belonged to us as part of this flat. Secondly, your daylight wasn't obscured by those shrubs. Ours was. Thirdly, we have paid for everything so I don't see that you have anything to complain about.'

'We actually have a lease that requires us to cooperate in living in this house together,' said John firmly. 'We have to ask each other if we want to change things that affect anyone else. You had absolutely no right to do this.'

'Believe me, when it comes to rights, I know what's going on. Feel free to consult a solicitor if you want but it won't alter the situation.'

'But it's in our leases,' John remonstrated, enunciating every word very specifically.

'Listen to me,' replied Mark. 'I assure you I can do what I want with that area out there. And if that has offended other residents, then I'm sorry but that's the way it goes. It's my wife and I who have to live here. Now if you don't mind . . .' He stepped back into his flat and held the door, signalling an unequivocal end to the conversation.

Everyone had been shocked. There was a lot of talk and complaining but no direct confrontation after John's attempt.

At the time, Clare had felt something in the atmosphere change – as if people were a little more wary of each other – which was why she felt relieved to see that there was still some friendliness in evidence. Maybe they would survive the Allinsons' arrogance after all.

17

The next morning, Clare rang and left another message for Sophie to call her back as soon as possible. As she drove to Harwell House she couldn't stop thinking about her. The usual old spectres of the past floated through her mind: how Sophie had got herself pregnant when she was nineteen with a current and, in Clare's opinion, disastrous boyfriend in tow. The pregnancy had ended in a miscarriage. Sophie had been utterly devastated although Clare had been privately relieved.

Clare would never forget the dreadful time after that. Sophie became depressed and stopped eating. Communication between them had degenerated to little more than polite conversation. It had been one of the hardest and most powerless experiences of Clare's life, unable to get through to her own daughter because of some invisible wall she sensed was only partly due to the medication.

Sophie had recovered in part but Clare felt she hadn't eaten properly since then. She still believed that, even after six years, her daughter hadn't fully recovered. Her former sparkle had never returned.

Still preoccupied when she arrived to start work, she had to make a real effort to put it all to one side.

18

Feelings and Emotions – A Preliminary Guide

Most of us have become so accustomed to aggression that we find it impossible to distinguish it from anger. Angry feelings are often designated as negative so we try to suppress them. The more we suppress them, the more we encourage others to do the same so we never find out the difference between being angry and behaving aggressively.

To understand anger more clearly, we have to look at it in the context of other emotions. As an overview, it's useful to see emotions as belonging to one of three families or groups. These groups of emotions are related to three polarities of need as human beings. A polarity is an imaginary line between two points. These points are not opposites (right-eye vision) but complementary and of equal importance to each other: one of the many paradoxes of left-eye vision.

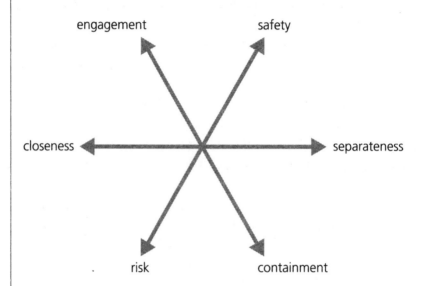

The three polarities

Each of the polarities connects two 'poles', between which we move throughout our lives depending on our particular needs at the time.

1. Closeness – separateness

Closeness ⟷ separateness

This first polarity connects the two poles of closeness and separateness. These are needs which affect us from birth to death. They change of course – our actual needs for closeness as infants are different from adult ones – but all our lives, we need some measure of closeness with others. At varying ages, then, we might meet this need through sharing affection, cuddling a pet, being rocked to sleep, holding a parent's hand, making love, talking with a friend.

Separateness is the complementary need that – again at any age – we meet through experiences of chosen solitude: getting lost in a book, going for a cycle ride, playing alone, writing a diary, pottering in the garden. Whenever we move towards closeness we need contact with others; whenever we move towards separateness, we need a bit of space from everyone else so that we can get back in touch with ourselves. Later, we move back towards others ... and back again to solitude when necessary. All the time, there is a constant movement, back and forth, between the two poles.

2. Engagement – containment

Engagement ⟵————————————————⟶ containment

The second polarity connects the poles of engagement and containment. Imagine the energy involved in achieving a difficult task, overcoming an obstacle or meeting a challenge. Imagine the momentum you need to wrestle with a difficult problem, score a goal, take part in a good argument or debate, to express and stretch yourself to the full: these will give an idea of how we meet the need to engage.

The need for containment is met through an experience of boundaries. These boundaries can be human (a parent saying no), social (accepted rules about behaviour) or legitimate (legal restrictions). As a child, we need the containment of parental discipline against which to exert our own will; as adults we need the emotional containment provided through clear boundaries set by other adults. We need something or someone to push against in order to know who we are, where we are in relation to others, how far we can go: we need consistency.

We need both sides of the polarity at different times throughout our lives, in differing ways. When we need to exert our will, we move towards engagement; when we need the security of a boundary, we move towards containment.

3. Safety – risk

Safety  risk

The third polarity connects the two poles of safety and risk. Again, these poles exist in equal relation to each other throughout our lives, changing form but always there. Whenever you receive a smile of recognition, feel 'at home' or a sense of belonging or 'family', you are meeting this need. You appreciate your own familiar things around you; you enjoy speaking the same language; you feel truly confident in a certain task. These meet our needs for safety.

The complementary need for risk is met whenever we leave our personal comfort zone. Whether getting on to a bicycle for the first time, reaching out to a stranger, getting out of a rut in life, standing in the minority because of your beliefs, or aiming high even when you're afraid, any risk entails a personal challenge.

We move towards safety when life feels a little too uncertain and insecure; we move towards risk when life lacks stimulation and we feel stuck in a rut.

The key to understanding how emotions function within our bodies and minds is realising that emotions prompt us (we are literally *moved*) towards one pole or another, even though we may not be fully conscious of this process. As these three polarities interact at the same time, all the time, you can see that as a human being, we can be drawn this way and that way in any one of six directions. We move in response to emotion: this is a vital aspect of the word e-motion itself.

Our needs and our feelings along the first polarity

When our needs for *closeness* or *separateness* are not met or remain unfulfilled, what do we feel? At the core of feelings in this group we find *love* and *grief*. The right eye sees these as opposite emotions, but the left eye perceives an essential link. It sees love and grief as bound to each other, aware that they are not separate experiences. We feel love *or* grief at any particular time but the depth of love will inevitably be reflected in the depth of grief if and when the loved one dies. The stronger the presence, the more we feel the absence. We often express the two emotions through tears.

Death is one of the major ways in which our need for love and closeness is interrupted. Other experiences include endings of all kinds: withdrawal, rejection, lack of response, being far away from someone you love, being turned away, being ignored when ill or in trouble, having no one to confide in.

When we are feeling miserable, have a hard time at school or work, or feel unwell, we move towards solace and comfort: we turn to someone else. We seek the comfort of another body or the presence of someone who cares. This need is what moves us along the polarity, but it is not always met. Many times, for many reasons, the need goes unfulfilled. So what happens? We feel sad. We feel unhappy and lonely and cold. These same feelings occur when we experience significant endings of closeness (death, divorce, departure): loss, grief and deep, deep sorrow.

Sorrow is also felt when our complementary need for separateness is unfulfilled. Monocular vision has persuaded us that we can only be happy when we are in a relationship with someone else, obscuring the *equally* vital need for separate time, for space away from others. Many professional carers, for example, recognise that exclusive involvement with the needs and welfare of others will take its toll somehow: as tiredness, going through the motions or not having your heart in your work any more.

All of us, at all ages, need time to be alone and to nourish our own being. When this time is denied us in the long term, as children, we don't get the chance to develop a sense of comfort in our own company. Too much preoccupation with parental needs or siblings' demands can stifle the opportunity for the seeds of self-love. An appreciation of being one's own person, so essential for establishing healthy relationships later on, gets little chance to develop and flourish. This loss, often too deep to put into words, lies at the heart of many relationship problems in adult life.

What do we feel when our needs for closeness are met by contact with others? We respond with feelings of comfort, warmth, affection, love or tenderness. Imagine the happiness of all those times you've been hugged or felt cherished, been given a special present from a child, received words of wisdom from a friend, embraced a lover, been welcomed home.

When we are able to find the time and place to be separate (when we *want* to be) the feelings are similar. We feel a love and acceptance of ourselves; we feel comfort and pleasure and a different kind of happiness and peace in solitude. This renews our capacity for love within the experience of closeness to others.

Our needs and feelings along the second polarity

When our needs for *engagement* or *containment* are not met or are blocked, what do we experience? In this family, feelings are related to the emotional core of *joy* and *anger*. Imagine how you feel when your will is blocked. What is our response when our efforts are thwarted, when our opinions are ignored, when we are robbed of something precious or prevented from having a vote? What do we feel when choice is taken away or when freedom is restricted, when we encounter injustice or lies, when a personal, social or professional boundary is transgressed? We encounter frustration, irritation, resentment, fury, rage, annoyance – all related to the emotion of anger.

Less obviously, we have these same feelings when we are denied our complementary need for containment. One aspect of human development and functioning is the need for consistent boundaries. Boundaries are essential. We need to push against them and challenge them and test them but we actually need them in place. A young plant in a small pot will grow more vigorously if its roots are confined, not excessively, but enough to promote healthy development.

What happens when nobody says a clear 'no' to us? Or when rules are inconsistent and unpredictable? The anger prompted by someone 'moving the goalposts' is a simple illustration of our need to have certain predictable constraints within which we can operate. We get understandably cross and feel mistreated when they alter randomly or without warning.

We also get angry in response to a total absence of boundaries, even when we are not conscious of it. Children who are given insufficient consistent discipline (boundaries) often end up expressing their accumulated frustration in delinquent behaviour.

We often fail to appreciate that boundaries are an essential aspect of loving. When nobody *cares* for us sufficiently to say 'no', 'that's far enough', 'this is the limit', and, of course, to *mean* it, our frustration accumulates and can be expressed quite destructively, towards ourselves or to others. When boundaries are inconsistent, too flimsy or non-existent, we feel desperate and angry. We sometimes lash out to provoke a limitation. If we don't encounter it then, we lash out again, going further and further until we meet a boundary that deep down we actually need and yearn for.

When our needs for engagement or containment are fulfilled, we experience feelings related to joy. These might be pride in achievement or sheer elation at overcoming a problem; excitement at breaking through a barrier, the exhilaration of being stretched and meeting a challenge. These are all aspects of the dynamic of joy.

We experience similar feelings when equally met and matched by another person: the thrill of an equal tussle. There is also a real joy to be felt through surrender: choosing to submit to a discipline or regime or acquiescing to a higher order. When we make a willing sacrifice, when we choose to obey or put someone or something else first, we can feel pleasure and peace. If it strikes you as odd that there should be anything at all joyous about discipline, obedience or surrender, you'll begin to understand how the up/down mindset of aggression corrupts so much of human transaction with its obsession about winning.

Our needs and feelings along the third polarity

Finally we look at the third family of feelings, related to our needs for *safety* and *risk*. The core emotions are *trust* and *fear*. When our need for safety is not met, what do we feel? What do we feel when we get lost, when someone hasn't returned home, when we feel pain for which we have no explanation? If your child is sick and the doctor ignores what you're saying or when we're faced with aggression and intimidation, we feel scared and frightened. All these kinds of experiences elicit anxiety, panic, alarm, terror and fear.

The same feelings are aroused when the complementary need for risk is blocked. When the risk factor in our lives is curtailed, being overprotected as children, for example, or when we're constantly told 'you couldn't', 'you can't', 'you'll never make it', we stop risking. Our need to try and experiment, to make mistakes and learn from them, our opportunities to get it 'wrong' so we can get it 'right', are severely restricted.

When this happens, instead of feeling safer, which we might assume (and is after all the aim of avoiding risk), we feel *more* frightened. This is because we never get the chance to go through the anxiety: in other words, to experience it and come out the other side. Anxiety is regarded, by the right eye, as a negative state, to be avoided. The left eye tells us that anxiety is to be experienced and lived through so it will then dissipate and be transformed into an energy that can be put to effective use.

Anxiety can be a real friend to us, signalling the unknown, warning us of the unfamiliar, to be vigilant and take care. It can prompt a sudden suspicion, a wariness that leads us to take another route or an extra precaution.

Our relationship to anxiety is crucial because we can learn to sift through what is real, what is exaggerated and what is groundless. This helps us, through the experience of risk, to understand the nature of our anxiety. Without this experience we don't get the chance to become acquainted, and so anxiety becomes more an enemy than a friend.

When our needs for both safety and risk are fulfilled, we feel trust. Trust incorporates feelings of confidence, relaxation, calmness, excitement, ease, peace. The ability to trust *others* is developed by meeting the need for safety. It comes from knowing through experience that you can be sure of certain things and routines and people: in other words, that you have enough consistency. Trust is reinforced whenever we find someone to support us if we feel frightened or scared, when those we depend on prove to be reliable and predictable enough, when we can be certain that those in power will be behind us when we need them.

It is in the other direction that we have to travel to build up a trust in *ourselves*. We move towards risk when we feel ready to, knowing that fear is an integral part of the process, continuing to move through the fear and survive it. We learn that fear is a necessary aspect of taking a risk and that we have to risk if we are to move on to the new. The feelings of trust then extend to a different kind of confidence: an awareness of an inner resilience and resourcefulness that give us courage to get through times of being alone.

19

'I need to stop for a minute,' said Helen and left the room.

Clare waited, looking blankly at the words on the screen, until Helen came back and proposed a break.

'How long have you been working on all this?' Clare asked when she joined Helen in the kitchen.

'Some years now. It's grown and developed over a long time – that's why I've got so many bits and pieces of paper!'

'It's making me realise that writing is just like any other craft, isn't it? Just using words instead of fabric or whatever.'

'Yes, I think it is,' agreed Helen.

'Have you always been good with words?'

'Probably.' Helen smiled. 'It's a bit of gift and a curse at the same time.'

Clare looked puzzled.

'Well, words have quite a power, you know. I've hurt people in the past, just underestimating that power. It makes you careful.' Helen put their mugs of coffee on the table.

'I've always admired people who were really articulate. I feel quite clumsy in comparison.'

'So do I, believe it or not!' said Helen.

'I *don't* believe it!'

'It's true. There are many times when I've envied people who express themselves seamlessly and unemotionally. They speak as if there could never, *ever* be any doubt or question as to their absolute authority!'

Clare smiled in recognition.

'And what I hate even more is that this reinforces their power because we believe that articulacy is a prerequisite for the truth. And it isn't.'

'What do you mean?'

'I mean it's easy to say the words we want to believe, or that we've been schooled to believe or that we think will make the right impression. But when we're trying to express something truthful, we need time and safety and frequent pauses.'

Clare thought for a moment. 'You mean the deeper the thing we're trying to say, the harder it is to find words for it.'

'Precisely. You see, you *are* good with words! Come on, we'd better get back.'

20

The Need for Balance

With each polarity, there is a need for balance between the two poles. This is why we move first in one direction and then the other, depending on our needs at any particular time. One side without the other always produces rigidity because each 'pole' is necessary to the functioning of the other.

We need *closeness* with others to develop our skills in interacting lovingly with others; we need *separateness* to develop our self-love. Through our need for *engagement*, we experience the joy of self-expression; we learn to stretch and challenge, to discover who we are as individuals. Through the need for *containment*, we develop an awareness of limitation, teaching us how to negotiate, to cooperate and coexist equally with others. We learn the scope of finite power, in other words the limits of perpendicular power, and this teaches us the value of our own inner, personal power.

Through our need for *safety*, we have first to learn through others whether we can trust them. If there is enough safety, and therefore enough trust, in the outside world, then we move towards *risk*, which teaches us how to trust ourselves on the inside. Balance teaches us the value of instinct and intuition; it helps us develop the necessary wisdom of knowing when to protect ourselves and when to trust and take a risk.

The effects of imbalance

The principle of balance at the core of left-eye vision is essential to our emotional life. If one side of a polarity dominates, emotional perception and behaviour will become distorted because of being unbalanced.

When loving others, for example, is unbalanced by self-love, care becomes compulsive: we try and bury our sadness by being excessively and often inappropriately caring to others, sometimes denying others their own emotional space as we do so. Conversely, if there is no opportunity to share love with others, self-love easily degenerates into self-centredness, even ruthlessness.

Engagement unbalanced by containment leads to an obsession with 'me, me, me' and a corresponding inability to be vulnerable. It is hard from this self-centred position to be anything other than arrogant. We become unable to take responsibility for our actions because of a lack of consideration for, or even awareness of, the sensitivities of other people.

On the other side, containment that suppresses engagement becomes oppression. Engagement encourages us to exert our will and find the limits of our power in order to develop and flourish. Exposed to excessive restriction, the flowering of the self will be stunted. We need the impetus of engagement to experience ourselves fully; we need containment to experience ourselves fully in relation to others.

When safety isn't balanced by risk, or vice versa, we can become paralysed by excessive dependence on others' opinions of us or stuck in petrified attitudes and prejudices. Our eyes close because we don't want to see anything that doesn't fit in with the closed system of our concepts. Every new idea or impulse is ignored or resisted.

Similarly, risk without sufficient safety is distorted into reckless and dangerous behaviour. We ignore our inner warning systems. We place trust in individuals whom it would be safer to avoid; we risk damage to ourselves with substances we would be wiser to avoid.

Although the emotions have been described in three 'families', related to three distinct polarities, our feelings (when we experience them) are often a mixture because all three polarities interact constantly with each other. Our needs are dependent on each other.

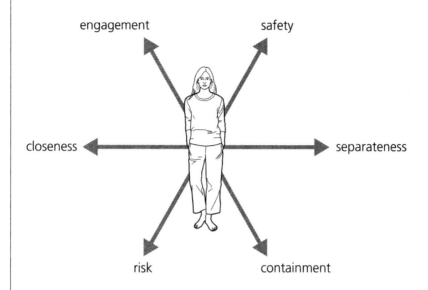

engagement safety

closeness separateness

risk containment

The three polarities

Containment, for example, is just as important to love and trust as it is to joy. Boundaries, as the left eye sees them, are not shackles or chains but provide a needed stability within which risks can be taken. Take away consistent boundaries and security is reduced so it will be hard to establish trust.

A single key event can cut across all three polarities. If your husband leaves you suddenly, after twenty years, for a younger woman, imagine the different feelings involved. There would be sadness, loss, shock and hurt because you have to deal with an ending of a close relationship. You could well feel angry or outraged (second polarity) at the unfairness of being 'dispensed' with, of having your trust betrayed, at having no choice in the matter. Then you might feel also scared of the future, worried about money, frightened of being alone (third polarity), and that's before we take into account feelings about any children involved! Even though you may feel more angry than hurt, or vice versa, at any particular time, a combination of feelings is always involved.

The main emotions – love/grief, joy/anger, trust/fear – are at the root of all feelings. Emotions are forms of primal energy that are universal. Wherever or whenever we're born, whatever kind of upbringing or cultural conditioning we have, we'll be subject to these three core emotions simply because we're human.

Feelings, on the other hand, function like satellites around the main emotions. This is because we *learn* feelings. We copy them. They come, literally, with the territory. Not every culture, for example, knows or feels jealousy or envy. Everyone experiences grief in response to death, anger in response to invasion of boundaries, fear in response to danger, but not every culture knows or feels guilt or loneliness.

This distinction is crucial for understanding the difference between anger and aggression. Anger is a universal emotion and therefore an intrinsic part of being human. Aggression, on the other hand, is a feeling that we *learn* within a monocular culture.

21

Clare lay in bed, tired but unable to fall asleep. Her head was full of thoughts about feelings and emotions and aggression and her body was churning in response to what had occurred earlier that evening.

It had been the first annual meeting for all the residents since the 'front garden' incident. Everyone had gathered, as usual, in the Hadleys' flat. As usual, too, Jane had prepared some little things to eat and other residents brought wine or cake. But the moment the Allinsons arrived, the tension had been palpable.

John Hadley acted as chair and went through the business items of the meeting. Nothing really happened until they reached Any Other Business. Mark Allinson then took an opportunity to propose that all vehicles were left in the road, not in the driveway. This was a clear though indirect reference to Moira, who staunchly challenged him: 'If you're talking about me, then address me directly,' she said.

'All right, I will. I'd like you to leave your motorbike in the road because that's where it ought to be and it's a bloody nuisance where it is.'

'But you don't have to pass by it to get to your entrance.'

'That's not the point.' Danielle Allinson joined the argument. 'It is unsightly and in the way of everybody else; it's not just us we're thinking about.'

'That was hardly in your mind when you dug up our garden,' retorted Moira.

'I don't think that's relevant,' said Danielle icily.

'It was not your garden,' said Mark.

'It belonged to everyone,' said Moira. 'You ask Ellen; she planted it all, years ago.'

Ellen was startled at being mentioned by name. Everyone looked at her. She looked helplessly at Mark, who stared at her with obvious impatience. 'I do miss the garden,' she said quietly. 'I used to enjoy looking at it every day from my window.'

'I honestly don't think there was that much to look at. You could always get some plants and put them on your windowsill,' said Danielle, in a bright and patronising tone. Clare felt herself stiffen.

'We're getting away from the point,' said Mark. 'I am talking about the motorbike.'

'*My* motorbike,' said Moira.

'Yes, your motorbike. So please would you keep it in the road where it belongs?'

'The reason I keep it where I do is because, as anyone who has a bike will tell you, if you leave it in the street, some idiot motorist will knock it over. This is why I'll carry on keeping it where it is. I always make sure that it's not in anyone's way.' Moira stopped and looked evenly at Mark.

'Well, then I shall have to move it myself,' he said threateningly.

'Over my dead body,' replied Moira, still looking him in the eye.

'Listen, everyone,' said John. 'I really think there must be some sort of compromise possible here rather than a fight. Perhaps you could talk about it later when you've both had a chance to reflect.'

'I don't need time to reflect,' said Mark. 'And I do not intend to change my mind.'

'Neither do I,' said Moira.

Everyone waited.

It was Jackie who broke the silence. 'Actually, Moira, I think it would be better if you did put it in the road, you know, because it is a bit dangerous . . . I worry sometimes that it will fall on one of the children.'

Moira looked at Jackie, open-mouthed. Clare felt for Moira. She could see the look of disbelief and betrayal on her face.

'I think Moira has a point,' Clare ventured, desperate to show some support, but Moira leapt up from her seat, holding back tears, and was out of the room and through the front door before anyone could stop her.

'She's right. Bikes do get knocked over,' Clare continued in the ensuing silence.

'But she has to take others into consideration,' said Jackie.

'Quite,' agreed Mark.

Clare didn't say any more. She was aware that they were talking about Moira as if she were a child in need of correction. She also recognised that the policy of taking others into consideration seemed to apply only when it suited one's personal needs. But she didn't have the energy to challenge the Allinsons. Was it energy she lacked? She didn't know. Perhaps she was too much of a coward.

Was this what Helen meant by aggression? It had never struck her before that this might be aggression because it wasn't violent. But it was, she now realised, a sort of bullying on the part of the Allinsons: no concern for others, doing things without consulting, overriding others' wishes and needs. There were Ellen and now Moira, both hurt in different ways, and it was easy to see Ellen's powerlessness. She was old and on her own and unable to defend her corner. Although Clare didn't know whether Moira would continue to stand up to Mark, it was clearly going to be 'war' between them.

When John closed the meeting, the Allinsons excused themselves and left. Jane popped upstairs to see how Moira was, but she'd gone out. Those who were left made an effort to chat but Clare could almost see people closing up. Everyone was a little less warm and a little more polite. This small community was now divided into two sides.

She turned over on to her other side and tried to get comfortable. For some reason she couldn't relax. Was it the tension in the house? Between Moira and the Allinsons? Clare was confused. Her mind wouldn't think clearly any more. All she knew was that she was quite deeply disturbed by it all and she didn't like that. It worried her. Sophie worried her. She stayed awake worrying for a long time before she finally fell asleep.

22

The next morning, Clare was about to leave for work when the phone rang. It was Sophie.

'I'm sorry I didn't get back to you sooner, Mum. I haven't been that well.'

'What's the matter?'

'Nothing much . . .' Sophie hesitated. 'I've been a bit down and tired, that's all.'

'Why didn't you phone and tell me?' asked Clare, uncomfortably aware of the true answer even as she asked the question.

'Oh, I don't like to talk to anyone really . . . you know what I'm like. Listen, do you want to meet? I'm back at work this week and we could get together in town sort of early evening for a coffee or something.'

'I'd like that. When would suit you?'

'Thursday. I've got to see Tricia later on but early evening's OK.'

They arranged to meet in the Cagey Parrot at 6 pm and said goodbye.

23

How the Healthy Flow of Anger Becomes the Swamp of Aggression

If we look at anger through the left eye, we see a powerful and *necessary* emotion, without which we would be unable to recognise or negotiate our own and others' boundaries: physical and psychological boundaries, social and geographical ones.

Through the left eye, anger is seen as a necessary complement to love. Love invites in, encourages closeness and merging; anger signals how far that closeness goes and limits it. Anger helps us spell out limits: 'No'; 'I don't like that': 'Don't treat me in this way'; 'Stop'; 'Back off'; ' I want to make my own choice/decision/statement'; 'Don't touch me'. Anger tells us who we are in relation to others. Through the left eye, this is a process of equal negotiation.

Unlike anger, aggression is not a fundamental energy that comes from within us: it is what we learn as a tool of self-defence whenever we are vulnerable. We learn aggression, as we learn a language, very early in life. Our experience of vulnerability is never so extreme, physically and psychologically, as when we are children.

The concept of power is pivotal to this process. Any child is lower down the ladder in terms of perpendicular power: status, age, physical power, conceptual ability, resources and expertise. Given that, for a time in our lives, we idolise those we depend on, even charisma is likely to be an aspect of adult power as well. So, a child is very low down the ladder in relation to a parent.

How is the adult going to use this power? External power is a real commodity in this world and it comes with a responsibility. It is a power we can choose to use or abuse, to manage with care, to neglect or wield with devastating effect. How we handle power will depend on how we *see* it. With binocular vision, the left eye has a chance to balance the right eye, so that two realities go together.

A binocular perspective of power

With both eyes open, imagine how we would see both kinds of power at once: different positions on the ladder *and* equal as human beings. An adult sees his or her greater power over the child, a power that is both an authority *and* a responsibility.

Power is seen in an immediate (perpendicular) context: 'Right now it is my responsibility to say no to you and you have to obey me because I have more power in this situation than you do.' It is also seen in the wider context: 'We are also human beings together and my role now in your life is to guide you. Although you can make some choices for yourself, I won't allow you a choice in this matter because you are too young to make it. If this makes you angry, it's understandable. You have the right to express your anger towards me for not giving you a choice in this, even though it won't alter my actual decision. I have to be strong enough within my own boundary to let you fight with me and be angry with me because this is how you will learn the limits of your own power and mine.'

These lines of imaginary dialogue may sound stilted and unusual because they are probably unfamiliar to our ears. This is because binocular vision has for so long been unfamiliar to our eyes.

A monocular perspective of power

This is more familiar. Close the left eye and look through the right eye exclusively. We again see the same child on the same lower rung for the same reasons as before. However, the adult now has no reference point other than the up/down framework of the ladder. He has to make the choice for the child because this is his right or duty in the superior position. The child must learn the rules of hierarchy, one of which is to submit simply because of occupying a lower position. No questions, no protests.

Any protest is unacceptable because it constitutes a threat. Threats have to be eliminated: protest has to be punished so that it will not happen again. Anger on the part of the child will be seen through the right eye as aggression and interpreted as a refusal to submit. This will progress to a conflict from which only one contender can emerge as winner. In this instance, the adult has to use whatever means are available to ensure a win.

Depending on circumstances, the child may respond by escalating the battle or submitting because of the inequality of power. However, there will always be feelings in response to this submission: powerlessness, fear, anger at the injustice, hurt and bewilderment. This is a potent emotional brew. Multiply this experience a thousand times or more and the brew becomes lethal.

If expression of feelings brings further punishment, we learn to keep quiet. But feelings don't go away. As children, we cannot rationalise or comprehend the situation because we cannot see the greater picture. Even so, we experience this huge and powerful emotion of anger (all the more huge and powerful because of our actual physical smallness) but have nowhere to express it safely. Being simultaneously so angry, vulnerable, and without the capacity for articulation, we face an unbearable psychological impasse.

How do we escape? We identify with the parent/person/adult and internalise the model of up/down in order to survive psychologically. In other words, we learn the basic rules of aggression. Win or you will lose. If you lose, you'll be hurt; so make sure you win.

Take the accumulated experience of being directly on the receiving end of aggression as a child and as an adult. Add the indirect experience of witnessing its devastating effects and the reality of being surrounded by the promotion and acceptance of aggression all around us. Top this with the fact that we have very little real understanding of our feelings anyway and it's hardly surprising that we are afraid of what we call 'anger'. It gets lost with the aggression. This is why we end up not knowing the difference.

Unfortunately, this means that our anger, that wonderful, dynamic emotion which helps us negotiate, cooperate, coexist and which, most vitally, is a huge force for change, simply goes underground. It becomes lost from view.

Vulnerability reviled

There is one particular psychological twist that affects the majority of those of us brought up in this system. Stored up anger easily converts into aggression, starting in childhood and continuing for the rest of adult life. We find an outlet, if we can, to mete out this same treatment. A child who is 'down there' at home often endeavours to be 'up there' at school. We find opportunities to hurt someone else in the same way, by rendering them powerless, in turn giving them neither voice nor choice.

But what do we do with the energy of aggression if it is unsafe or impossible for us to direct it outwards? We direct it inwards and target our own powerlessness. We blame ourselves for being vulnerable. A teenager who fears being down there in the eyes of his/her mates may lash out to establish 'superiority' in the eyes of those who matter; but a sensitive individual can crumple, become depressed, even commit suicide.

Seeing only one kind of power in place in the world teaches us to despise (and never stop despising) this state of vulnerability. Being vulnerable, we learn, equates with being powerless and these lessons make their deepest impact on us while we are naturally vulnerable as children. They create a warning for life: vulnerability must be avoided at all costs.

This is why aggression has little real relation to anger. It doesn't even come from the same core emotional source. Aggression actually belongs to the third polarity, between safety and risk, because the emotional root of aggression is not anger at all: it's *fear*.

24

Aggression in Thought, Word and Deed

Aggression is born of fear of powerlessness. This profound fear has made aggression into an immense force in our world, encouraging individuals and nations to wield power as a weapon, a weapon that variously hurts or gags, conquers or eliminates.

The following examples of aggressive behaviour are extreme but so commonplace that we wouldn't recognise the world without them: bullying, coercion, rape, emotional abuse, physical abuse, torture, sexual abuse, mutilation, murder, war, slaughter, intimidation, imprisonment, genocide, damage or violation of property or territory belonging to others, suppression of rebellion, destruction of the natural environment.

Most of us manage to avoid overtly aggressive actions but will probably channel our aggression indirectly, typically through sarcasm, deflation, put downs, excessive control, withholding information, second-hand criticism, gossip, taunts, denying rights of expression or choice, withdrawal of vital resources, manipulation, neglect of responsibility, collusion, sabotage.

With all the above examples, the force of aggression is directed towards a target outside oneself, towards someone or something else. In the following examples the target towards which the aggression is directed is *oneself*: self-mutilation, addictions, eating disorders, punishing regimes of work or diet, self-criticism, self-loathing, self-abasement, self-blame, cosmetic surgery, suicide.

Aggression makes the (monocular) world go round, so much so that it's hard to register its full impact. Some of the more extreme instances we may only hear or read about but none of us is likely to get through many ordinary days of our lives without an instance of competition, self-criticism, sarcasm, self-blame, revenge or a mild misuse of power. And even if we're not generating aggression, we're likely to be on the receiving end.

But how do you tell when you're being aggressive yourself? How can you be sure whether you're expressing anger or aggression? After all, anger can be loud and vigorous and powerful as well. The difference is that anger can be expressed and released *harmlessly*: as one equal human being to another. Unlike aggression, anger doesn't require an outside object upon which to vent itself.

Aggression, in *all* its forms, always needs an object. Once we fully understand this, we can see the difference between anger and aggression in every single transaction of our lives. As soon as the left eye closes and monocular vision takes over, other people cease to be human beings. Each person becomes a *thing*. A stereotype. A commodity. A consumer. A fuck. An obstacle. A piece of shit. A nuisance. An accessory.

The most heartbreaking aspect of this one-eyed monster is that the preoccupation with coming out on top precludes feeling, which is why aggression is often a cold-blooded, emotionless state of mind. We have to stop feeling because as soon as we allow ourselves to *feel*, the left eye opens and we see human beings, in the round. So in order to maintain a linear (ladder) perspective, mentally we must make the 'other' into an object, an 'it'.

This practice is so endemic that it has become utterly normal and ordinary; it has given rise to the invisible cult of *objectism*.

25

Objectism

The practice of objectism, like any other 'ism', is an example of oppression. In fact, objectism is a prerequisite for all the others: to treat anyone as inferior because of their gender, race, nationality or disability, first you have mentally to turn them into an object.

Objectism describes the end result of objectifying others. It is different from objectivity in the same way that the creeds of racism and sexism are a world apart from the act of distinguishing people by race or gender. Classification is one thing; applying an up/down judgement is quite another. Being objective is an aspect of compromise connected with binocular vision; objectism is the outcome of monocular vision. Objectism has become entrenched and underlies our attitudes, fantasies, language and consequently our behaviour. Whether hidden or obvious, it affects us all.

So what exactly is an object? An object is a thing. A thing has specific qualities that can be compared with those of other things. Boats and hats and cheeses and tables are examples of thousands of objects that can all be selected or rejected for their qualities. These we are happy to treat as objects. Then there is a middle area where there is disagreement. Some people talk to plants because they believe that plants and trees are more than just inanimate objects, while others consider this attitude eccentric.

Cattle are chosen for their breeding or milking qualities or their suitability for producing a profitable supply of meat. Here a degree of objectism is acceptable but, every now and then, we are made to feel uncomfortable. Television images of the abysmal conditions of the factory-farming of chickens or pigs and the scale of the more extreme and unnecessary slaughter touch something in many people who don't normally give much thought to the welfare of farm animals. Faced with shocking images, it is impossible to keep denying the reality that animals are regarded as disposable objects in a disposable world.

The perpendicular ladder is crucial because the relationship of subject to object implies an upper to lower position – never equal. Human slaves were selected for qualities of strength and health, like cattle, so that they would serve their owners well with their labour.

Before we can treat humans as objects, albeit useful or hard-working ones, we have to think of them as objects. Before we can think of humans as bestial, we have to *see* them as bestial. This is an example of the extraordinary power of monocular vision. How you see something is how you treat it: if it is lower down, you treat it accordingly. If it behaves as it should, all is fine. If it protests or disobeys or threatens your assumption of superiority, you discipline, punish or get rid of 'it'.

Depending on right-eye categorisation, an object is negative or positive. If positive, it becomes an object of desire, invested by the desirer with the power of beauty or glamour or symbolic of prestige or status. We learn to desire an object because we learn to associate certain objects with an image of power. We seek (and are sold) good, desirable (because powerful) images and reject bad, undesirable (because powerless) images.

In this way, manufacturers of diamond jewellery, cars, stereo equipment, designer clothes, watches – to give just a few examples – have created markets to convince consumers that such objects are associated with status and wealth, through specially contrived images of power that are used repeatedly in advertising. Without the belief, there would be no market.

One essential aspect of an object is that whether it is desired or rejected will depend on the whims of external judgement. Therefore, in the eyes of the viewer, an object has *no inner existence*. This is an important feature of the practice of objectism. An object has nothing abiding within, no permanent qualities unique to itself, no intricacy, no choice, no 'subjecthood'. It is just a thing. A thing is a thing, not a self.

This remains unchanged by labels of negative or positive. Whether you are a desirable or undesirable accessory, a 'goddess' or a 'slut', you still remain an object, beautiful or ugly, attractive or repulsive. A delicacy on one man's plate will be repugnant to another. The object doesn't change, just the viewer's eye.

What makes us blind to someone as a whole person, seeing only what we want to see? Part of the answer is our own past experience. We all treat others as objects at times because, somewhere along the line, we have been treated as objects ourselves. A woman who has been raped describes feeling like a soiled object. A patient in an overcrowded hospital ward complains of being treated like a body, not a human being. A long-term employee who is sacked in an unfair and inhumane manner resents being dispensed with like a thing, not a person.

As we learn the language of aggression, we are taught its main grammatical rule: aggression always needs an object. So when we get desperate, when we feel threatened, when we want to avoid powerlessness, we use others as props or scapegoats, appendages or whipping posts. At the time, we think only of our own needs and, looking resolutely through the right eye, we discount the other person. We block out what we don't want to see. We have to. If we were to see equality, we would behave differently. But we close off the other as human being, temporarily making them non-existent. He or she becomes an 'it'.

Bosnians and Serbs, Shi'ites and Muslims, Protestant and Catholics, Indians and Pakistanis, colleagues in the same office, members of the same family, can all interact harmoniously for years as human beings – in the round – until aggression contaminates the emotional climate. The label is fixed in the context of the opposing side. The object becomes the enemy in sport or war, in business or law.

Neighbours, friends, customers, relatives, colleagues, who were previously seen as *people*, are then set against each other in a struggle for power. Power may be access to economic advantages, promotion within an organisational structure, political survival or often sheer physical survival. The multifaceted possibility of human relationship is diminished to instant and defensive surface assessment. The whole person becomes identified by one aspect and thus becomes an object.

This happens even in intimate relationships. How many partners are left bewildered when years of commitment, concern and cooperation suddenly seem to change overnight when one party leaves? The one left behind feels less than human, a failure, rejected as a not-good-enough object or one now past its sell-by date.

Of course, relationships of all kinds often reach a point when it is time to move on, when what initially drew two people together has evaporated. The sinister effect of objectism is that, through the right eye, we avoid what we don't want to face or deal with. We trash the relationship ('it never meant anything anyway') or trash the other person ('you were always hopeless in bed'), denying any love or responsibility. This is to avoid feeling the pain of separation or the fear of moving on without sufficient 'leverage'.

With the left eye open as well, you would see the person in the round. You may still decide that, for you, the time has come for a separation but if you see a human being in front of you, you behave differently. This eye shows you two equal human beings. You see that, whatever the current problems and dissatisfactions, responsibility must be *equal*.

The right eye sees differently. We seek an object to blame. Aggression fuels battles about maintenance and custody because we are intent on winning instead of losing.

The bottom line is that looking through the left eye, we would inevitably *feel* something. We would care. This is precisely what we don't want. We want to avoid the need to feel – regret, concern, sorrow, anger, fear, even a sense of failure – all those things we experience naturally as human beings at times of significant change. Feeling would mean being vulnerable.

The mainstays of objectism

There are four kinds of behaviour which sit, like carriage lamps, on each corner of the vehicle of objectism as it conveys the forces of aggression around the world. These are labelling, fragmenting, denial and splitting.

Labelling

Labels help us to distance ourselves from the other person. They can be neutral – she's just a secretary, he's the boss; derogatory – she's a tart, he's a loser; or positive – she's a cracker, he's what I've been looking for. As soon as you label someone, you know you are looking through the right eye.

The person becomes one-dimensional. The 'beggar' on the street makes us feel uncomfortable; the child is a 'nuisance' and irritates; the friend is a 'drain' and exasperates; the husband who is a 'bore' or the wife who is a 'nag' cause resentment; the daughter is a 'problem', making life difficult.

Labels help us to distance ourselves from the whole.

Fragmenting

Using labels leads to the practice of fragmentation. This furthers the practice of objectism in two ways. First, it reduces the *power* of the other. If you reduce anything into its constituent parts, it cannot function as a whole, reminiscent of the 'divide and rule' policy of government.

First, isolate the fragment from the whole: for example, skin colour, dress, age, uniform, size of breasts, political or sexual orientation. Then assess it on an up/down scale. The corresponding positive or negative fragment can be easily used to maintain the object as desirable or otherwise as in 'a bit of all right', 'Paki git', 'cunt', 'terrorist', 'wrinkly', 'faggot', 'nigger' or 'shag'.

Denial and splitting

When the right eye shows us evidence of a quality (fragment) that is labelled undesirable in *ourselves* – vulnerability, inadequacy, envy, ugliness, dependence, powerlessness, stupidity, loneliness, timidity, disability – it causes us distress. We often respond by splitting off, in our minds, the offending fragment so that it is isolated from the whole, thereby reducing its potential for causing emotional havoc.

Our minds come up with all sorts of ingenious solutions for dealing with this unwanted split-off part. The most common ploy is to conceal it — certainly from others and possibly from ourselves. We deny its existence. Sometimes we manage to disown it completely. If it rattles the door of its hiding place and causes disquiet, we can always divert attention by identifying this quality in other individuals and becoming extremely critical and intolerant of anyone who mirrors our unwanted fragments back to us.

It is well known as a dynamic of therapy that we have first to embrace rather than reject any aspect of ourselves that we wish to change, in other words to reconnect the split-off part to the whole.

The attraction of continuing denial is we can continue to suppress our feelings and risk vulnerability. The right eye encourages us to deny our own wholeness so we deny it in others as a consequence. With the left eye resolutely closed, these four strategies enable objectism to flourish.

26

The Cagey Parrot was humming. It had a predominantly young clientele, but not so much that Clare felt out of place. She ordered a glass of house red, feeling the need for a little alcohol even though she had to drive home.

Sophie, as ever, was late. It was almost 6.30 when Clare saw her crossing the street and running towards the café. Her heart leapt at the sight of her daughter. She looked so thin and fragile. She arrived and greeted her mother with a kiss on the cheek and an apology. Her short-cropped bleached blond hair emphasised her hazel eyes as she looked squarely at Clare. 'What time did we agree?'

'Six o'clock,' Clare answered.

'Oh dear, I'm later than I thought then. Sorry.'

'Don't worry. What are you going to have?'

'Um, an espresso please.'

A waitress appeared and Clare placed the order.

Sophie was wearing a baggy beige jumper with a flower pattern around the hem that Clare recognised from years ago. 'You've had that jumper a while, haven't you? I remember it from Morton Road.'

'I know,' Sophie agreed. 'It's one of those things I can't bring myself to throw out. I expect it looks terrible but it's still warm and I'm very fond of it.'

'How have you been, Soph?' Clare's concern was evident in her tone.

A short pause. Sophie looked down at the table.

'I don't know, really. I've been a bit run down, that's all, but I'm on the up again.'

'What's the matter? Have you been to the doctor?'

'No, course not. They can't help,' said Sophie, with more than a touch of impatience.

The espresso arrived.

Clare took a sip from her now almost empty glass and wished she hadn't brought the car. 'Look, Sophie, we haven't got long if you've got to go out later. I don't want to push you to talk if you don't want to but I am concerned about you, obviously. You look as if you've lost weight again and . . .' She stopped as Sophie bristled visibly.

'Don't start, Mum. *Please.*'

Clare saw her eyes filling with tears; her own eyes prickled with tears in automatic response. 'What's the *matter*, Soph, love?' She reached across the table and touched her daughter's hand. Sophie didn't respond but she didn't move her hand away. They sat there like that for a couple of minutes, in silence, Clare looking at Sophie and Sophie looking at the table top, tears trickling down her face.

Sophie shook her head. 'It's no good, Mum. I can't talk about it. Not because it's you, it's just that I can't seem to find the words.'

'Is it Phil? Is something wrong there?'

'No, Mum,' Sophie sighed. 'Phil's OK, as OK as he'll ever be anyway. It's not him and it's not work either. It's nothing in particular. I just don't feel like doing anything. Haven't got the energy. I feel sad all the time; I cry a lot for no reason. I did go to the doctor a few weeks ago and she gave me anti-depressants which I hated. They made me feel sick and completely out of it so I ended up throwing them down the toilet.'

'Why didn't you go back and tell her and get something else?' Clare asked.

'There's no point, Mum. They haven't got the first clue about anything. She actually asked me if I'd like to make an appointment to see the counsellor. But I know, from before, that counsellors are hopeless. They don't listen: they sit there and look sympathetic but they don't *listen*. They seem to have some ideas of their own already in their heads that you have to fit into.'

'Well, you've got to see someone, love. You can't go on like this. Have you thought of giving Angie a ring? She'd know of someone who knew what they were doing.'

Sophie shook her head and drank her tiny cup of lukewarm coffee. She saw the clock on the wall and looked startled. 'Is that the time already? I've got to go soon, Mum. I'm meant to be going to Tricia's for supper. She's had a baby, a little boy, you know. She and Gary split up but she seems really happy.' She stopped. 'How are *you*, Mum, anyway? I haven't even asked how you are.'

Clare told her about starting to work with Helen. This was really her only news.

'What does she write about?' asked Sophie.

'Difficult to say. It's basically psychology, I suppose, but very easy-to-read stuff. I can understand it anyway. I find it interesting because it makes me think about things I've never considered before. You might find it interesting yourself.'

'Maybe I'll have a look when I come round some time,' said Sophie. She started to look for her purse.

'It's my treat,' said Clare, though not much of one, she thought to herself.

'Are you sure?'

'Yes. If you're in a hurry, you go and I'll wait to get the bill.'

Sophie kissed her mother on the cheek and said goodbye. Clare watched as she left, feeling very sad and helpless.

27

She drove home, continuing to feel sad and helpless. She poured herself another glass of wine and put a frozen pizza into the microwave with little relish at the prospect of eating it. There was a message from Angie on the machine. The tone of Angie's voice was uncharacteristically subdued, as if she were really disappointed that Clare hadn't been in. Clare tried to call her but there was no reply.

She settled in front of the TV with her supper. Apart from cooking or gardening there was only a documentary about child prostitution in south-east Asia. She started eating with little appetite and, as she watched the programme, she found she was even less hungry.

Someone, under the guise of being a punter, had smuggled a hidden camera into the compounds where these little girls were housed and kept. All aged between eight and eleven, they looked so sweet and so young. Clare found herself frowning with bewilderment at the possibility of actually seeing these little girls as *sexual*.

They showed one man, an ex-headmaster from England, who had been caught making pornographic movies with young girls. Apparently, he had tried to bribe the officials as every other man did – to avoid jail – but his bribe had been too small so he was now imprisoned.

The whole trade was maintained by Western male tourists on the buying end, who wanted sex without the risk of Aids, and impoverished parents who, in exchange for their daughters, were paid money they desperately needed to live on. In between were the agents earning their fortunes.

They really were objects, she thought, those little girls. To everyone involved. The reporter seemed to be genuinely appalled at what he had found and also that there was no indication of what could be done. Trade, after all, was trade. Customers with the money and eagerness to pay for unspoiled goods ensured booming business. Booming business seemed to be the acme of life, mused

Clare. As she registered this thought, she wondered whether reading Helen's words was making her more cynical.

She threw the half-eaten pizza away, thought about the dishwasher and then decided to wash up what little there was by hand. As she was doing this, Angie called, phoning on her car phone so Clare couldn't hear very well. Angie asked if she could come round. 'What, *now?*' said Clare, seeing from the clock that it was already 9.20.

'Is it too late?' asked Angie. 'I can be there in twenty minutes . . . I won't stay long.'

'No, it's not too late. I was just surprised but it's fine. I'll see you soon.'

Clare went back to finish clearing up, wondering what on earth could be wrong. Angie tended not to let things get her down. She'd certainly been through difficult times. Her first marriage had been a mistake and didn't make its first anniversary. Her second husband, Derek, whom Clare had known and liked, had become an alcoholic. Angie had struggled with this for years before finally giving him an ultimatum. He chose to continue drinking; she chose to separate.

She'd also had problems with pregnancy. While married to Derek, she'd had two miscarriages and then never conceived again. Now, of course, on the rare occasions it ever came up in conversation, Angie would declare her lack of children to be a 'good thing', considering her feckless husbands and her unsuitability to be a single parent, but Clare suspected that, deep down, the sadness was still there, even though Angie's lifestyle was quite different to Clare's own. Whereas Clare felt she tended towards sexual apathy after Len's death, Angie had always been more outgoing and adventurous. She was so much more forthright than Clare but their differences didn't seem to weaken the bond between the two friends.

28

A little while later, Angie arrived. She said she just wanted a cup of tea – which was unusual – so Clare switched on the kettle.

They chatted about nothing in particular and then went to sit down in Clare's front room.

'Clare, do you mind if I have a cigarette? I really need one.'

'Heavens, things must be bad. I'll go and get the ashtray.' She came back, put it next to Angie and opened the window slightly. 'You haven't smoked in years,' said Clare.

'I know. I bought a packet on the way here. I promise I'll *only* have one, and if I need another I'll go outside the front door.'

'What on earth's happened?'

Angie lit her cigarette. 'Well, it's something at work, which happened this afternoon. It really upset me and I don't know what to do about it. I needed to talk to someone. That's why I called you.'

Clare listened.

'I was giving a lecture – second-year psychology class – I'd left about fifteen minutes for questions. I answered one question and then Brian McCarthy – he's the new protégé of the Dean – who'd been sitting in on my lecture, put his hand up. He asked if he could come up and put something on the board because his question would then be clearer to everybody.

'I wasn't at all sure what he was going to do but I agreed, so up he came and, as he did, I saw he was carrying a roll of paper. He stood by the board, attached the paper and then proceeded to give a mini-lecture . . . all of his own! I couldn't believe what was happening. Not only was he taking over my role but he was contradicting a lot of what I'd just been saying.'

'What a cheek,' said Clare.

Angie gave a little snort of agreement. 'I mean, he could have contradicted from where he sat – I wouldn't have minded that because it's all part of a discussion – but actually to come up and stand there and take over . . . I was speechless.'

'Didn't you say *anything*?' asked Clare, knowing Angie could be very forthright when she wanted to be.

'No. Not a *word*. And that's the bit that I've been crucifying myself with since. I don't know why or how but I just stood there and let the whole thing happen. He ended his own lecture and looked at me for a response, but by then we'd run out of time so I dismissed the students. He came up to me as I was packing up my things and said, "I hope you didn't mind me doing that?" but I was too choked to reply. I couldn't even look at him in the eye, Clare. Isn't that awful? I feel so embarrassed.'

'Embarrassed? Why?'

'Because I said nothing. I went to the staff room, simmering inside, and a colleague was there so I told her what had happened and her response was, "You'd never get that happening to a male lecturer. They wouldn't have the nerve." And I think she's right but there's no comfort in that, for me.'

'Because . . . ?' asked Clare.

'Because it's not the point. I've been thinking about it all for hours now. I sat in my office not knowing what to do with myself. It's really made me see the whole picture at work in a different context, I suppose.' She flicked some ash from her cigarette. 'You know, I'm sure that Brian is after my job. I've had a feeling for a while and put it down to paranoia but I'm sure there's something going on. Nobody says anything, of course, but each term they keep increasing my workload a little more. Just a little extra, they say, but I'm sure they're pushing me to a limit that they hope will finish me, you know, that'll force me to a place where I simply cannot cope so I'll opt for early retirement.'

'You really think that's what's going on?'

'Yes, I do. It made me think of Suzie Thomkins. Do you remember her?'

Clare nodded.

'She got really high up, you know, assistant director of Social Services. She completely dedicated her life to her career. We bumped into each other at a conference a month ago and she was about to quit! She said that they kept building up pressure on her and then, when the director's job was coming up, she'd heard that someone with very little experience was to get the job. There was no question of her being incompetent. She was the wrong gender at the wrong age. She was devastated by it all.'

'I certainly remember that happening at school: the head of Drama was ousted by a young man with virtually no experience. But I can't believe it's only women, Angie.'

'Well, let's just say that as women get older they are less likely to achieve the senior posts that men seem to occupy, regardless of age. I honestly believe that older – middle aged – women are not wanted, however competent, hard-working or dedicated they may be.'

She stubbed out her cigarette and looked at Clare. 'I really do think women in middle age are increasingly vulnerable. You know, we give our all, we're committed, we work hard – I've just thought of another woman this happened to – and there's a subtle increase in pressure of workload . . . and it never lets up. It takes its toll. You see younger men being encouraged and valued, even promoted over you: you see the writing on the wall.'

Angie stopped and shook her head. 'I don't know. There's nothing we can do about it.' She paused. 'You know, Clare, what gets me more than anything, right now, is my own silence. That's what infuriates me. I can't believe I said nothing. Why didn't I say, "Excuse me, you're out of order," or something? *Anything*. What stopped me?'

'I don't know,' ventured Clare, who privately was also surprised that Angie had said nothing.

'I've been trying to understand it. If I saw anyone else behaving like I had, I'd say they were lacking in confidence.' She caught Clare's eye. 'I know, you don't associate me with lack of confidence but in that situation, when you're feeling undermined generally by the department, and insecure, it makes a little more sense, doesn't it?' Angie smiled at Clare. 'I'm trying to make myself feel better by finding a reason for it.'

'It makes a lot of sense,' agreed Clare.

'I've never really thought of myself as a feminist, but it makes you wonder. I really don't think I'm paranoid any more. In fact, I know I'm not.'

'Are you going to say anything to him?'

'To Brian? I don't know. It wouldn't make any difference.'

'Well, you could tell him what you thought.'

'I could,' said Angie doubtfully.

'Why are you being like this, Angie?' said Clare suddenly. 'I'm the one who's usually too anxious to rock the boat, not you.'

'I know. I'm surprised myself. I think it's because I'm still too shocked by my response. I don't understand it yet. It's more than just lacking confidence. There's something else . . . perhaps there's a dormant cavewoman gene in me that still *expects* to be treated like that, you know, a genetic throwback that suddenly kicked into gear and had me behaving in a way that my normal self would be appalled by.' Angie laughed. 'I *hate* it, Clare. I really hate my subservience to that little upstart!'

Clare smiled. 'It sneaked out before you could stop it.'

'It certainly did,' said Angie. She gave a big sigh. 'It's good to talk about it. You're great, Clare.'

Clare looked surprised. 'I've done nothing,' she said.

'You've listened and cared. That's what it's all about,' said Angie, giving Clare a warm smile.

Angie announced she was going outside for her second (and positively last) cigarette. When she came back, Clare asked: 'Would you like a drink now, a real one?'

'I'd love one.'

As Clare looked in the cupboard, Angie asked about the new job and wanted to know what Helen was like to work for. Clare then told Angie of her concern and sadness about Sophie. They talked for a long time, so Angie ended up staying the night.

29

Helen's car was missing when Clare arrived. For a moment uncertain, she checked that she'd got the right day and the right time. She had. She'd no idea where Helen was but she was happy to wander round and wait in the peace of the garden. It was a lovely morning, gentle and warm.

She was still thinking about Angie's story from the night before. It brought back memories of her own last years of teaching. There had always been individual members of staff who thought only of their own careers, but the general atmosphere had been coopera-tive. People used to help each other out. Despite the perennial horrors and villains, there'd been a climate of tolerance, humour and a real sympathy. This generated a feeling of camaraderie in the staff room that she felt had completely disappeared by the time she retired.

The change at school had been gradual. She had hated the way the children had become less important as individuals while the numbers of passes and high grades – statistics really – became the priority. Members of staff started to watch their backs, trying to ensure the survival of their own departments. She'd felt very uncomfortable with the ruthlessness of some of her colleagues . . . and their dishonesty. This was when she started to lose confidence.

Everyone complained about the workload and impossible dead-lines; inspections and the incessant fault-finding of those governmental reports took a huge toll on morale. Suddenly she remembered Tim. Her heart dropped and she felt very sad. She'd liked Tim. There hadn't really been anything to dislike about him. Committed, enthusiastic, a real vocational teacher. He loved the kids and loved the job and was very good at it. He wasn't even thirty, she remembered. He'd committed suicide by taking an overdose, a couple of days before an inspection. He'd told Julie, his wife, that he was sick to death with worry about failing. Clare had been completely shocked. She had talked about it with another colleague who also felt terrible, especially since Tim had been talking to her about the inspection a few days before his death and she felt she hadn't given him enough time. She'd been too busy with everything else.

Tim had been with the school five years and many of his pupils were devastated. It had been one of those final straws for Clare, listening to the headmaster talk about Tim's death. He had spoken a few kind and predictable words at the assembly and then briefly addressed the teachers in the staff room, to boost 'morale'. 'Of course, it's a tragedy,' he said, 'but you do have to be able to cope with the stress of this job and, unfortunately, Tim just couldn't handle the pressure. It's not at all productive to start thinking we could have done something to avoid it. He was probably the wrong sort of person for this kind of job so we mustn't blame ourselves. It is sad, I know, but we simply have to get on with our lives.'

The sheer heartlessness of his words had made Clare very angry, an emotion she couldn't identify in herself very often, even after reading Helen's pages. She didn't say anything because she knew it was pointless. There were too many others who shared his attitude.

She remembered taking to her bed with back pain. She'd been in so much pain those last six months of school, actually having to take days off, which, for her, had previously been unheard of. A specialist had diagnosed a slipped disc and suggested physiotherapy and exercises. She'd relied on painkillers to mask the pain sufficiently for her to carry on. On that particular day, thinking about Tim and the tragedy of it all, she had lain in bed in agony and had finally reached her decision to opt for early retirement.

She heard the sound of Helen's car in the driveway.

'I'm so sorry,' said Helen as she got out of her car. 'I had to go to the vet unexpectedly and I thought I'd be able to get there and back by the time you arrived. That's why I didn't phone you.'

'It doesn't matter,' said Clare. 'I've enjoyed wandering round here. Was it anything serious?'

Helen opened the front door. 'Oh, no, not really. Just his ongoing ear problem. Look, Clare, how are you placed for time? Do you have any flexibility the other end? We're obviously going to be starting late and I'm desperate for a coffee first . . . '

'That's fine,' said Clare. She followed Helen into the kitchen and sat down. Helen did seem a bit distraught. Clare didn't say anything while Helen prepared the coffee but, when it was ready, Helen suggested they sit in the garden before rushing to start work. Helen sat for a minute, maybe two, without saying anything at all, giving a deep sigh and gazing ahead.

Although this struck Clare as unusual, she didn't feel uncomfortable with the silence at all. She quite admired Helen's ability just to sit and compose herself, without feeling she had to speak.

'That's better,' Helen said eventually. 'I'll be ready to start in a few minutes.'

'Can I ask a question?' asked Clare tentatively.

Helen looked at her. 'Of course.'

'It's about the left-eye/right-eye vision. If we get so used to looking through the right eye, how do we really know when we are looking through the other eye, the left eye?'

'For one thing, it has a different quality to it, simply because it is not exclusive. It's both a distinct way of seeing things and, because of its very nature, it allows the other vision to exist alongside. So it's inclusive . . . more democratic, if you like.'

Clare listened so Helen continued. 'But in terms of what you actually *see* through this eye, apart from its "attitude", there are clear distinctions. You can take anything – food, politics, education, medicine, money, sex, the natural world – and compare the views from each eye because there will be two ways of seeing. But then we find that the right eye dominates because it needs to be exclusive and has designated its own view as the *only* view.

'So what I'm trying to do is to prompt, or reawaken, if you like, our awareness of the vision through the left eye, because this has been eclipsed. It's not that we don't see through this eye – it's that we either don't register it or ignore it or pretend we haven't seen what we've seen. We've got so used to living our lives through the view of the right eye that we treat anything else we see as inferior, silly or childish. We tell ourselves it's nonsense.'

Clare was fascinated. When Helen spoke she was quite compelling. Clare sensed somehow that what she said seemed to come from a place somewhere deep inside, and was not just words out of her mouth. She was glad she'd asked.

'Is it really true that we are born with binocular vision?'

'Yes. I found this out from a visit to my optician. He explained it all when I asked him why the right eye so often becomes the dominant one. It is connected to why we usually become right-handed but he said the answer lay deep in the workings of the brain. Apparently, the brain starts relying more on one image than the other. It then selects the clearer image of the two and this becomes habitual. It doesn't suppress the image of the weaker eye for a while; it continues to fuse and create binocular vision unless and until one image becomes so weak that the brain eventually shuts it out. The vision becomes what they call "amblyopic", but I coined the word "monocular" because it adds a whole new dimension!'

Clare smiled at Helen's obvious delight in her discovery.

Helen got up. 'Are we ready to start work?'

30

Sexuality – How Do We See It?

Sexuality provides a useful illustration of the different character-istics of right- and left-eye vision. Whatever our individual experience, there are norms and general assumptions – certain 'givens' about sexuality – that we tend to take for granted. Identifying these will give us an idea of the extent of monocular influence.

The popular view

Let's start with the definition of the word. Sex is generally under-stood to describe what we do, as if the word sexuality were a condensed form of *sexual* activity. In other words, the emphasis is almost exclusively on *doing*; it implies engagement in some kind of sexual activity, solo or with others. It then follows that one is sexual only when doing something sexual with a (real or fantasy) partner.

The emphasis on activity leads inevitably to the how/what/when – the mechanics – of sexual performance. How frequently do you have sex? How long does it take you to have an orgasm? How long can you sustain an erection? Can you get an erection in the first place? How many times a night, the range of your repertoire, whether or not you are a satisfactory lover or doing it 'right' are all typical concerns. Within sexual activity itself, we find the implicit goal of orgasm for at least one of the people involved. We assume a well-defined (linear) path of progress from cold through warm to hot: foreplay to serious stuff to bingo!

The up/down positioning of sexual status is very visible. Heterosexual is higher than homosexual in the culture at large. The young and beautiful occupy higher rungs than the older (shouldn't they be past that sort of thing by now?) brigade. Orgasm is higher than no-orgasm but mind-bending multi-orgasms attain higher standing than damp squibs. More frequent and a longer duration of intercourse are placed over less and shorter. This is before we even touch on the relentless cultural preoccupation with penis size, constituting a ladder unto itself.

Another clue to monocular influence is the use of sexual labels. Permanent fixed labels of either hetero- or homosexual are defined by the gender of the *other* with whom one engages in sexual activity. These labels convey up/down status: normal/deviant; right/wrong; natural/unnatural. Whenever we feel uncomfortable about sexual relations between two people who are elderly, perhaps, or whose intellect is considered to be inadequate, we uncover the presence of a fixed frame of reference for entitlement to sexual activity.

The ingrained habit of dualism – for example, men need sex/women need love or men are naturally polygamous/ women are naturally monogamous – provides another clue to the influence of the right eye. Women's sexual stereotypes have been split into Madonna and Eve since that famous first occasion in the Garden and, even though women's sexual expression has undergone enormous change, women (as Eve) are still subject to the charge of being irresistible and dangerous temptresses. The most popular and effective rationale for coercing a woman into unwanted sexual activity remains 'look what *you've* done' and the often-cited argument in defence of rape – 'but look what she was wearing/how she was behaving' – shows Eve's influence is alive and well.

The practice of fragmentation is generic: when it comes to sexual stimulation, it is easy to assume our genitals are the only parts of our bodies with any nerve endings. Within the genital fragment, we find another incidence of upper/lower status: the penis enjoys a higher profile than … what? The 'vagina'? The 'vulva'? The lower status of this particular fragment accounts for the difficulty in finding a label that is neither anatomically incorrect nor socially offensive.

We respond to clear, if unwritten, rules and goals that determine our sexual activity. A great deal of behavioural sex therapy deliberately concentrates on 'sensate focus' (more akin to the left eye) when problems occur with following these rules. This approach guides a couple to bring the rest of their bodies into the sensual/sexual experience so as to bypass the pressure of the goal of intercourse and orgasm. However, this is regarded as a therapeutic and *temporary* measure before 'normal' relations can be resumed.

Many clients and their sex therapists still assume that sexual problems, described variously as 'lack of arousal', 'lack of orgasm' or 'lack of sexual interest', are isolated from the whole of our relationship to our bodies, our emotions and the rest of our lives. Dysfunction of the higher-profile fragment is treated as mechanical failure. With drugs like Viagra now available, the fault in the equipment can be remedied without reference to any other aspect of a man's life – stress, emotions, work, relationship problems or outside pressures – or even possible risks to other parts of his body (his cardiovascular system, for example).

There is widespread exposure in magazines, television and the internet to ways of improving and enhancing sexual technique and performance. Women's sexual pleasure has become an equally important goal to men's, which marks a huge shift in social thinking over the last hundred years. The former prime objective of a man's release has disappeared from sex manuals, and, in California, lessons, with the aid of plastic genitalia, are now available for young men to practise their technique of cunnilingus. Soon it will be possible to resort to an electronic implant that is said to deliver the 'ultimate' experience for women who have difficulty 'achieving' the goal of orgasm naturally. At the touch of a remote control button, 'the device provides sexual ecstasy without the hassle of sex'. Despite the shifts of social change, the monocular mindset – mechanics split off from the context – continues to dominate.

A further split occurs between sexual activity and the rest of life. A man with public responsibilities may need to dress up in baby clothes or pay a prostitute to throw grapefruit between his legs to obtain his sexual release but this isn't considered in *any* way an adverse reflection on his ability to administer judicial, clerical, educational or governmental power. Until very recently, even paedophile practices were seen as a man's private affair and completely irrelevant to his suitability for employment in a position of authority over children.

The power of monocular vision is such that we believe there is only one way of looking at sexuality. We hardly ever question it or take the time to ask ourselves what we believe and why. Through a combined process of actual experiences and what we absorb from our culture, we all come to accept certain norms, which harden like concrete over time. So the assumptions which govern our behaviour – what constitutes a sexual encounter; how long it should last; the differences in sexual response between men and women; the relevance of masturbation; the relationship of emotion to sex; the role of fantasy – are never questioned. The right eye rules OK.

31

A Different Perspective

The usual way most of us discover an alternative is when we find ourselves feeling inadequate in the prevailing sexual culture. This can be prompted by physical disability or injury when we suddenly have to rethink and adapt to different circumstances. It can also be in response to an ongoing sense of not fitting in to the mould.

As anyone who has attended a sexuality group will know, there is an important moment when participants realise – through sharing their personal thoughts, experiences and needs – that they are not alone. In this way, the participants discover the existence of a distinct model of sexuality, which, though hidden, has definitely shaped their expectations and attitudes towards themselves and their partners.

When we see that our sense of 'difference' is not just a personal aberration but a common condition, it means that, somewhere, there has to be *another* way of looking at sex and sexuality, even if we are hard-pushed to say what it is.

If we were to open the left eye as well, how would the picture change? First of all, we would see sexuality as a *state*, as a permanent aspect of being, whether or not there is any current activity or partner. We would define sexuality as an intrinsic facet of a person, regardless of appearance, age or sexual status.

The left eye perceives sexuality as an integral part of the rest of human life. It is one aspect of our power and our emotionality. Sexuality appears within a context of sensuality and eroticism: an energy which exists in us all the time that can be expressed in many ways, sometimes in activity, sometimes in loving, sometimes in creative form. From this perspective, we are sexual beings even if we are not *doing* anything sexually. Sexuality exists as a potential to be experienced as a subdued or dominant force in our lives depending on change and circumstance and choice.

We see that sexual desire and arousal are subject to cycles that fluctuate, not only from day to day and month to month but even while actually making love. This offers a strong contrast to a system where the goal of orgasm and a fixed directional activity make it virtually impossible to 'change your mind' once you've pressed the start button.

If this model sounds rather vague and dreamlike, it is because here, in contrast, the whole concept of sexuality is more fluid, more abstract and less concrete. Not preoccupied with mechanics and performance, it describes an experience in which the whole body participates. Seen through this eye, sexual and physical release is connected with meeting emotional and spiritual needs as well.

Although at first sight this view of sexuality appears gentler, the power of sexual experience is undiminished. Sex is, after all, a force that compels us for many reasons. It pushes us to the limits of our physicality. We can experience out-of-the-body sensations and moments of fusion with another human being through sexual experience which undoubtedly evoke primal feelings and spiritual longings. Sexual activity is one of the ways in which we are able, as humans, to experience our physical limits and transcend them.

We find that experience of sexual fantasy can also involve abstract images of colour and sound, emanating from the experience of being totally absorbed within the sexual activity itself. This body-mind experience is quite different from the mainstream definition of sexual fantasy that infuses all forms of pornography.

The dominant right-eye approach to sexuality is most starkly obvious where pornography is concerned. Statutory ingredients are an absence of context or care; sexual activity is mechanistic; there is a linear goal and an almost exclusive focus on genitals, either huge and thrusting or wet but decorous, depending whether they belong to a male or a female.

The connecting theme from frame to frame in film after film is sexual conquest and the cult of the object. This theme is reflected in millions and millions of images in hard- and soft-core videos, 'girlie' magazines, literary texts and the 'normal' media.

Opening the left eye adds a different dimension to the nuts and bolts of sexual activity. What is missing from pornography? Humour, talking together, wrong turns, wrinkles, semi-erections, spare tyres, bald heads, stops and starts, giggles and farts, and most importantly, affection and care. The left eye provides the human facets of sexual experience. Binocular vision shows us an image of sexuality in the round.

32

'Are you sure you're able to stay on?' asked Helen.

'Yes.' Clare looked at her watch. 'I can certainly do another hour.' She hesitated. 'If there's time – after we finish – today, I'd like to have a quick word with you about my daughter, Sophie. Would you mind?'

'Not at all. Let's get the next two chapters done and then we can stop.'

33

Objectism v. Intimacy

Within a monocular system, where acquiring power is highly competitive, with a winner or loser, sex has become a marketable commodity and a desirable goal in itself. Sexual power is a sought-after commodity as an important aspect of external status: having a sexual partner or making a sexual conquest illustrates 'pulling' power (over others). We are persuaded that those who have access to sex are powerful: able-bodied, young, beautiful, heterosexual, wealthy. Those without access – the aged, the unattractive, the disabled, the sad – are consequently powerless.

Pulling power will depend on being sexually desirable; we

have to attract a sexual partner who will prove our sexual viability. The cult of objectism thrives. With the possibility of sexual conquest in mind, we objectify others. Every time we isolate the 'mega tits' or 'nice arse', we fragment the whole body/person into its parts. We regard our own bodies as objects too.

Sexual activity then becomes split off from a context of care, let alone love. By choice and by mutual consent, sexual activity is experienced in isolation from our emotional needs for safety, trust or affection: we deny them for the sake of sexual conquest. As with the attainment of any other kind of perpendicular power, sexual conquest admits no vulnerability.

When we develop a taste for any kind of perpendicular power, we get greedy. We get addicted to the quest for 'more and more, bigger and better'. This applies equally to acquisition of possessions and status symbols as well as to intensification of bodily experiences. Sexual stimulus is like any other ladder: the highest rungs are always just beyond reach. There are always higher/ bigger/better possibilities of orgasm to be reached with the aid of exotic, tantric, sado-masochistic, drug-enhanced or fetishist practices.

In an interview during a recent TV documentary about the pornography industry in California, one successful mogul described how his sexual tastes kept pushing the barriers. He refused to have his face filmed because he didn't want to risk his wife and family finding out about this (denied and split-off) part of his life.

He candidly acknowledged that, having run the gamut of sadistic practices with women and pushing his young actors and actresses ever further and further, he found that he could only get a *real* high now by strangling a young woman at the same time as fucking her. He went on to describe the thrill of feeling his hands around her neck and the power of knowing he could actually stop her breathing. Such *power*. So chillingly ordinary and unchallenged in a monocular system.

What is disturbing is that sexual objectism has entered the mainstream. A monocular outlook persuades psychoanalysts to maintain that sexual attraction is simply not possible without making the desired other into an object. Within a linear frame of reference, sexual arousal has only one place to go: towards the goal of sexual activity and release. Through the right eye, sexual attraction always indicates the possibility of sexual activity with and sexual release through the object of desire.

One of the most significant contrasts between the two perceptions of sexuality relates to the definition and nature of sexual attraction. If we want to counteract the habit of objectism, we have to open the left eye. The left eye sees sexual energy as part and parcel of inner personal power, abiding within oneself. It is not static or fixed but fluid and changing. Though responsive to outside influences, sexuality is not dependent for its actual existence on the presence of an external assessor any more than the fragrance of a flower depends for its existence on contact with someone's appreciative nose.

So sexual attraction (the arousal of sexual sensations) is interpreted more widely through the left eye. Sexual energy can emanate from an individual without it necessarily meaning an automatic invitation to sexual activity. Sexual energy fluctuates in response to hormonal change, physical exercise, emotional needs and fantasy as well as the desire for actual sexual engagement.

With the left eye open, acting on sexual attraction becomes an option: a question of exchange and negotiation, with an equal human being. This is because sexual activity now belongs within a context of closeness, contact, release or procreation. It requires us to be vulnerable because sexual experience with another person then involves a temporary loss of boundary as we let down our normal physical and psychological defences. To do this, we need safety, trust and, at the very least, affection. Sexual exchange through this view is embedded in the context of trust.

In a context of trust, there is the possibility of the transformational power of sex, for giving yourself up to the richness of your own emotionality and sexuality, jumping into the water, risking, opening, diving deeply, disappearing, letting go and riding to the surface, renewed in heart, body and soul. A process of death and rebirth. A process that requires intimacy.

Intimacy and sexual activity are inseparable in the left eye. This requires the consensual encounter of two subjects. Two equal subjects. Intimacy requires openness and risk; risk requires letting go of control. For a while, therefore, when we are aroused, we are not fully conscious of every dimension of the other person. Some aspects of consciousness inevitably recede as we lose ourselves in physical sensations and sexual arousal.

If this encounter is based on trust and intimacy, the other person, even at the height of 'orgiastic delight', does not become an object. He or she is still there, just a little removed. If you care for the person, you see their vulnerability simultaneously with your desire. You cherish this because you too are open. Any encounter (sexual or otherwise) based on equality leaves no possibility of the up/down mode of power necessary for objectism.

34

Clare drove home. She'd found it easy to talk to Helen, easier than she'd imagined. It had been Angie's suggestion. Helen offered to meet Sophie so that she could get a better idea of what was going on. She insisted that Sophie phone personally to arrange a meeting if she wanted one and hadn't thought that the fact that Clare worked for her should present any problems.

She turned on the car radio and heard an old seventies song playing. She found all the words coming back as easily as if she'd been singing it every day for the past thirty years. One associated memory floated into another.

She remembered the early days of her marriage to Len and making love in a small hidden dip along the clifftop during a coastal walk. Hardly surprising that I'm thinking about this today, she thought.

She felt her own sex life had been rather dull. She'd never been to bed with anyone before Len. It had been all quite straightforward and she had loved Len and he had loved her and there hadn't been any problems, until he was ill, of course, but that was different. Only once in all the years since his death had she ever been out with another man. She had felt that part of her had died with Len and she'd never given much thought to the possibility of someone else.

A couple of years ago, Angie had generously paid a dating agency fee as her birthday present, saying that she shouldn't spend the rest of her life shut away from people. Clare had found the whole thing slightly awkward. She'd met six men in all. They'd all been pleasant enough but only one, Peter, had struck any chord in her at all. Peter was divorced, a personnel manager, and they went out a few times before going one evening to dinner at Angie's, where Simon, Angie's man at the time, made up the foursome.

It had been Simon, she remembered, who had brought the video to watch after dinner. Clare had felt embarrassed and cornered Angie in the kitchen. 'What are you doing, Angie? I've hardly even kissed this man, let alone anything else!' she said in as loud a whisper as she could manage.

'I didn't know Simon was going to bring it. He likes to watch that kind of thing, that's all. They're not hard-core, you know, or anything nasty.'

'That's not the point. It . . . just makes things awkward. I mean, what happens if Peter thinks he's being set up or something?'

Angie looked at her friend squarely. 'Look, Clare, you're still attractive and you're not past it so what would be so awful if things did develop a bit between you? You seem to get on together . . . you know, you've got to take the plunge sometime.'

Clare was still doubtful as they went back to join the men. She settled on the sofa beside Peter but couldn't bring herself to look him in the eye. She watched the screen feeling a little irritated with herself for not being more laid-back about everything. While they watched the first one, she vacillated between being curious and feeling detached from it all. She felt certain sexual stirrings in her own body; these made her feel even more uncertain.

Before the second one started, Peter stood up and, looking at Clare, suggested they made a move as it was getting late. She was happy to go so they said their goodbyes and left.

In the car, Peter asked how she felt about the videos. She described her mixed response of curiosity and detachment.

'Did you find it arousing?' he asked suddenly.

'A bit,' she said.

'We haven't really talked about this side of things, have we? I don't know how you feel about me but I'm willing to give it a try if you are.'

Clare thought hard but couldn't find anything clear to say. 'Well, I don't know really . . . it's been a long time.'

'Why don't we go back to my place and just see what happens?'

'OK,' she said, rather amused. The whole thing seemed so strange to her but she liked him and she didn't feel a definite 'no'. After all, she said to herself, remembering Angie's words, I've got to do it sometime.

They arrived back at Peter's house and she decided to be less hesitant. She said she'd like a shower so she went upstairs and put on his bathrobe. Clare could still recall every detail because it had been her first sexual encounter since Len and Len had been her only previous point of reference. So it had been a very new experience for her.

While Peter showered, she lay on his bed in a sort of daydream. In a little while he lay down beside her. He was being very unpushy, she thought, so she reached out and initiated a kiss. She was faintly aware of an unfamiliar taste and smell and feel. She felt vaguely turned on as Peter stroked her breasts and belly. She moved her hands over his body, feeling his surprising hairiness.

They didn't speak. She could feel his erection against her and felt his fingers go to her vagina. It was a little wet. She would have liked to go on getting acquainted, stroking and building up a bit longer, but he suddenly seemed more insistent. He turned her over on to her back and, leaning on his elbows, lay over her, looking down at her face, his penis touching her between her thighs.

In a few seconds, after her initial tightness and discomfort, and some conscious relaxation of her vaginal muscles, he was inside her. He had closed his eyes now so she was looking at his face as he withdrew into himself. She still felt a little absent from it all although she was happy to go along with it. There was a point at which she started to feel some genuine arousal: this lasted a few seconds before Peter came, with a moderate sigh. He stopped moving and opened his eyes. He looked at her and smiled. 'Are you OK?' he asked.

'Yes.' She smiled back.

He moved to lie beside her, his arm lying loosely across her body. She lay there feeling a little numb. Peter shook her body gently: 'Are you sure, you don't want anything . . . ?'

'I'm fine,' Clare replied, knowing she wasn't but not knowing what the matter was. After a minute or so, Peter turned over and got out of the other side of the bed.

'I'm going down to get a drink. I'm parched. Do you want something?' he asked.

'Yes, please.' He left the room.

As she listened to him downstairs, she was suddenly engulfed with a huge wave of sadness. She burst into tears, really sobbing, and feeling a spasm of pain right through the middle of her body. She instinctively curled inwards, holding herself, and cried and cried, forgetting for a moment where she was. She felt enveloped by whatever it was, so much so that she was quite surprised to see Peter standing at the side of the bed, holding two mugs of tea, clearly alarmed at her state.

'What on earth's the matter?'

'I don't know,' she mumbled.

'Did I hurt you?'

'No, no . . . it's not that. I don't know what it is . . . or was.' She felt she had to reassure him so she moved into a sitting position to collect herself. 'It just came from nowhere. Don't worry. I'm fine.'

She reached for a box of tissues on the floor, took one and blew her nose. Then she sipped her tea and was glad of its warmth. She said she should be getting home. He asked her to stay the night, without any real enthusiasm, but she knew anyway that she would be happier to sleep in her own bed. He checked she didn't mind if he didn't take her home and ordered her a cab. She couldn't think of anything more to say so they drank their tea together in silence.

When she said goodbye to Peter at the door, she knew they wouldn't be meeting again, even though she was too exhausted to analyse exactly why. As soon as she was in the back of the cab she relaxed, feeling lighter somehow and happy to be on the way home.

35

For a while after Clare left, Helen sat at her desk. She thought over their talk about Clare's daughter. At this stage of her life, Helen was able to consider her own relationship to motherhood with a wistful sadness. It hadn't always been so.

Helen had got pregnant at eighteen and, in those days, there was no acceptance of illegitimate children. Her mother had refused to have her in the house and her father had arranged an abortion. It was a very expensive (because illegal) operation in a private clinic but it had gone wrong nevertheless and left her unable to conceive again.

That simple fact of her life had left permanent emotional scars as well. She had raged and stormed and wept about it all many times over. Every now and then, even after all these years, she would indulge in a fantasy about how her life might have been, had she been able to be a mother. She had considered the possibility of adoption but the combination of her own psychic fragility and the non-appearance of a likely helpmeet had prevented her from following such a single-minded path.

Her recurring periods of depression had been a strong deterrent to prospective partners. She was not an easy person, she knew that, but neither was she, by nature, a loner. She loved solitude but was not temperamentally inclined to life as a hermit.

With the realisation that physical motherhood would always be an impossibility, she had rather given up on a conventional lifestyle. She had had lovers, both men and women; since sexual consciousness had first dawned in her, she had fallen in love with the being of a person, not the body.

Helen had always lived through her heart. She had come to terms with childlessness enough to keep in touch with her need to love, and was able to direct some of her unused mother love towards those adults who approached her for help. She knew she offered a safe place to contain the love and loss and rage that couldn't be expressed with the real-life individuals.

She found herself wondering if she lived too unreal a life without the mainstay of family that most others had in their lives. She knew, though, where these thoughts would lead so she stopped. She started rummaging distractedly through her desk drawer until she came across a tiny crumpled-up newspaper cutting. She smoothed it out and read it again.

Twenty-five Burmese girls, all HIV positive, were executed with cyanide injections by Burmese authorities after being sent back from Thailand where they had been forced to work as prostitutes.

She'd written the date in the corner – now nearly nine years ago. When she'd first read it, she remembered, there had been something about the insignificance – as an item of news – that had chilled her: anonymous young lives and deaths as objects. She knew there were literally countless other such anonymous examples, over here, over there, everywhere. So much so, it was scarcely worth mentioning.

She had intended this book to be a kind of 'wake-up' call to anyone who might also be aware of the same dangers of monocular excess and the urgent need for change. Did anyone else see what she saw? Did anyone else *care*?

Right at that moment, she doubted that anyone cared enough

actually to confront the system. There were challenges from environmentalists, ecologists, 'holistic' practitioners, but nobody seemed to see the bigger, interconnected picture. Or maybe those who saw had no access to an audience . . . or went mad.

Heavily, she got up. She went downstairs and into the garden; it was a grey day but not cold and she lay down on the grass. Rusper appeared, sniffed and nuzzled her, then lay down alongside, leaning his small body staunchly against her own.

As soon as self-doubt crept in, she was in danger of sinking into depression and losing her clarity. She was familiar with the private prison of depression, that loveless space where time passes numbly and all you hear is the familiar blame: there must be something the matter with *me*, it must be me that's wrong, not the system.

After a while, she sat up. Difficult to distinguish sometimes between real sorrow and self-pity, she thought. They often merge together.

She remained there, absorbing the stillness of the garden, until eventually she decided she needed a diversion. She looked at her watch and stood up. She'd phone Don and Pam and invite herself to supper. They were the kind of friends who were genuinely happy for her to invite herself over, even at short notice. They were really welcoming and down to earth; she'd be able to forget about everything for a while and have a laugh with them. She phoned and Don responded with an immediate and cheery, 'Come on over.' She was delighted. An evening with them always did her a power of good, and right now it was exactly what she needed.

36

When she got home, Clare left a message for Sophie to ring when she got back from work. She'd brought back the last chapter to read at home. The content reminded her about the TV programme and she wanted to have time to take it in. She decided to put her feet up and read straight away while the ideas were still fresh in her mind.

37

Inequality and the Potential for Abuse

Whenever sexual activity occurs between two adults who are not equal (who hold different positions on the ladder of power), there is always the potential for abuse. When a doctor or psychotherapist has sex with a patient, a boss with an employee, a lecturer with student, anyone with power (over) with someone correspondingly 'under', the dynamic is unequal. There can be no genuine choice for anyone on the lower rung any more than for a woman married to a man who will beat the hell out of her if she doesn't 'consent' to sex.

But how do we explain those times when a patient is willing and eager; when a participant in a group makes the first move; when the man declares he was seduced? Isn't the other person then making a choice? To understand what choice is really about, we have to open the left eye.

We then see two important features. We see that sexual attraction is more than a straightforward matter (stimulation, arousal, sexual activity and release); it is made more complex by emotion. Sometimes when we are sad or angry or afraid, when we want to be loved and held and don't know how to ask for this, we get ourselves into a sexual encounter which may ease the pain of the underlying need for a while. We all do this at times. This is because, in a binocular reality, sexuality is part of a whole-body experience and cannot be split off entirely from emotional needs. Many tangled past and present emotions become 'sexualised', in other words, displaced through sexual activity.

Next we see that anyone in the lower position in an unequal relationship is vulnerable (powerless). When we are physically ill, lack adequate intelligence or information or are undergoing psychotherapy, our powerlessness increases because physical or psychological dependence mean we need protection. These two features mean that *however* seductively a child or dependent patient is behaving, when we are in position of power over this individual we have a choice: we look upon the other as a person or an object.

If we choose to keep both eyes open, we see sexual energy/attraction *and* our responsibility simultaneously. This can be tough because the seductive behaviour is sometimes extremely persuasive and disturbing, playing on all sorts of our own susceptibilities and needs. Ultimately, however, integrity demands that we maintain a safe boundary for those in our care. This is our responsibility because they have placed trust in us.

Alternatively, the left eye closes: vulnerability and inner life disappear as the other becomes an object of sexual attraction. Once we step over that line into objectism, we turn our backs on the possibility of trust and care. Short-term gratification wins over longer-term consideration. Denial of responsibility is a recognisable feature of objectism. Monocular thinking can be ingenious in its rationalisations: sexual relations were in 'the best interests of the patient', constituting a beneficial part of therapy, we're told. But the truth is that abuse of power (aggression) is only ever self-serving.

Children, power and sex

When we put child and adult experience of sexuality side by side, we have a clear contrast between the left- and right-eye perspectives. A childhood experience of sexuality accords entirely with the vision of the left eye: a child's sexuality is all-pervasive, diffuse, whole-body-centred, unstructured, unfocused, non-specific and unbounded by concepts. It lacks genital focus and the hierarchical, symbolic (in terms of sexual power) and linear characteristics of the right eye.

For children, whether male or female, their 'intactness' means that their body is not yet split into fragments, each with a separate symbolism and meaning. Most of us can remember the moment in puberty when we became aware of a part of our body that up until that moment had been an insignificant part of the whole. Henceforth, though, these fragments – breasts, genitals, faces – are seen in the new light of self-consciousness and sexual power.

A child's sexuality is naturally a state of sexual *being*, not doing. It isn't naturally based on a sequence of object, attraction, arousal and release. Experimentation with masturbation, even with peers, occurs in the absence of this sequence. Even when hormones necessary for physiological arousal are present, the psychological capacity for negotiating a sexual encounter is absent.

The taboo on incest offers a physiological and psychological protection because a child's mind/body is not ready for sexual engagement. A daughter may touch her father's penis in curiosity; a child may mimic a provocative stance or sexy walk or expression of flirting without understanding the full implications or consequences of sexual activity.

The left eye loves shadows and the spaces in between the obvious and emphasises the power of the threshold: neither completely one thing nor the other. The period when pubescent girls and boys are on the cusp, as it were, between childhood and adulthood, can be a time of particular sexual power. They can emit a strong sexual energy, often unknowingly, that is hard for an adult to ignore.

When we experience attraction to someone who, for whatever reason, is taboo, like one's own children, we normally feel embarrassed, ashamed and guilty at such implications. Remember, it is alien to the monocular view to consider the possibility that we can respond to sexual energy without the need to *do* anything. We can't imagine that we can feel sexual attraction in a way that doesn't demand our active participation.

The left eye helps by highlighting the paradox between internal power and external vulnerability, showing us the need for protection through clear and caring boundaries. A father, looking through the left eye at his young daughter, can acknowledge to himself the startling impact of this sexual power, quite different from sexual attraction to another adult. He will see it as his special responsibility (as currently the most important man in her life) to enable her to become the subject of her body, in preparation for a world which will inevitably see her as an object. He will realise the importance of instilling a sense of pride and beauty in her woman's body and perhaps encourage her to be circumspect in her choice of future sexual partners.

Above all parents can understand that there needs to be a crucial *transition* from child sexuality to an adult sexual framework. Without this transition, the meeting of child and adult in a sexual relationship always represents a clash between two very different models. Remember, a child's sexuality is all-pervasive, unstructured and unbounded by concepts. A child's body is, as yet, bounded by a need for integrity until the body and psyche are fully developed. Through the left eye, we see that an individual needs a context of psychological, social *and* physical maturity to be able to enter into any sexual encounter as an *equal*.

No encounter is equal without choice and no choice is possible without equality. The adult brings to any sexual encounter with a child a dominant view, a right-eye view, of sexuality. He sees premature body development as a sign of sexual maturity, isolating one aspect from the whole picture. He has a goal – along the lines of tension/ejaculation/release – and he imposes his own concepts and needs on the child. The child becomes an object. As an object there is no choice because there can be no equality. Looking at any single aspect of perpendicular power, it is immediately obvious that the adult is on a higher rung.

Many adults justify sexual activity with children on the grounds of the apparent sexual maturity of the child, on willingness to participate or, at least, on the absence of a clear refusal. Once again, these rationalisations come straight from the precepts of monocular vision: sexual maturity is assessed via external appearance and knowledge of what to do; the inner psychological state is split off and ignored. The right eye's resolute focus on sexual release splits off the context in which the child is 'consenting' to sexual activity; the adult denies the physical and psychological powerlessness of the child in the pursuit of his own goal. Aggression always needs an object.

Another plea of justification, similar to that used for the

defence in many rape cases, is the apparent pleasure experienced by the victim. However, even in the absence of obvious coercion and with the apparent consent of the child, there is still no context. A child has not yet learned to focus sexual feelings towards a goal of release. A child has not yet established personal boundaries; physically or mentally, so has no context for sexual activity. Therefore no real choice, on the part of the child, is possible. The encounter remains unequal. Inequality of power always leaves the one on the lower rung vulnerable to abuse.

38

Clare came to the end and sighed. It really made everything so clear, so why did people keep on doing these things? She went into the kitchen to do something about supper.

The phone rang.

'Hi, Mum. You called.'

'Yes, I did.' Clare took a couple of seconds to refocus and took a deep breath. 'Soph, I phoned because I . . . I talked to Helen a bit about you today.'

'Who's Helen?' Sophie snapped.

'You remember, the woman I work for.'

'Why on earth did you talk to her? What *are* you doing, Mum? I haven't asked you to do anything. Who says there's anything the matter with me?'

'You said yourself when we met that you'd tried to get some help but nobody had been able to do anything. So I talked to Angie.'

'Angie as well!'

'Angie is very fond of you, Soph, and has known you a long time. She was the one who suggested I talk to Helen.'

A little pause. 'So what did this Helen say?'

'She said she'd be happy to meet you and talk to you.'

'What about you?'

'What about me?'

'What about you working there?'

'Well, obviously I wouldn't be involved. You can make your own arrangements. All I wanted to do was give you her number and leave the rest to you. I'm trying to help, Soph. Surely you can understand that.'

'I know, it's just that it feels like you're interfering.'

'Well, it may feel like that, but ...' Clare didn't quite know what to say. She felt too stung. 'Look, do you want Helen's number or not?' she continued, more guardedly this time.

'You can give it to me, if you want, Mum, but I'm not likely to do anything.'

Clare read out Helen's number, which Sophie repeated as she took it down. There was now too much awkwardness to have a simple chat, so they both said goodbye and hung up.

Clare felt tears in her eyes as she put the phone down. From somewhere just below her ribcage a sensation of acid heat spread upwards to her chest. She hated this sensation. She knew she was hurt by Sophie's manner but she could also recognise that she was angry at the unfairness of everything and her helplessness. Suddenly, a thread of words – I only want to love you – swam through her mind and, as the words registered, she burst into tears.

The phone rang again. Clare let it switch to the machine, but when she heard Angie's voice she picked it up and said 'Hello' rather lamely.

'What's the matter?'

'Nothing really. I'm a bit upset about Sophie.'

'Did you talk to Helen?'

'Yes, I did. That's why I phoned Soph, to give her Helen's number.'

'And she wasn't exactly grateful.'

'Not exactly,' replied Clare, relieved to have cause to smile at Angie's irony.

'Look, why don't you forget about it for now? You've done your bit and you've done your best. How about coming with me to a concert tonight? One of my students gave me a couple of tickets and it's not Geoff's thing at all.' (Geoff was the latest man in Angie's life.)

Clare wasn't sure. 'When does it start?'

'Eight o'clock. I'll pick you up at six forty-five.'

'That's soon!' said Clare. 'Less than an hour.'

'We've got to get there early, apparently, because our tickets aren't numbered: you have to find your own place to sit. Why don't you come?'

Clare felt a sudden surge of warmth for her dear friend. 'OK then. I'm sure it'll do me good to get out. See you very soon.'

39

As they drove to the concert, Clare asked Angie if she'd said anything to Brian about 'the incident'. Angie reported that she hadn't yet; she'd decided to bide her time until she was clear about the whole work situation and what she wanted to do about it.

There was already a queue when they arrived. Once they got in, they found it was surprisingly crowded in the body of the hall. Their tickets were for the upper gallery so they climbed the stairs and strolled around until they found a small space against the wrought-iron balustrade from where they could see the stage.

Angie, as ever amazing, thought Clare, had brought a small picnic: smoked salmon, salad, buttered bread rolls, grapes and a bottle of wine, even two glasses and plates. They sat and ate while waiting for the actual performance to begin.

When the music started, people around them either watched the stage below or settled themselves in a comfortable position, sitting or lying down on the gallery floor, to listen. Nobody spoke. There was a myriad of people there: scruffy students, smartly dressed businessmen, one elderly couple sitting on the floor nearby, with their eyes closed and tenderly holding hands, intently listening and oblivious of everyone else. Everyone was revelling in the music in their own way. No one person's enjoyment detracted from anyone else's pleasure: in fact, Clare thought, it seemed to enhance it.

She loved the whole atmosphere as much as the music. She enjoyed the commonality and the differences, the simplicity of sharing pleasure with so many different people through the connection of the music. Occasionally she looked down at those below, sitting in fixed rows, and felt glad to be less restricted physically. She glanced over at Angie, who was lying next to her with her eyes closed, and then leaned back herself and surveyed the whole scene. She felt strangely happy.

40

Emotion and the Mind/Body Connection

Just as with sexuality, our beliefs about emotion are constructed along certain lines. We absorb, directly and indirectly, certain 'facts' that we rarely question. The world of emotion is going to be more at home in a left-eye perspective because of its fluid, changing, dynamic and cyclical nature. However, when we look at the prevailing cultural assumptions, it is easy to see that monocular vision once again rules our way of thinking.

We generally accept that feelings are negative or positive and that negative feelings are best denied. Expression of feelings gets a low rating: messy, childish, dangerous or self-indulgent. Most of all, we judge them to be a sign of weakness and inadequacy so we are fearful of these unwanted experiences. Fear leads to defensiveness and blame as we try to deny or suppress our feelings.

The left eye would show us a different reality: emotions are forms of human energy, existing within us and triggered by outside events. There is no split thinking so feelings are simply feelings: neither good nor bad. We are responsible for how we *act* on our feelings, not for the emergence of the feelings themselves. Through the left eye, emotions are inevitably part of the whole context of life, not split off and marginalised and, instead of being feared, emotion is regarded as an essential and enriching aspect of our lives.

Once we see – and accept – that emotion is a potential within us individually that can be aroused by people and external circumstance, a crucial turnaround occurs in our thinking. Instead of assuming feelings are directly and entirely caused by outside agents or events, binocular vision also takes into account the interior context: how we respond to an experience of rejection, for example, will depend on our vulnerability, our sensitivity and perception of the experience. What we feel is in response to a stimulus but not caused by it.

This is why we don't all respond in the same way to an identical stimulus. The process of emotion is much more akin to a labyrinth, interweaving past and present, than a straight line of cause and effect. The left eye acknowledges the threads of connection between past and present emotional experience.

Above all, the left eye shows us that emotion is experienced in our minds and bodies simultaneously, which is why emotional, like sexual, experience can be so powerful. This power can be handled with responsibility and respect or controlled by suppression and fear.

Binocular vision favours a psychosomatic approach to emotion because the body is seen as integral to our emotional experience: when permanently suppressed, feelings have mind/body repercussions. We then understand that while self-control is essential in the short term, physical release and catharsis are also vital aspects of healing.

Instead of being fearful, we could learn that emotions can be communicated and released appropriately and harmlessly. This requires the process of personal emotional clearing to be private and not for public consumption or display. It also demands that we take responsibility for what we feel, instead of using others as convenient receptacles (objects) for whatever unwanted emotions we don't want to acknowledge (split off) ourselves.

The left eye makes it clear that both emotional and sexual

experience function through an indivisible mind/body connection. Thoughts and sensations weave together in an extraordinary process of reciprocal stimulation – perceptions arousing sensations, feelings affecting perceptions – so that even if we are conscious of only one aspect, two are always involved.

A mind/body connection paints a very different picture from that of the monocular higher/lower split. Since cultural beliefs and attitudes towards sexuality and emotion stem from monocular beliefs about our bodies, it is difficult to imagine the change that would come about if we started treating our bodies and minds as totally integrated aspects of the whole. Most of us have become so accustomed to this split that we forget that it isn't natural at all: it is an aspect of our conditioning.

Mind over matter

Watching small children move and enjoy their bodies – while the connection between mind, body, emotions and spirit is unbroken – reminds us that we are naturally at one with our bodies.

As the right eye comes to dominate, self-consciousness takes over and our all-inclusive world changes. We learn to assess. We look at ourselves as we are looked at, or as we imagine we are looked at, by others. The image of ourselves comes from *outside*.

Our physical and psychological image – our personal identities – are, from now on, shaped by external reflection, immediately incorporated into the up/down system of assessment. The body is invested with the status of an object within a system that will forever deny the mind/body connection.

The whole is reduced to an assemblage of parts, most of which – breasts, thighs, calves, necks, folds and wrinkles, bellies, baldness, noses, eyes, chins and bottoms, genitalia, lips, hair, feet, teeth and nails – can be removed, reduced, implanted, expanded or streamlined. In order to be controlled, any natural condition such as mess, chaos, dirt, age or pain must be suppressed.

Binocular vision offers an approach of mind *and* matter and shows us the possibilities of the body as a living whole, accommodating all natural bodily processes. We still see the obvious yardsticks against which we are measured but see a different reality alongside. The body is beheld as a miraculous system to be listened to, cherished, lived with and through from birth to death. Here there exists integrity, the key to personal power.

Binocular vision allows these two contrasting images to merge. To survive with integrity, we must look beyond the collection of fragments, beyond perpendicular assessment and temporary reality, to an interconnected whole. In this place, the internal and external self are indivisible and an abiding beauty exists, untouched by perpetual change.

41

The Place of Suffering

In the absence of a hierarchy, it is possible to see a cyclic nature to pain and pleasure, allowing a place for suffering. Monocular thinking has persuaded us that suffering equates with weakness and vulnerability and so pain is generally disowned (split off) as an unwanted aspect of life.

Medical trends encourage us to repudiate pain – with anaesthesia, analgesia, antidepressants and the routine prescription of painkillers – but if the left eye opens, pain appears in a different light. We see that a function of pain is to tell us when something is wrong and needs attention: it acts as a signal, part and parcel of the process of being alive. The meaning of suffering expands to include letting things take their course: accommodating, acknowledging the truth of an experience even if it is 'painful'. We see the possibility of allowing and going with instead of instant suppression and control.

The left eye doesn't promote pain. Torture or mutilation and flagellation of the self – intended pain – have no place in this view. Nor does it encourage suffering for its own sake. Binocular vision allows for relief of pain as well as the value of suffering: a perspective, as ever, of balance. But instead of a blanket rejection, it reminds us that pain isn't always just pain: it varies. There's the kind that we need to go with, for example, the contractions in childbirth, and the kind caused by injury from which we instinctively recoil. Sometimes, we can learn something from it.

Since the mind/body continues to be interrelated beneath our awareness, *despite* the denial of monocular thinking, there exists a close parallel between our automatic rejection of physical pain and our resistance to suffering emotional or psychic pain. When we feel emotional pain, this is also a communication.

Love may tell us to comfort someone. Trust tells us we are safe. When a need isn't met, we feel something that informs us of an imbalance. Anxiety may warn us to be vigilant. Anger may tell us a boundary has been crossed. Irritation can communicate the need to leave a situation before we do something we regret.

These signals are automatically rejected instead of listened to because we experience feelings as *painful*. We don't understand that emotional pain is caused when we go *against* our feelings instead of going with them.

When you go with your mind/body, you do not experience immense pain. Pain is intensified when we tighten a hundred different muscles and ligaments in the diaphragm, the eyes, the jaw, the abdomen, the ribs, the thighs, the arms, the hands, the buttocks, the shoulders, the neck and throat to do *battle* with our feelings.

This simple truth has been lost. Through the wisdom of the left eye, we see that allowing or suffering a process uses less energy, tension and strain than fighting it with denial, conquest, eradication or burial. The response to fight against what we feel is so automatic we don't know we are doing it. Even when we register the accumulated effects in a variety of psychosomatic illnesses – our bodies continually send us symptoms (messages of pain) to alert us that something needs attention – we don't stop to hear because we are too long accustomed to regarding our bodies as objects.

Objects are supposed to act efficiently and productively and without problems. The response to the experience of pain is more likely therefore to be a wish to eliminate the specific fault than consideration of the message of the *whole*. This loss of connection leaves us vulnerable and out of touch with our bodies as our outer selves. A relationship with our bodies that could be described as cherishing and mindful of the body's wisdom cannot possibly develop unless monocular vision is challenged by the left eye.

42

Later in the week, Clare was catching up on her reading; she was due the next day at Harwell House. She quite enjoyed the discipline of keeping abreast of the work they were doing. Funny how she felt they were working together instead of her working *for* Helen.

She found she had lots of questions about feelings: about tears and why they came, and what was actually being released, and why some people seemed to be very emotional and others completely the opposite.

Clare didn't think of herself as particularly emotional. She hadn't come from an emotional family. She had a sister, Ruth, who was three years older and who now lived in Canada, to whom she'd never been particularly close. Sophie, for some reason, had always been sensitive, even as a child, and had seemed to feel things far more keenly than Danny, far more than other children, even other girls. Now, am I stereotyping? Clare wondered. She thought about it and decided she really did believe, on the whole, that women felt more than men did.

Len hadn't been unfeeling but had never talked much about that kind of thing. He'd told her he loved her and he told the children the same. Feelings hadn't come up much at all. It struck her now that this had, in fact, been one of the things she'd found hardest in their whole marriage: her isolation when Len was ill. Every time she'd wanted to talk about the seriousness of the illness and how she felt and about the children, Len would close up.

He simply refused to talk truthfully about what was happening. He'd get irritated with her and insist there was no point in talking as it would only make things worse, so she felt she had to keep silent for his sake. She felt this silence had infiltrated the whole family. She didn't know if the children had talked to each other but they hadn't talked to her.

There'd been times when it had been almost unbearable for her. Seeing him in such pain, and knowing that the painkillers would only take the edge off it and, even then, only for a short while, had been agony. She had felt so powerless. She'd talked to Angie occasionally but it had been one of those periods in their friendship when both of them were going through difficulties – she with Len and Angie with Derek's drinking – and there hadn't been much opportunity or energy for them to support each other.

The very worst thing had been the loneliness of being separate from Len. She'd wanted so much to tell him how much she loved him or hold him even if it did make her cry. She'd wanted him to be close to the children. Sometimes she'd wanted to protest at the unfairness of it all.

As she thought about it now, it crossed her mind that she had, in fact, been quite angry with Len for not letting her talk, although she could hardly blame him. There was a large part of her that would always regret that the last couple of years of their time together were spent so separately. They'd shared such a lot in the past together. His refusal to share then meant they both had to deal with everything alone.

By the time Len died, she had felt quite distant from him, their former intimacy eaten away at the edges by unspoken thoughts and feelings. She'd never talked about this to anybody, nor even thought about it much.

43

Clare was typing the next day when she was startled by the sound of the phone. She realised this was the first time it had occurred. She'd wondered vaguely why there were never any interruptions but assumed that people knew not to phone Helen in the mornings. It was clearly a bad connection and from abroad because Helen was enunciating with extra care. Feeling slightly awkward, she went downstairs. In a few minutes Helen joined her in the kitchen.

'You didn't have to leave. It wasn't private.'

'I wasn't sure . . .'

'Since we're here, why don't we have our break early?'

'Fine.'

While Helen prepared coffee, Clare decided to ask a question.

'There's something that confused me in the last chapter. Is this a good moment to ask you about it?'

'Sure. What is it?'

'Well, it's about feelings. A couple of things. First, what do you mean exactly by "release"? It sounds quite special and I don't know whether you mean just crying or if it's more than that. And the other thing is about pain: are you suggesting pain is a good thing?'

Helen didn't respond until a few minutes later, when she had sat down facing Clare at the table.

'I'm not suggesting pain is a good thing, more that pain is neither good nor bad, but exists as a natural phenomenon which we could learn from if we didn't insist on trying to "kill" it straight away. I'm describing a very different way of seeing things, Clare. The way this connects to our feelings is that we have been taught that feelings are painful, that crying for example is a painful and therefore a *bad* experience. This makes us very afraid of doing so.'

She paused. 'Can you remember a time when you released any feelings, as an adult, I mean?'

'Yes, I remembered quite recently an occasion when I suddenly started crying, really crying, but I didn't know why it was happening. I couldn't explain it then and I still can't.'

'We often don't know why. But did it hurt? Was it painful?'

'No. It seemed to come from nowhere and then it went away again.'

'Well, that's a form of release. Many people just wouldn't be able to let it happen. They'd hold tears back, swallow hard and keep everything in.'

'So is that wrong?'

'It's not *wrong*, it's just not helpful. It doesn't matter keeping things in for a while – we all have to – but over a period of time there is an accumulation. You asked what release was. When we feel something straightforward, like anxiety when we're lost or angry . . . being stuck in broken-down train, let's say, or sad when you say goodbye to someone, you can recognise the link between the feeling and the event, the stimulus that triggers the feeling. Do you see what I mean?'

Clare nodded.

'Physical sensations – feelings – are telling us something – that we are lost and need to find our way home or that we'll miss the meeting or we care about the person who is leaving. At this stage, you don't need to go any further. You can manage what is happening. You can still function. You can talk to people and be reasonable. You can still control yourself because you need to.

'But problem arises when this particular stimulus reactivates a whole pile of other stuff that is already there, but hidden from view. If you think of sadness like water, you can picture how a movement of water stirs up another current or something lying deeper down. Or imagine anger like a fire emitting sparks that set ablaze something close by.

'You don't see this happening so you have no idea of this in your head. Because of the split between mind and body, we only believe what we can put into a logical sentence. If we can't put something into words that make sense to our *own* minds, let alone to someone else, then we're told it doesn't have any validity.

'The thing is, these connections exist. The truth is that your head *doesn't* operate in isolation from your body. They are functioning together the whole time. So, unbeknown to our heads, there is a system constantly in operation and every now and then, usually when something happens to disrupt the normal order of things, it shows itself.'

Helen sat back in her chair and then continued. 'For example, we find ourselves reacting excessively – when instead of being a little cross with someone, which would be appropriate, we erupt with immense fury –' Helen flung her arms wide in emphasis – 'or when feelings seem to come out of the blue, from "nowhere". Both these signs can alarm us and that's why feelings get a bad press, as it were, because we think we're being ambushed out of nowhere. We've come to believe they're dangerous.' Helen paused. 'Am I saying too much?'

'Not at all,' said Clare, who had been listening intently. 'I'm fascinated.'

'So back to the nature of release. It's really easiest to understand the process by imagining a child who falls over or is being taken unwillingly to bed or gets frightened by a loud noise. This stimulus causes the child to feel something – pain, hurt, anger, fear – and these feelings, once aroused, will reach a point where they are released somehow. What would you understand by release in this context?'

Clare, initially taken aback to be asked a question, thought about it and replied: 'Tears, I suppose, and kicking or screaming and crying and shaking, depends on how frightened the child is.'

'Right. So this is release. What is being released? The chemicals in the system. The chemicals in the body caused by the arousal of feeling: chemicals from hormonal changes, like adrenalin, lots of stuff in the body which is produced in response to how we see – interpret – the things that actually happen to us. This is why once you know what a firework is, for example, you don't get as frightened as you might the first time when you have no idea what it might be. Without information you have to rely only on your imagination, which fills us with all sorts of incorrect ideas, making us far more terrified than necessary.

'With tears, vigorous movement, shaking, all the chemical stuff in the body, due to the arousal of emotions, is cleared. It is the mind/body system's way of getting itself back to normal. Getting back to a position of balance or what is called homeostasis. Do you remember how quickly this process is over for a child?'

Clare smiled. 'Yes, and even when you think it's the end of the world, they actually get over it more quickly than you do sometimes.'

'Exactly. They are young enough to do this. But what happens later? We learn that to grow up, we must exercise self-control, which is fine, but self-control, in a culture that splits mind from body so completely, means not just necessary restraint, but ruthless control and, as you know by now, having typed it so many times, elimination. We learn through instruction, correction and example that feelings are dangerous and are best avoided.

'A firework is a good example because it *is* a dangerous object, so here you have an illustration of the difference between helpful fear that warns you to be careful and the sort of disabling fear that occurs when there is no information to balance it. You learn to treat the firework with due caution because you learn through experience. If you don't get the information and just imitate others who are afraid, what will happen?'

'You get more frightened?'

'Exactly. Your anxiety grows and grows, fuelled by imagination and fantasy into a completely unrealistic and therefore inappropriate fear. So we end up being afraid of anything to do with emotion, and ignorance breeds an awful lot of fantasies.

'Just think about it. We have this huge and natural part of human experience completely ruled by fantasy and fear (a bit like sexuality). What we do learn is skewed and we end up with rigid but crazy rules that have no base in reality. We don't even understand the basic differences of release: that tears release sadness and grief, that anger is something different, needing sound and movement and space, and that fear is different again, being released in sweating, trembling, shivering, shaking.'

'So, is it one thing at a time, like when I was crying?'

'Not really. We can release different feelings close together, so when adults release feelings, they can go, within a short space of time, from tears to shouting to trembling to tears again.'

'Do you actually feel better physically?'

'Yes . . . you do feel better, if you let it happen. What I mean is that release doesn't happen in one go because the body/mind, as a system, couldn't cope with it all at once so what emerges for release is just so much and no more. This is because some things that happen to us are so traumatic that we have to close them off in order to survive. Especially when we're small and vulnerable and can't make sense of things.'

'So is it OK to stay closed or do we have to open things up?'

'It depends. It depends on the circumstances. As long as we are in danger of any kind, we are protected by a natural mechanism. You know how the body naturally prevents a woman from psychosis while she is pregnant, well, it's that kind of protective mechanism.

'When you need all your energies for survival – whether in childhood or in famine or war or when you need your skill and clear-headedness to survive in a crisis, you don't have time to feel. It's only when it's over that you can have your feelings. After the trauma or danger has passed, then we allow ourselves to feel and release them.'

'But how do you know when something needs release?' asked Clare.

'Our mind/body systems tell us – they give us clues which come through the mind or the body or both. When we get the clues through the body, they come through headaches or stomach aches, tiredness, numbness – a whole variety of bodily symptoms – that tell us, if we listen, that something is needing our attention.'

'Would you include backache there?' asked Clare.

'I would. Does that ring a bell?'

'Yes. I had dreadful back pain during my last months of teaching. To be honest, I didn't connect it with any feelings till afterwards. It was amazing how quickly it disappeared after I retired. Every now and then I get the odd twinge but nothing like it was.'

Helen nodded. 'Our bodies give us so many clues. They come through the mind, too, like when we find ourselves depressed, you know, unable to find enthusiasm for anything. Moods are a great indication of the need for release. Whenever we get into moods of martyrdom or self-pity or resentment or recklessness, you can guarantee that we've accumulated enough emotional debris to get in the way of normal functioning – or soon will do.

'Then there are so many behaviour patterns which signal that the system is overloaded: we find ourselves working, drinking or eating to excess or the reverse – not eating at all.' Clare instantly thought of Sophie but didn't say anything.

'It shows in excess of all kinds, when we get cravings for sex or spending money or when we've any kind of appetite that can't be filled. The orgasm or the bags full of new clothes don't quite touch the real spot, do you know what I mean?'

'I certainly used to eat more when things were bad at school.'

'There you go,' said Helen. 'We all find something, believe me.'

Something in the tone of this last remark intrigued Clare. 'How did you get into all this?' she asked.

Helen regarded her levelly. 'My own experience. To start with anyway. For many years I drank far more than was good for me.'

'What happened?'

'I saw the light!' said Helen flippantly.

Clare waited. 'Is that all you're going to say?' she asked.

Helen shrugged her shoulders. 'There's not much to say, really. I grew up with alcoholism in the family and I followed suit until I learned a different approach to dealing with my feelings. That's it in a nutshell. Since then I've spent an awfully long time working with these things. Is that answer enough?'

Clare nodded, although she was curious to know more.

'I think we'd better get back to work, don't you?'

'Fine,' agreed Clare. 'I'm sorry if I've made you talk too much. It is all quite new to me.'

44

Our Capacity for Care

When the right eye dominates, we become preoccupied with the up/down aspect of power and our response to all feelings is coloured by blame and aggression. By splitting our minds from our bodies and by the suppression of the physical aspect of feeling, we restrict our emotional capacities. Monocular vision encourages the heart to close.

Imagine for a moment (through the left eye) every aspect of our relationships – whether meeting, loving, fighting, challenging, bonding with, separating from, caring for, depending on, learning from or yielding – without the need to win or the need to exorcise our own hurt through objectism.

Imagine being able to relate to others from another, gentler place where our emotional capacities could evolve naturally. Each of the three polarities offers us the opportunity to evolve an emotional capacity. The polarity between closeness and separateness offers us the capacity for care; the polarity between engagement and containment offers the capacity for power; the polarity between safety and risk offers the capacity for trust.

The left eye sees these as fledgling capacities present in us when we are born, providing us with the essential tools of relationship that we can learn to work with through interpersonal experience. With these tools, we construct our sense of self, of others and the world at large.

The chance to evolve each capacity depends on the flexibility of the psychic mechanism. Maintenance is made possible through the necessary release of the emotional build-up because this will keep the mechanism unblocked and clear. As release occurs, insight allows us to achieve a point of balance again.

We start by looking at the capacity related to *closeness* and *separateness*, the capacity for care.

This capacity describes the urge to give and receive love, an ability to reach out and exchange care with other creatures; an inborn talent for tenderness, an eye for concern, an ear to distress, a sensitivity and the instinct to *respond*.

The capacity for care extends equally to self-love, for there has to be a balance. Through giving and receiving, we learn about closeness with others; through permission to be separate, we learn about care for ourselves.

How does our capacity for care become distorted? Whenever our boundaries are unclearly established and our feelings accumulate as a consequence. Without release, though, the mechanism becomes blocked. This is because the free-flowing movement (the e-motion) between the two poles is impeded, like the slow silting of a river, imperceptible in its process but indisputable in its eventual effect.

When we suppress sadness and grief over a period of time, our capacity to give or receive love is diminished. Our capacity to experience joy in human relationships becomes restricted and confined to a tiny fraction of its potential in our lives. Over time and with reinforcement, the psychic mechanism loses balance: we become obsessively close and possessive or excessively remote and detached.

These positions make objectism possible. We either get so close that we see only one fragment, which becomes distorted, or so far away that we see nothing but an indistinct shape, number or statistic. It is only when separate and close are *balanced* aspects that we can relate to the other in the round.

A common feature of imbalance is the emergence of compulsive care. This develops as authentic care for others and is gradually eroded by the build-up of resentment that will be felt when giving becomes one-way for too long. We find it hard to admit this to ourselves so we deny it, but these feelings don't go away: they emerge as compulsive care. We start caring on automatic pilot. If this goes on over a period of time, the natural capacity for care is distorted into a psychically imposed obligation or even a mission, tinged with hidden bitterness: far removed from its nature of reciprocity and balance.

If we are to develop fully our capacity for care and fine-tune it, we have to see (through a binocular perspective) that we need as much to receive love as to give it. This is a simple truth but what happens to many people, over years of compulsive care, is that they lose sight of it.

We get stuck in dualistic thinking, identifying with the rejected lover, not the loved, the giver not the receiver. Giving out of a sense of duty or debt is a similar distortion belonging, as it does, to a system of hidden strings of perpendicular power. So does being a martyr or receiving with bad grace. In the left eye, refusing a gift is no less unloving than refusing to give. We experience the paradox of giving through receiving and, through giving, learning to receive.

Taking this a step further, we see that ultimately the dual categories are meaningless. The less rigidly we are fixed on either giving or receiving, the more the distinction becomes blurred. We begin to realise through experience, in a personal or even work situation, that officially being the helper, carer, giver (on a higher rung) is little more than a convenient label. We see that giving entails receiving and that receiving is a gift in its own right.

Emotional distortion affects our capacity for self-love as well: we become excessively dependent on others to give us the power and affirmation we cannot give ourselves. The capacity for care is balanced and reciprocal: the condition of 'loving aloneness' allows us to move towards 'loving fusion' and vice versa. The wisdom of the left eye shows us that no amount of love from anyone else can ever compensate for lack of self-love in the long term.

45

Helen got up to see whether Rusper was outside, as it had started to rain. Clare looked out at the trees. She felt inexplicably sad. 'There's another question I have,' she said as Helen reappeared, 'but you don't need to answer it right now.'

'Go on,' said Helen. 'We can take a moment. What is it?'

Clare turned round. 'What exactly are you meant to *do*?' she asked. 'I mean, how do you actually *do* it . . . how do you release whatever it is you're meant to?'

'Well, there are ways you can learn to do this like courses where adults learn to read these clues for themselves and to release their emotions in this way. But you have to be careful because it isn't so much a doing thing, more a question of allowing it to happen. The best way to start is by simply allowing what is already happening to *happen* . . . in yourself or in anyone else. Just starting there would make such an incredible difference.'

Helen sighed. 'Do you know, Clare,' she continued in a weary tone, 'how many times, in ordinary lives, a human being – young or old – begins to express and release feelings but is *stopped* from doing so by a parent or friend or colleague or even a partner? Doctors stop their patients, even therapists stop their patients. It can be a complete stranger or your spouse of many years – it makes no difference. They start to express something and we stop them. Why do we stop them? Because we are so afraid of feelings that, at the very moment someone opens a door and shows themselves to be vulnerable we close it. We shut that door because we cannot bear the fact of someone else's vulnerability. I find that so sad.'

There was a pause. Clare wondered whether Helen was waiting for her to say something. But she couldn't speak. She was thinking about Len. Her own eyes brimmed with tears and she looked down, embarrassed. The silence continued. Clare knew Helen was looking at her.

'It's OK,' said Helen, in a different and gentler tone. 'It really is all right, you know. You can never talk about these things without feeling them. That's the beauty of the system. Don't explain. Just stay with whatever you feel and you'll understand. I've probably talked too much.'

Clare shook her head but couldn't find any words. She sat without speaking, resolutely looking at the rug on the floor. She could feel Helen's gaze and she could also feel a great ache around her forehead and eyes as she tried to fight back her tears.

Suddenly she felt Helen's hand gently on her own and heard Helen say, 'Just let go.'

A sob seemed to come up which she held back.

'You'll feel silly and embarrassed, Clare, and think this is not why you're here, but trust me, just let it go. Trust your body at this moment. You're quite, quite safe.'

Another sob came up, from her chest this time, followed by a few more and some more tears. Clare felt Helen's arm lightly around her shoulders. She knew she was being ridiculous and stupid and, at the same time, something in her responded to the touch and she felt something give inside. She was aware of making silly sounds, of the heat of the tears as they fell on her cheeks, and of being somewhere suspended between Clare sitting at the desk and Clare somewhere else, with pictures of Len's face appearing and disappearing as she cried.

The tears stopped and then his face would come back into view and a really painful spasm caught her just under her diaphragm. She bent forward automatically and, somehow, Helen's arm pushed her slightly forward and persuaded her to rock. Her body seemed to move into a rocking motion and now she heard even stranger sounds coming from her. Intermittent thoughts about what Helen might be thinking and worry about appearing ridiculous flitted through her mind, but at the same time she remained in this suspended halfway place.

Suddenly she felt a huge wave of heat rising from her abdomen and her body tensed. She stopped rocking. 'You may need to do a little shouting,' she heard Helen say gently. Clare looked up at her. She didn't know what she expected to see but she was struck by the look of complete and utter acceptance in Helen's eyes.

'What do you mean?' she mumbled.

'Well, you may need to stretch and move as well as cry. Sometimes it helps to walk about and make a noise. Why don't you try it?'

'Now?'

'Yes, now.'

Helen helped her up. She moved stiffly and stretched her arms. She felt awkward and clumsy and her body ached. Helen spread her arms out widely and, looking at her, said, 'You may need to roar. ROAR!' she shouted. 'Go on, make a noise.'

'I can't,' said Clare pathetically.

'Yes, you can. Try it. Give it a go.'

Clare gave a feeble roar, more like a groan.

'Try again,' urged Helen, laughing. Clare laughed too and then gave another roar, louder than the first, but still quite timid. She laughed at her puny sound. Helen roared again, a ferocious sound that amazed Clare. She tried again but felt her throat hurt. 'Don't force your throat. Try getting the sound from below, somewhere in your belly.'

Clare tried again a few times but she just ended up laughing.

'How are you feeling now?' asked Helen, looking at her intently.

'I'm fine. I don't know what happened. I was a bit somewhere else. I'm sorry . . .'

'Clare, the one thing you don't have to do is apologise, especially here, with me. No apologies.'

Clare smiled. 'All right, but thank you anyway. I don't know what it was all about.'

She realised that wasn't completely true. 'At least, I don't know all of it but I do know what started it, I think. Do you want me to tell you?'

'It's entirely up to you. I don't need to know at all. If you want to put some of it into words now, then I'm happy to listen. Let's go downstairs. The rain seems to have stopped for a bit.'

They wandered round the garden under a still-heavy sky. Clare told Helen about Len and the sorrow she had felt because she couldn't talk to him when he was dying. At one stage, she found tears coming up again and Helen suggested that they stopped talking about it for the time being.

'Do you understand what I mean now? About simply letting something happen when it wants to happen? We have so many opportunities to do this, without setting out to be therapists. It will come up of its own accord.'

'Yes, but not everyone knows what to do,' said Clare. 'You know what you're doing.'

'When you learn more about this, you'll understand what I mean when I say that doing is not the operative word. It is more *being* there and you discover how to be, by experiencing this first hand. There is no other way. It doesn't come from books or observation or training or lecture. It comes only through the body. That means you have to learn to trust, to jump and risk and swim before you can have any genuine understanding. You have to know the currents and the medium to be able to navigate yourself, before accompanying anyone else. And this, Clare,' Helen said with an exasperated grimace, 'is what people don't want to do. They want to talk about feelings but without the risk of losing control. Did you get a glimpse of that? Just letting go?'

'Yes, I did. You can't explain it exactly. It's not the first time I've felt that. Something like that happened when I was alone once.'

Clare described the experience of the evening when she had sex with Peter. 'That really was out of the blue,' she said. 'At least this morning I could make a connection but I didn't know what was going on then. But I do remember feeling better afterwards in a funny way. What was happening then, do you think? Or maybe I've asked you enough. I don't want to take advantage of you.'

'Don't worry. I'll answer this and then we ought to go and start again. Let's go in.' It was starting to rain again.

'Do you remember,' Helen continued as they went upstairs, 'what I said about how a multiplicity of feelings can get triggered even though, in our minds, we've shut all the doors and "forgotten" about them?' She didn't wait for Clare reply but went straight on. 'Well, when we get sexually aroused, we let go a bit of our usual control. There is a very close link between sexual arousal and emotional arousal because they both require us to go into our bodies and lose ourselves for a while. When sexual release occurs, emotional release can occur at the same time.'

'But the time I'm talking about, Helen, I wasn't really that . . . you know, excited. I certainly wasn't anywhere near an orgasm.'

They both stood at the top of the stairs.

Helen thought for a moment and then asked: 'Did you say that this was the first man you'd been to bed with since Len died?'

'Yes.'

'Ah, well . . . it's possible that the sexual/physical contact with this man triggered something else in you. Mind and body working together, remember?'

Clare nodded.

'Let's consider the possibility that when Len died you were left with lots of feelings, especially after what you were saying earlier about not being able to talk to him. So you're left with those feelings and you're also left with the hassles and loneliness of being a widow with two young children and then there's everything else that's happened. There must have been hundreds of times when you missed Len consciously and even more when you missed him without being aware of it.

'Now imagine your mind/body holding all of this inside and, meanwhile, you function and work and bring up your children. When Len died, you had to survive. You put all your energy into your children and your work and that's how you managed.

'Your psychosomatic system can continue like this for ages, years sometimes, until something gives. Then we notice a bodily symptom or tearfulness, depression . . . that sort of thing. You mentioned your backache, remember?'

Clare nodded.

'This is the body's way of informing us that things have reached overload and we need some kind of release of tension. But we still keep going because we have to. And you probably didn't get close to anyone else in all that time, somehow knowing the limits of what you could manage.

'Then, years later, Peter comes into your life. As he does so, those emotional depths are going to be stirred up, even if you are not conscious of them. Why? Because being close to another man again will revive memories and associations. Then, you actually go to bed with him.

'At this point, you experience even more tweaking of body memories and sensations and with those come the feelings: the longings, the ache, past intimacy with Len all triggered by touching another man's body. All those things that you've kept at bay until then. Peter's presence emotionally reactivates Len's absence, do you see?'

Clare was totally absorbed.

'This doesn't mean that you can't be happy with Peter, or whoever, but to experience fully someone's presence, you have to experience, in some measure, Len's absence, in both your mind and body. This means experiencing grief, anger, fear, God knows what, but once you've let that go, released it, you are then more open to taking in the present.

'As long as we carry round a pile of past feelings, our bodies cannot respond fully to the present because they are too full already. In a sexual context, especially, you cannot let in sexual pleasure and arousal fully until your body is empty enough. And even when you do let things in, something, probably unexpected, will come out! Do you understand any of what I'm saying or does it all sound too complicated?'

'No, it does make sense,' said Clare.

'Ah, well as long as it makes "sense", then it's all right,' said Helen teasingly.

'You know what I mean.'

'I do. In fact, you remind me that through the left eye we make an entirely different sense of things.' Helen looked at the clock on the desk. They had been standing this whole time and now moved to their working positions.

Clare turned round to face Helen before starting. 'I really am grateful for your time. I've never thought about any of these things before.'

'It's a pleasure. As you may have gathered, once I get started on these things, it's difficult to stop me!'

'I feel I've had a free therapy session.'

Helen shook her head. 'It's not like that,' she said. 'Come on, let's get this section finished.'

46

Our Capacity for Power

This second capacity relates to the polarity between *engagement* and *containment*. Power in this context is defined by the left eye: our inner power that waxes and wanes but never leaves us completely.

This emotional capacity is, in essence, reciprocal. It demands the effort of will, developing and stretching our individual power, as well as encountering and merging with that same quality of power in others through relationship. Between the polarities, there is the possibility of balance of power: when the internal power of the self meets the internal power of another, we experience peace.

Peace is impossible within monocular culture; the very best we can hope for is a truce. When power can only be measured in terms of hierarchy, there is no point of balance because of the constant movement to acquire or preserve one's position on the ladder.

The seesaw swings between up and down with no possibility of equality. Each position is held in place by the other so only reversal is possible, never resolution. Hierarchical power, as we've seen, is forever unequally distributed, so, depending on our own relative position, we respond with aggression or futility.

In contrast, personal power is developed both by asserting one's will and by the less obvious path of acquiescence. Will power is balanced by acts of obedience and accommodation in respect for others' boundaries or greater needs. Developing this capacity teaches us to allow, to suffer, to bend and accept the will of another. We learn, through experiencing the movement between these two poles, to yield.

This movement is maintained by the emotional release of anger: without this, the psychic mechanism becomes impaired by the pollution of aggression. Flexibility becomes rigidity and we find ourselves somewhere between the two extremes of dictator (imposing our will without any regard to others' boundaries) and doormat (refusing to set any boundaries in the first place).

Aggression, as we've seen, doesn't release anger, so this emotional energy remains trapped, turned inwards, causing mild or suicidal depression and, more generally, chronic apathy and a sense of powerlessness.

If anger were experienced and released (without an object), we would understand it in its proper place. We would see the value of others' anger and our own. Anger informs us when our territory is invaded, when someone has come in too far or inappropriately. This process is reciprocal. Someone else's anger gives us information about their boundaries. This is crucial information in any meaningful relationship. Without it, we can never feel the edges of our own power: we cannot gauge how far to go unless we learn by going too far.

As fear of anger diminishes, we realise that the split between anger and love is a monocular imposition. We know we can love and be angry at the same time and more than this. We discover that far from the 'if I love someone, I shouldn't feel angry with them' belief, anger is in fact a *vital* aspect of loving, if we are to keep seeing the loved one as a person in their own right, not as an object.

Without the up/down seesaw, the expression of anger communicates from a position of equality. You have a self and you recognise the other person has a self too and is not merely a reflection of your own identity. This is how we avoid the dynamics of objectism.

It works both ways: being on the receiving end is also a

different experience. Instead of having to hide or cower, anger means we *matter*. The fact someone bothers to challenge at all means they care, that they feel equal and, even if we resist listening at first because of the previous fears of injustice or punishment, that loving confrontation will get through to the heart. We learn that seeing and hearing someone's anger is a completely different experience from being battered over the head by indiscriminate aggression. The experience of healthy anger is liberating. Fear of aggression in a relationship makes us afraid to risk being fully ourselves – to risk being powerful – so the self remains a shadow of its potential.

When self-worth becomes solely dependent on reflection from outside, personal power dwindles. The dictator depends on others' submission; the doormat depends on avoiding real or imagined sanctions. We lose the balance with our own internal power.

Without balance, even love is worth less. Without the possibility of anger, love degenerates into a sentimentalised blur. We lose our identities in others. We lose touch with our own boundaries. We give up responsibility for our needs, our feelings, our choices, and when this cycle ends, we sink into blame and bitterness.

Willing surrender requires a measure of personal power. Then we can see yielding as an aspect of power rather than defeat. As long as monocular values dominate, submission is little more than a posture in self-defence, accompanied by little grace and a great deal of self-recrimination. Such feelings sow the seeds of revenge and future aggression.

The capacity for power is maintained by the release of anger which puts us back in touch with that power of 'me'; this allows me to be able to see 'you'. It allows us to be challenged ourselves and it transforms our approach to confrontation.

With the ladder in mind, we often hesitate to challenge because we don't think others could 'take it', if they're lower down the ladder than ourselves, or through fear of repercussions if they're higher. Personal power alters the view: we see ourselves entering a dance rather than a fight. It gives us the opportunity to submit, if necessary, not as a gesture of degradation but as an encounter with an equal. Power ceases to be a commodity and becomes an evolving process of human relationship.

47

As Clare parked outside the house, she noticed Moira's motorbike against the kerb in the rain and wondered what had become of the conflict. There was a postcard from Danny in her mail; also a small parcel that was addressed to Ellen. She didn't want to talk because she was tired so she propped it up against Ellen's front door.

Danny's card was from Hawaii – he and BJ were on vacation and having a great time. That was about the sum of it! She smiled and once again the idea of going out there crossed her mind. She made herself some lunch and then lay on the settee to gather herself after the extraordinary events of the day.

Her head was full of thoughts and impressions. Helen really was very stimulating. And the way she'd reacted to the emotional 'episode' . . . Clare felt touched and puzzled. She realised it was Helen's line of work but there had been more to it than that. In fact, that was probably the point. Helen had never appeared professional. She hadn't been overdistant or oversympathetic. There had been no reference to anything once they had started working again; Clare understood what Helen had meant when she'd told her it was safe.

Maybe this was a new dimension of safety, to trust someone in this way. Even with Angie, whom she trusted more than anyone, she would have felt less secure. Why? Because somehow letting go physically was so new and you wouldn't want to risk anyone else feeling awkward.

It was all a bit of a mystery to her. And yet Helen had been so laid back about it all, so simple and gentle as if it were the most natural thing to do to burst into tears, in response to something that happened over fourteen years ago, when she was meant to be there doing her job. Clare hadn't even put in more time at the end to make up for it. It had all been so . . . ordinary. Like being in another world.

She hadn't met anyone like Helen before. It frustrated Clare a little that Helen seemed to want to keep their relationship strictly professional. She respected the reasons, of course, but she found herself wanting to know more about what made Helen tick. Even though the boundaries between them had been stretched by what had happened today, Clare had been the focus of attention so she herself was none the wiser about Helen.

Thinking about safety brought back bits of the last chapter they'd done. She got up to find it so she could read it through with more concentration.

48

Our Capacity for Trust

Related to our complementary needs for *safety* and *risk* is our emotional capacity for trust. A prerequisite for the unfolding of this capacity is the ability to withstand a measure of fear as a natural process. Fear, through the left eye, is a necessary experience.

This emotional capacity helps us, through the experience of fear, gradually to build an internal reference point of balance that acts as a home base. We need this base to return to time and time again, whenever we get caught up in the tangles of deception and fantasy, in order to establish a point of personal truth. This isn't truth in absolute terms, but it's the base of what some people call an inner guide or inner wisdom. It is how we establish trust, how we build it or acknowledge its absence, protecting ourselves accordingly. The healthy development of this capacity helps us to distinguish, through trial and error, what and whom we can and cannot trust.

This requires us to be open to risk and, unless we are either fools or robots, we simply cannot take a risk without being vulnerable and therefore without eliciting some degree of fear. Once we see fear as a process, we do not have to become paralysed by it. We can experience fear by acknowledging and moving through it: surviving the body/mind experience, we are able to re-establish a point of balance that allows for emotional evaluation. This is how we build our own inner integrity in relation to others.

This emotional capacity, again, has a reciprocal dimension which means we see the importance of being trustworthy for others. With binocular vision, vulnerable becomes a transient state – not a permanently assigned derogatory label. Openness is regarded as a virtue but binocular vision allows us also to register that, in our monocular world, openness is a risk. So instead of turning away, we can respond with appropriate care.

The condition of vulnerability applies to a period of time – moments, months or years – when someone needs extra protection. Whether this condition is due to having a fragile personality, being at a certain stage of one's life or undergoing a traumatic or stressful experience, we are happy to take the role of minder and protector. There is no sense of innate superiority because we are human (and equal) and know, from within, the need to have someone to trust.

The maintenance of the psychic mechanism depends on the experience of fear and anxiety. Anxiety is stirred up in the shallower waters of the deeper emotion of fear. It acts as an early warning (mind/body) system, helping us to be alert to possible danger. It can be elicited by a specific stimulus: a stab of pain or the failure of someone to return home. It can also be felt in response to something less tangible: a sense that a reasonable proposition is not quite what it sounds; a feeling that there is something wrong with the attractive plateful of food in front of you.

When we do deny or repress this emotion, the flexibility of the mechanism is damaged. As the chemical levels of unreleased emotion increase, anxiety becomes chronic and unhelpful: we get anxious about feeling anxious. Instead of usefully informing us of possible harm and raising our awareness, it confuses us, depletes our mental and physical energy and robs us of clarity.

We then label anxiety as the enemy, and try to find a magic strategy that will prevent us from feeling it. While residual fear clouds our perceptions, we lose our inner reference point and our contact with instinct and intuition. The more distanced we are from our instinctual wisdom, the more vulnerable we actually become. We end up by putting our trust in the 'wrong' people; we allow ourselves to be persuaded that a no-risk policy in life is really possible, if we care to pay the premium.

We deny what we see and hear and know to be at odds with our own inner truth because *doubt becomes destructive*. We find it difficult to open up and acknowledge uncertainty because this would prompt more fear and, with so much accumulated in the psychosomatic system already, it is easier to shut down against any more. This makes us increasingly susceptible to 'virtual reality' and to the spin of the media; real life and fiction become dangerously blurred.

Repressed fear tightens the hold of monocular culture. Advertisers, insurance companies and security firms persuade us to buy their products by offering a guarantee against a multitude of fears: sudden death, poverty, robbery, accident, illness, old age, being unattractive, alone, dependent, a failure. The strength of their persuasion feeds on our fear of powerlessness.

Our capacity to be trustworthy has been profoundly damaged by monocular insistence on repression of fear. Vulnerability is not only uncherished: it is open to neglect, punishment and abuse. Children, the elderly, the mentally and physically infirm have no guarantee of protection. The cult of 'blame the victim' takes over as confidences and trust are exploited with impunity for personal gain.

The knock-on effect

Damage to any one emotional capacity affects the others. Accumulated fear stifles our capacity for power. We become too fearful to confront, to challenge, to say 'no'. We stop asking questions because the answers could present us with a choice, so it becomes easier to deny what we see and to pretend everything is fine. We disclaim personal responsibility while acquiring as much access to hierarchical power as we possibly can to shore up any weakness.

While anger is kept at bay by aggression, our deepest sorrow stays locked away beyond reach. In this way, fear also stifles our capacity for care, narrowing it to a safe and controllable few individuals whom we call our own. Chronic mistrust of others encourages us to snuggle down more comfortably under the quilt of dogmatic beliefs and the safety of 'them/us' prejudices; *different becomes dangerous.*

Emotions are experienced as obstacles only because we have not been taught to use the potential energy. Fear is uppermost and is the most accessible emotion: this is why the response of aggression is universal. Whenever we go through the fear, it diminishes: what we are left with is a new emotional vigour and vitality. Self-limiting fear can be suspended and our personal power restored.

This energy would then be available for transformation through a gentleness that touches all realms of being in the service of love. This is the power of the heart. It is the most potent antidote to the exclusive domination of monocular vision.

49

A few days later, Clare arrived for work, preoccupied with a conversation she'd had with Sophie earlier that morning. She'd phoned because she hadn't heard from her. Sophie sounded dreadful, really low, and, of course, automatically rejected any suggestion that her mother made. Clare didn't know what to do next; she felt quite desperate about it all. She sat down at the desk, moving aside a large folder entitled *The Bonbon Effect*, and switched on the computer.

'I'll take this,' said Helen, picking up the folder.

'What on earth does it mean?' asked Clare, intrigued.

Helen smiled. 'Do you know what a bonbon is?'

Clare shook her head.

'It's the French word for a small, round, wrapped sweet.'

'Oh yes,' said Clare, nodding in recognition. 'I remember it now from school.'

'Well, a dear friend once told me a story of a trendy and extremely popular homeopath who travelled round America and Europe giving lectures and drawing huge crowds of devoted female followers. Apparently he was very charismatic. Playing the "star", he would begin all his lectures by standing on the podium and throwing showers of bonbons in the direction of the audience. In response, his fans would shriek and leap around like little girls to catch one or scramble on the floor to get hold of one as a treasured keepsake. It sounded hysterical.

'The story made me smile because it seemed a lovely metaphor for those two vital assets that belong to our opposite gender but, of course, are absent from our own bodies. The bonbon *effect* – that we're going to look at later – describes the repercussions of this absence, you know, how it's shaped our attitudes, as women, both to ourselves and to men as well.' Helen ended with a mock flourish, as if to rousing applause. 'So now you know.'

'I certainly do,' Clare replied. 'Thank you.' She turned round to face the screen. 'Ready when you are.'

50

The Dynamics of Domination

How does a dominant culture become dominant? The dynamics of domination are the same, whether between individuals, groups or nations, in the sense that there is always a two-way relationship. Every dominant group has to have a lower group over which to dominate. Examples of lower groups, in the past and present, are: Black Americans, peasants, Native Americans, the working classes, the poor, the Irish, mulattoes, the lower Hindu castes, the Jews, the mentally and physically disabled, Asians, Aborigines, the Incas, the Hutus, Afro-Caribbeans, and gypsies.

So what makes a group dominant? Is it larger? Not necessarily. Nor is it necessarily better armed, more advanced, more resourceful or better organised. What is essential, though, to the dynamic is that the dominant group *assumes* superiority. This means it operates on an assumption that such superiority is unquestionable, simply 'Godgiven' or part of the natural and fixed (hierarchical) order of things.

Correspondingly, the dominant group assumes the natural or 'God-given' inferiority of the lower group. In the course of history, this inferiority has been labelled heathen, godless, primitive, underdeveloped, quaint, backward, naive or even cute: but always inferior.

To maintain dominance, the culture of the lower group is also labelled 'inferior'. The word 'culture' here means beliefs about the meaning of life, from birth to death and everything in between. Culture includes codes of dress, rituals, social and domestic practices, the structure of social, family and national life. It also includes language, music, literature, art, food and customs. Culture describes how we see ourselves in relation to each other and the world around us.

Whatever the culture of the lower group, the dominant group demands that it be, at the very least, superimposed upon or, at worst, exterminated. The Bushmen of the Kalahari desert, whose culture has existed for thousands of years, are currently under threat of such extermination by the dominant group in Botswana, keen to profit from the diamonds found in the Bushmen's ancient land.

When a lower group loses its own culture, a new culture is imposed: a new language; a new dress code; new social practices; new diet; a new deity; a new way of life. This group now becomes *muted* by the dominance of the other.

Historically, it is interesting to note that many cultures that have become muted were not built around monocular beliefs. The examples of Mayan, Maori, Native American and Aboriginal cultures would be far more at home with left-eye vision. Sometimes a muted culture goes underground: a language, religious practice or social custom is kept alive, secretly, to avoid sanctions by the dominant group. Often, these cultures die out for ever.

Once any dominant group is in power, how does it stay in power? It needs to gain access, by force if necessary, to all other facets of perpendicular power: resources, wealth, territory, expertise, governmental or military control. Then the dominant group has to hold on to them by any means that 'justify' the end. Unsurprisingly, justification can always be found.

Dominant cultures have a common *modus operandi*: aggression. Archaeologists have long believed that war has been and is the impetus behind the process of civilisation. The need to band together to fight a common enemy produced the transition from small, autonomous, self-governing and self-sustaining communities to a much larger population governed by hierarchical rule.

Dominance and gender

It takes a leap of imagination now to see how the dominant/ muted dynamic relates to gender. We know of no moment in history when women were colonised by men in the same way that we identify other 'coloniser'/'colonised' relationships. We can't define an actual process of colonisation, and yet we are often aware of a supposed 'natural' order of things, of an up/down system in which women find themselves in the lower position.

One glance at the ladders of the monocular system in every country and every nation in the world shows us that those on the higher echelons of hierarchical power each have a pair of bonbons. There may be the odd and pronounced exception, with metaphorical bonbons only, but let there be no doubt that the higher rungs are top-heavy with individuals who are endowed with the genuine articles.

This applies to the upper echelons of the hierarchy in government, corporate, scientific, commercial, academic, medical, financial and religious institutions, the armed forces and the civil service. Look at the 500 richest, most 'powerful' people in the country, in Europe, in the world, last year, the year before, next year or the year after and you will conclude without doubt that bonbons rule OK. Look at the hallowed traditions of revered composers, scientists, painters, inventors, sculptors, explorers, architects, philosophers and poets, and the same feature applies.

The exceptions to this norm – those famous and infamous women who have made it on to higher rungs or ruled nations for a while and are constantly trotted out to pre-empt any current complaint – usually appear so cold or fearsome or corrupt that we really don't want to be reminded of them.

Now how do we explain the remarkable absence of our gender in these upper echelons? What puts men higher up the ladder? What keeps them there? How come that being born with bonbons means that you are automatically placed on a higher rung than being born without? Is it that women are inferior in some way, perhaps less intelligent, less hardworking, less competent or less enduring? Is women's role in the world better served elsewhere? Does gender inequality matter? Would women really achieve a greater sense of fulfilment if they were more equally represented in the higher strata of power?

These questions and their repercussions for our lives have been discussed by women and men for over two hundred years. Millions of words and years of time and energy have been dedicated to challenge and counter-challenge; efforts that have inspired many of us to see differently.

The precepts of feminism have encouraged us to move upwards, each gain marking another higher rung on the ladder. The past 150 years have seen a huge change in women's status throughout most of the world. Many young women today take for granted rights that were not available to their mothers and that their grandmothers could only have dreamed about.

So much has changed for the better that it has become less fashionable these days to talk of inequality. While men yawn when the issue is raised, women look faintly embarrassed and claim it is no longer relevant. Reference to gender issues or gender inequality – in *Western* culture – is regarded as outdated. People declare that 'Times have changed' or 'Young men and women are different from the past generation'. Even when evidence of sexism rears its ugly head in the media every now and then, its impact is offset by payment of vast sums in compensation for sexual harassment or discrimination; so it's easy to be sceptical and conclude women are hardly 'disadvantaged' any more.

Popular opinion is influenced by the higher public profile of women in positions of authority, usually in business or in government. This has a different effect from that of seeing women who are powerful through wealth or beauty – there are many stars and models or artistic performers in this category – because now women hold positions of some legitimate power over others. We're told that 'Women have the same opportunities as men now' by those who then trot out the usual examples of Margaret Thatcher or Hillary Rodham Clinton who, for some reason, are regularly cited as role models for the rest of us.

We don't look at the details of the bigger picture. Simply because there is the occasional woman approaching the top of her professional ladder and a smattering of women in senior managerial or directorial positions, we don't comment much on the imbalance or absence of women from the highest echelons. Now we believe we're getting somewhere, we don't like to draw attention to the downside. So it isn't newsworthy any more or worth questioning, as though previous grievances have been attributed to a problem of mere mismanagement that has now been addressed and corrected, once and for all.

Equality or emulation?

We could almost be persuaded that equality has truly arrived were it not for one small problem. Equality isn't quite what it appears when we look more closely. Somewhere along the line, the monocular system has taken over. The course of feminism has been determined exclusively by right-eye vision.

The goal of feminism has been to increase women's power: to the same power as men have. This includes material gains, increased status and improved access to educational and professional opportunities, all significant, but relating to one perspective only: the left eye has remained closed. Perpendicular power has become crucial to equality while personal power remains eclipsed. The achievements of feminism have moved the position of some of the players but the game remains the same.

If women are to be players, they must adapt to the rules of the game. For example, it is true that previously sacrosanct professions, which once stipulated the ownership of bonbons as a condition of membership, have now accepted a few bonbonless others. However, it is also true that these newcomers are required to display the characteristics associated with having bonbons if they are to be accepted, supported and seen on equal terms with the real guys.

To achieve 'equal' status, not just a title, a woman cannot continue to behave like a woman is 'supposed' to do. If you're not sure what constitutes such behaviour, try emotional, caring and attentive towards others; indecisive, unable to take criticism, susceptible; a tendency to be indirect and woolly minded and to exhibit little staying power when the going gets tough.

Pretending to have bonbons, therefore, means conforming to a particular style of behaviour: being determined and unwavering and unemotional. It requires us to be focused, competitive, tough, ruthless, self-interested and capable of putting others' needs and feelings right out of the picture if it interferes with the main goal.

It is clear that what we are describing as characteristic of a 'male' culture fits into the right-eye view of life. Seeing the system in place is not the same as liking it. Nor does it follow that women feel automatically more comfortable with the perspective of the left eye. Some women feel at home with the right-eye system and some men feel very much at home with the vision of the left eye.

Nevertheless, there *is* a dominant system. We can all see it in place. It is a system we have in common but experience differently. There are other factors – class, wealth, education – that affect our experience of the dominant system but the bottom line is gender.

Gender affects our response most fundamentally whether we uphold the system, challenge it, benefit from it or fight to overturn it. We see a system in place and, within the perpendicular, both men and women see the bonbons at the top. Whether we are born men or women, in other words, those precious two objets d'art will determine our relationship to this dominant system, as clearly as the colour of skin once determined one's relationship to the system of apartheid.

51

Helen put the coffee on the table.

'Thank you.'

They were quiet for a minute or so before Clare asked: 'Would you call yourself a feminist, Helen?'

'Well, I would, yes, but it depends on your meaning.'

'I don't know, really. I've never seen myself as a feminist. Just haven't been angry enough, I suppose.'

'What makes you think it's to do with anger?'

'Of course it is. That's what makes us protest because of inequality and unfairness. It makes us angry. Or it used to. I'm not sure that it seems as relevant now as it did perhaps a century ago or even thirty years ago. Don't you think things have changed?'

'Yes, at some level. But I still see young women today having problems with low self-esteem, you know, who feel powerless, who desperately want to be pleasing and attractive and—'

'That's not true!' Clare's vehemence came as a surprise – to them both – but she carried on. 'They've got so much more choice and independence. My daughter's not at all self-effacing like I was, she . . .' Clare's voice faltered.

Helen listened without speaking.

'I'm sorry,' said Clare.

'What for?'

'I'm confused, that's all.' She looked out at the garden. She didn't want to talk about Sophie because she was aware of the time they'd spent on her problems during the last session.

Helen sighed. 'These are difficult things to talk about, you know, they touch on very deep feelings. I'll just leave you with one thought about feminism and then we'll go back.'

Clare looked at her.

'I do regard myself as a feminist, very much so, but my beliefs stem not so much from anger as love.'

52

Something Missing

It is very hard to begin to contemplate the significance of what we see without some kind of metaphorical shutter coming down over our eyes. This is in response to a mixture of feelings, deep down, most of which are buried under many strata of denial and good behaviour. It is a reality that most women don't want to look at.

We work hard in all spheres of life, believing that being competent, successful, hardworking and honourable will prevail over any kind of prejudice. Yet it only takes one remark, one incident, one putdown or one rejection to remind us (and we are often genuinely surprised) that being equal actually means being equal in a man's world. Even when we adapt our behaviour along monocular lines, we are rarely forgiven by other women and often resented by men.

We tell ourselves it doesn't matter and, even if it did, what could anyone do about it? We remind ourselves that women are 'powerful' in the home – this is our sphere – and we can rule it, as we always have done. We make ourselves the emotional hub, the *heart* of the home, and, through love and a certain degree of manipulation, we exercise a considerable degree of control. We take consolation from the fact of having power indirectly over others.

This works well while we are 'in role', so to speak, while our partners and children need us. It is enough to love, which we do, and to devote our efforts to those we love. But there is often something else in the shadows, which may only become clearly visible when those we love cease, for whatever reason, to need our devotion. Then a feeling of disappointment appears, a sense of unfulfilled expectations, a loss of balance. We keep going with what we do and know best, while ignoring our inner voices. We keep quiet.

We cannot conceive of anything different because things have always been this way. One difficulty for all of us is that of sheer scale. If we ever allow ourselves to contemplate the existence of men's secret societies, clubs, cliques and exclusive organisations, or consider the dominance of 'laddish culture', it is unlikely we will feel anything other than an overwhelming sense of inevitability.

Even if we don't feel quite at home, few of us, as women, use our new and higher positions of perpendicular power to challenge the dominant culture. As aggression has become more widespread and 'normal' and the practice of objectism is increasingly unchallenged, we find ourselves more actively instrumental in maintaining the dominant culture. Our newly gained ground in the echelons of power gives us new (equal) opportunities, making us more visible in the front lines.

This is a change from the traditional place behind the scene where, even today, many of us still prefer to stand. We have a long history of passive collusion, if not active endorsement: we don't challenge, we don't confront, we keep quiet and we toe the line. Sometimes this can stem from a position of choice: we consciously decide to leave a situation or keep quiet because instinct tells us that our needs for self-preservation would best be served by doing so. Most of the time, however, passive collusion stems from a deep-rooted insecurity connected to an equally deep-rooted dependence on those in the higher position. This forms the essence of the *bonbon effect*.

When Freud described penis envy as a symptom of women's psychology, he was describing one tangible fragment, not the whole picture. Few women actually envy a man his penis or want to be a man. The majority of women have occasion to envy the privilege that goes with this fragment. Whereas jealousy is regarded as something elicited by a relationship, envy is understood to be related to other people's possessions or property: what they have and you don't, rather than who they are close to. This fits perfectly into the ladder perspective. Whoever is higher is envied because they have more power.

The bonbon effect describes a much wider, deeper and less obvious part of women's psychology. It describes a psychological syndrome constructed around an internal and invisible belief system that is an inevitable consequence of seeing our position always and for ever on a *lower* rung.

The bonbon effect describes a lifelong adaptation to living as 'mute' in relation to a dominant culture. At its core is our response to inhabiting a 'bonbonless' body and the effect this absence has on shaping *all* our relationships: to ourselves, to other women and to men.

53

As Clare drove home from Harwell House, she had a startling idea. She'd go and see Sophie. She decided to drive into town . . . no, she'd drive to Sophie's flat. Clare knew she'd be in because she'd said that she was taking the day off as she wasn't well, again.

Clare felt strangely out of character. It was unlike her to go anywhere uninvited, especially when she knew Sophie didn't really want to see her at all. But she felt emboldened by something, as if she'd taken some substance to give her courage. She realised that, for once, she didn't care that Sophie was going to be irritated if she went round: she knew that it was important to her, this visit. She was fed up with waiting and worrying and she needed to see for herself what was going on.

54

Forty minutes later Clare stood on the doorstep and pressed the bell, nervous but resolute. There was no answer so she rang again. This time there were sounds from inside and Sophie opened the door, clearly having been asleep. She looked dismayed when she saw her mother there.

'Sorry to wake you, Soph, but I thought I'd come round. I won't stay long but I just felt like seeing you.'

Sophie said nothing but sighed and opened the door wider to let her mother come in.

Clare took off her jacket.

'Do you want some tea?' Sophie asked.

'Yes, I'd love a cup, thanks. I'll make it if you want.'

'No, sit down. I'll get it.'

Clare looked around. She thought the flat was very gloomy. She couldn't see anything of her daughter in it; she remembered the way Sophie had decorated her bedroom at home with such care and enjoyment. It had been *her* room, so individually and completely, but there was no sign of her here.

'How's Phil?' she asked.

'He's fine. Well, he's not fine, actually. He sprained or did something to his knee playing football on Saturday so he's in a bit of pain at the moment.'

'Has he been to see the doctor?'

'I don't know. I don't think so,' replied Sophie with little grace.

A silence.

'Mum, why are you here?'

Clare thought. 'As I said, I suddenly decided to come and see you as I was driving home from work.'

'But why?' Sophie put a mug of tea down on the table beside Clare and sat down herself.

'Do I need a reason to come and visit my own daughter?' said Clare, knowing as soon as the words had left her mouth how very stupid they sounded.

Sophie looked at her and didn't say anything. She still looked thin, thought Clare.

'Soph, this is ridiculous,' she said suddenly.

Sophie looked startled. 'What is?'

'I don't know ... what's wrong.' Clare was groping for her words. 'I don't know how to talk to you without making you irritated. I'm worried sick about you ... and ...' She looked at her daughter. 'I love you, Soph, and I don't know what to do ... about everything.'

'What do you mean, "everything"?' asked Sophie in a guarded tone.

'Well, you're not well, Sophie. That's the truth. I can see you aren't. You know it too.'

'We've talked about this before, Mum.'

'I know we have and you don't want to do anything about it.'

'It's not that I don't want to do anything. It's because nobody can help.'

'How do you know that?'

As Sophie opened her mouth to reply, Clare said, 'And don't tell me again about those useless counsellors.'

'All right, I won't,' said Sophie somewhat bemused by the uncharacteristic, almost belligerent tone in her mother's voice.

Clare could hear this tone in her voice as well. She wondered at it and, at the same time, kept going.

'You know, Soph, as long as you keep dismissing everything, you can avoid having to take responsibility.'

'Responsibility for what?'

'Responsibility for your life, your feelings, your past, your present, your future.'

Sophie looked surprised. 'You don't usually talk like this, Mum. Is this because you've been working for that woman?'

'No, it's not as simple as that. Anyway, don't change the subject.'

'I don't know what you mean by responsibility.'

'I mean that you are an adult and already have a past. And you have a lot of feelings about things, about me, about your dad, about your dad dying, about losing your baby . . .' She hesitated and looked up to see how Sophie would respond to this but she was still looking attentively at Clare and listening.

'You are a beautiful young woman, Soph. No, I mean it,' she said when Sophie grimaced. 'You are very special and I'm not saying that because I'm your mother.' Something struck Clare and she paused for a moment.

'Look, Soph, I know we're not close. I . . . maybe . . . I don't know. Maybe I'm not good at being close. I know I love you but I know too that there are feelings, between us, that we've never talked about. But there are things that sit there, like a presence in the room. And I feel very sad about it. I don't know what I want, Soph, but I know that it seems such a shame to have a daughter like you and not be able to enjoy talking to you. I don't mean I want to be in your pocket or anything. I'm happy to be separate but that's the thing, Soph, we're too separate. We're never close. There's something in the way and I don't know what it is. I don't know if it's something I've done or not done but I know something is there, between us, and I'm tired of pretending that it's not there, when it is.'

She paused for breath. 'That was a bit of a mouthful, wasn't it?' Then she smiled at Sophie, feeling a little flustered after such an outpouring.

To her surprise, Sophie smiled back. Clare saw she had tears in her eyes.

'What's the matter?' she said, leaning forward and then, instantly remembering her experience with Helen, she sat back in her chair and said, 'You don't have to say.'

'I don't know, Mum. You're different today, that's all. You've never said anything like that before and I thought you were being really brave.' Sophie's tears spilled over and she started to cry. Clare did nothing but touch Sophie's hand. And be there. Her own eyes filled with tears too, of course, but it didn't matter. They just sat there together.

After a few minutes, Sophie got up to find a hankie. 'Here,' said Clare, fishing one out of her pocket.

'Thanks.' Sophie finished her tea and didn't say anything for a while. Clare was really happy to sit with this silence. She was finding silences more enjoyable these days, she noticed.

Eventually, Sophie said, 'You're right about things between us. Lots of things have got in the way, I suppose. What do you want to do about it?'

'I don't know. I'd like us to be able to talk when we can and to be more honest. But you still need to find someone else, you know, whom you can talk to and trust. There are things for you to find out on your own, not with me. You've got to get better somehow.'

'Do you really think this woman of yours would help?'

'I don't know. It would depend how you got on. I don't know Helen well but I like her and I would trust her. But you have to make up your own mind. Why don't you meet her and decide for yourself?'

'I'll think about it.'

Suddenly Clare felt that her purpose in coming, whatever it was, had been accomplished. She got up. 'I'm going now.'

'You don't have to, Mum.'

'No, I know I don't have to but I've said what I came here to say, even though I didn't know what it was before I came. You go back to bed. We'll talk very soon.'

'OK,' said Sophie.

Clare put her jacket back on and went to the door. She turned to say goodbye and Sophie suddenly kissed her cheek, really warmly.

'Thanks for coming, Mum.' She looked into Clare's eyes. 'I mean it. Thank you. I'll have a think and ring you later.'

''Bye, love, talk to you soon.'

On the way home, Clare wondered what on earth was happening to her and why things seemed different and where it would all lead. Whatever the answers were, she felt very glad.

55

The Bonbon Effect in the Workplace

To understand the enormity of the bonbon effect in the culture at large, we begin by taking a close look at one specific area – the workplace – because this serves as a microcosm of monocular culture.

All the familiar features are there: we see the bonbons occupying the higher echelons and the importance of competition and ambition; profit becomes the single goal to aim for. We see humans being regarded as objects, whether employees or those who make up the 'market'.

Markets and commerce are an integral part of society but, in the past twenty years, the business or executive class has bred a new 'royalty' in the workplace. Airlines, hotels, restaurants, telephone companies, car suppliers and travel companies aim at the business class so that its executives can enjoy the higher echelons of comfort and convenience. These modern-day princes of the boardroom demand 'executive' treatment – food, facilities, call girls, entertainment, personal mentors or coaches, services of all kinds – available from willing suppliers who want to gain access to the vast pool of expenses circulating around the corporate castles.

A psychological by-product of this phenomenon is that business (monocular) values have filtered down into large parts of ordinary life, previously outside this world. Sport, education, medicine, politics, broadcasting, the performing arts and publishing, for example, have been taken over (colonised) by businessmen and business ethics (or lack of them). Intrinsic values of gamesmanship, teaching, healing, governing, informing, entertaining and literature have been overlaid by the 'superior' values of business.

We are all encouraged to adapt to these values. During the privatisation of public companies, when the chance to purchase shares was offered to the public, an activity previously only available to a few cognoscenti was open to us all. We didn't need knowledge; we just had to jump on board. Ordinary men and women bought shares for the first time, made a few hundred pounds and were delighted with themselves while corporate executives made billions as usual without feeling a thing.

Business has become a metaphor for life in the Western world: the admonition to be more businesslike, streamlined, aggressive and profitable is regarded as a commandment from on high. These qualities depend on the most up-to-date technology, the right resources, a high profile, the right image, cost-effectiveness and, always, profit for the shareholders.

In business there are certain traditions, as in all long-established cultures. The main tradition is corruption. This includes lack of responsibility, lack of sanction for wrongdoing, financial reward for manifest incompetence, cover-ups, deliberate misinformation (lying) and lack of accountability. A second tradition is bullshitting, a familiar strategy deployed to cover up mistakes, liability, responsibility or ignorance. Together they form the modern catechism, handed down to us by capitalism, written in American and easily translated into any national language.

Women in the workplace

How do women negotiate the prevailing culture of the workplace? We are relative newcomers, after all. Although women have always worked, we have behind us no longstanding tradition of payment for our labour or experience of a business environment. Few of us are seasoned players.

This leads to a paradox: there are more women visible in senior positions in the workplace today but, less visibly, most of them lack confidence. Despite hard work, commitment, the best academic and business qualifications, and often a confident veneer, many privately suffer from a self-perceived feeling of inadequacy.

In every course attended by women who want to be more confident in the workplace, all sorts of skills can be learned very effectively, but at some point we encounter a deeper problem. When each individual woman repeatedly swallows back her feelings and reprimands herself for being oversensitive or over-imaginative, she loses the ability to distinguish what is personal from what is related to her gender.

When a group of twenty women, who don't know each other, discover that what each thought was a personal problem is shared or echoed by women, older, younger, higher up and lower down the ladder, then we begin to see that there is something else going on. We see that we are part of a much bigger and entrenched *system*. This is not cause for war. Knowing you're not mad and not alone is the most wonderful psychological tonic. It is a relief to see beyond the official line.

The official line declares that inequality no longer exists because of the equal opportunities provision in place: if disparity did exist, in the past, it has been talked about and dealt with and there are now more important things to focus on. One thing that makes us feel more powerless than *any* other experience is denial, knowing something is happening but being told or telling ourselves that it isn't. So the first step is to stop pretending it isn't there. It *is*.

It's not hard for us to identify the visible repercussions of having no bonbons in the workplace. Women are not blind to the way men are listened to, given preferential treatment, taken more seriously, lauded, rewarded and forgiven unpardonable sins – both by women and other men. We see the favouritism shown to our male counterparts. Even if we don't want to be included in the culture, we are certainly aware it exists and have to work alongside it.

Many women have studied hard, worked hard, have done everything right, put in the hours, taken the flak, hidden the hurt, imagining that they would be regarded as equal and treated as equal. Disillusion sets in over and over again when they finally see that nothing at all can make up for the absence of those two small spheres.

Accepting the presence of a system allows for two major insights. The first is that we have a tendency to perceive put-downs, patronising behaviour and experiences of being ignored, overlooked or intimidated as *personal* attacks. This is very understandable because you happen to be the person inside your body at the time. But in reality the presence of a system means that, most of the time, what happens to us is not directed personally. It's just that we happen to be seen as representatives of our gender. If you remember the monocular inclination to make others into objects, you can see how, within a work culture, this is going to be par for the course.

The second insight comes from understanding the dynamics of our usual responses to the above experiences. Two major stumbling blocks to challenging others are self-doubt and lack of confidence. One of the most common ways in which women undermine themselves is by failing to question or challenge unfair criticism. When we unravel the dynamics of why this happens, we find a small internal voice saying, 'Perhaps they've got a point; perhaps they're right.' This stumbling block undermines our ability to be authoritative when we need to be.

We also find out that we wouldn't be nearly so affected, wound up or demolished by others were it not for the existence of an inner conviction that, somehow, whatever happens to us is our 'fault'. It isn't logical. It isn't rational. But it's part of the powerful psychological mechanism of the bonbon effect.

The workplace is one small part of the system but it reflects what happens in the rest of our lives. The vast majority of inter-personal problems we experience result from this internal belief system. This, of course, is compounded by others' attitudes and stereotypical expectations, but acknowledging our own depend-ence on the system is the first challenge.

For the dynamic of up/down to be maintained, the dominant assumptions of superiority are only half the story. Clearly this is a complementary process. The lower group operates on a corres-ponding assumption (either/or): if the dominant group is superior, its own status is inferior.

If not exactly inferior, then, at the very least, members of the muted group have to have a sneaking suspicion that there must be some very good reason for the status quo to be the way it is. This assumption is born out of powerlessness to effect any change. We are born with something missing and this absence prescribes our future in the lower position. Believing this to be inevitable helps us to alleviate our powerlessness by rationalising our position in the system and enables us to survive within it.

56

Clare paused before starting on the next chapter. She still had a small pile to get through.

She wanted to read. She really wanted to make the effort somehow. It had gone beyond the stage of a mild interest and curiosity and had developed into an eagerness to understand what Helen was talking about. This was partly because of her own experience of Helen, as a person to work for, and partly because of something she felt occurring deep down in her self. Angie came into her mind: Clare felt there was a definite connection with Angie's situation at work, without knowing precisely what it was.

She remembered something else: a tiny incident that had happened the day before. She'd been in the supermarket car park, putting the bags into the boot of her car, when she'd witnessed a brief interaction between a young couple who had also come back with their shopping. Their car was next to hers. They were young, twentyish. It was the high-pitched tone of the girl's voice she'd first noticed.

'Oh, look! Isn't that pretty? Amazing colours!' Clare heard her say, immediately followed by a sharp slap of her boyfriend's hand crushing the small insect.

'What did you do that for?' she whined. 'It wasn't hurting anybody.'

'I don't want it messing up my car,' replied her boyfriend impatiently, ending the dialogue right there.

This little scene had stayed with her and she'd thought at the time that she'd scarcely have noticed it before. It wouldn't have made any impression on her, but now it did. She was thinking about things differently. She couldn't describe what the changes were but she was aware of some new energy in her, not frightening but certainly intriguing.

Things seemed to be happening. She'd had a long talk with Danny. He had asked her again to go out to California and this time she'd accepted his invitation, as well as his offer to pay. They'd agreed it would be a good idea for her to go in the autumn, or fall as he called it, about five months away. She'd go for a fortnight and maybe travel around while she was there. There were lots of details to sort out yet but she was pleased to have made a definite decision.

Then there was Sophie's decision to meet Helen. This was arranged for tomorrow. She'd offered to take Sophie there because it wasn't that easy on public transport and then she'd go off for an hour or so and come back for her. She wondered what they would make of each other. She also wondered if Helen would be able to help. She really hoped so.

She settled back to continue reading.

57

Vertical Vision

It is possible to identify certain characteristics from the interaction between any two parties where one is 'dominant' and the other 'muted'. Gender dynamics are no exception.

Looking up

We may wear trousers now, study construction engineering and initiate sex but despite any feminist advances over recent centuries, the vast majority of women still feel dreadfully incomplete without a man. It is not unusual for women to drop their girlfriends as soon as there is a man on the scene. Not only because it is sexual: gay men friends are often valued more than women friends. For many women, the man in her life becomes the centre of her universe with everything and everyone else becoming peripheral. On the other hand, a woman will often complain she is expected to fit in with a man's work and leisure activities and peer company.

Put a man in a group of women and he somehow takes all the attention. Either they fuss and cluck over him – if he's welcome – or they hiss and spit, if he's not. Either way the focus of the attention will be on him. Put a woman in a group of men and, unless she's stunningly attractive, she's hardly noticed, except perhaps when one of the men happens to swear.

We are rarely conscious of this higher value but it exists. There is something about a compliment or advice or criticism from a man – boss, father, lover – that has a special (higher) value. There's something about the approval (or disapproval) of a man – colleague, lover, friend, brother – that matters more. Women who are (more or less) happily married with children find themselves positively fluttering to the attentions of a younger male colleague (whom they know is immature and probably just using them) simply because he is a he, and a young he.

Why do we do this? We enjoy the reflected or vicarious power. Powerlessness, that we don't like, can be temporarily alleviated. Men's power rubs off on us and masks inadequacy. We want to have access to things in powerful places or friends to help us get up the ladders ourselves. If reflected power is all that's open to us, then this is what we fight for.

Looking straight ahead

Mistrust of other women is endemic and for good reason. This is not to say women are untrustworthy, far from it, but that as part of the lower group, we are long-term competitors for the same prizes of male approval, acceptance and a suitable (or even unsuitable) husband. We compete for all the dimensions of status predetermined for us within the dominant culture.

The ladders are prescribed for us: appearance, body shape, intelligence, attractiveness, articulacy, marital status, maternity, personality, dress sense. At work we can add competence, status, salary and position, which apply to ladders for men as well, except there is an extra edge to competition between women because high positions are far fewer in number.

We are wary of each other. We tell ourselves that men are more straightforward and direct and on the surface. Even though this can get a bit boring, you know where you are, whereas, with women, you're never sure. We 'know' men can be more brutal because they're physically stronger but women, we believe, can be deadly. We keep an eye on the competition, never missing a little weight put on here or a wrinkle there or too much make-up: 'What does she think she looks like?' 'Now why is he spending so much time talking to her?'

The ability to respond with warmth to other women is easily undermined by subconscious associations: we remind each other, by reflection, of our powerlessness. The very aptitudes and associations of femaleness are therefore often disliked. Infinitely preferable is the lean, muscular, taut, logical, unemotional, important, successful and powerful male.

We reject what the dominant ethos rejects even if we are not entirely sure we agree. If he complains about the 'hysterics' of the woman down the road whose husband has just left, it is easy to keep quiet. Men don't want women who are silly and they don't want hysterics. So we don't either. We don't bother to point out that maybe these hysterics are in fact emotions, and understandable in the circumstances. Even if we have an inkling that it would be more appropriate to offer support than criticism, it is easy to suppress it on the grounds that it would take too long and we couldn't make it sound logical so he wouldn't listen anyway. There is a hidden benefit to silence as well: it makes us feel safer when male disapproval is deflected on to a woman other than ourselves.

How do we see our own culture? What culture? Is it any different? Not many of us have — or even want — the opportunity to speak honestly with one another about something other than our children or, primarily, the achievements and shortcomings of the dominant group.

Looking down

The cramped position of powerlessness is often eased by looking down: a lower group always designates a further group below itself. Ladders exist within ladders. Middle-class women find working-class women, black women or coloured women (all labels) to work for them. When white American women presumed to speak for black women in the name of feminism, some black American women complained. They reversed the situation, putting white women lower down not only for being racist and bigoted, but for being intrinsically less able than black women to be 'real' women.

Who else occupies the lower rungs? Heterosexual women find lesbian relationships inevitably lower down the pecking order of status because there is not a bonbon in sight. Women without children are pretty much at the bottom of the pile in a monocular culture: fulfilling the criteria of the dominant group is all-important. If motherhood is designated as the most desired status, nothing else a woman achieves will come near to it in cultural importance; nothing will compensate for this lack in her own eyes or those of others.

We can always find someone 'worse off': less attractive, less competent, less sexy, functioning less well in the linear mode than ourselves. We have to make ourselves feel better somehow. We have to survive.

58

Survival Strategies Within the System

Remember that positions on the ladders are precarious. They can change quite suddenly, taking us by surprise. For women, it is a particular shock to be confronted by the unexpected because one of our major strategies, one evident in any muted cultural group, is that of monitoring.

From a lower position, we learn to watch. We learn to be vigilant and develop skills for detecting minute changes in atmosphere and emotional climate. We become expert monitors, wondering privately sometimes how we manage to pick up everything as soon as (or before) it happens, whereas men just don't seem to have a clue.

In some social systems, this vital strategy ensures physical survival: living under repressive dictatorship or an oppressive political or domestic regime. For most women, this strategy ensures our personal survival by scoring enough brownie points to make our presence and value continuously obvious.

Monitoring provides an early warning system. It enables us to spot signs of possible trouble ahead that we need to avoid if we are to fulfil our task of keeping everybody happy and the whole show on the road. This means we have to orchestrate largely from behind the scenes: if we see a problem, we learn to compensate.

In an unfriendly atmosphere, we try to soften the tone. We run after others to explain or comfort after someone else's thoughtless behaviour. If someone is overbearing, we shrink to take up less space; if someone expresses forthright opinions, we keep quiet.

If someone is unhappy, we try to cheer. If someone is shy, we become ebullient. We tailor our own feelings, needs, wishes and thoughts to those of others, depending on them to go 'first', so to speak, so that we can then react accordingly.

We become indirect and devious: we let the dominant ones think our ideas and suggestions are really theirs to avoid confrontation. For the same reason, we hide our feelings and we don't say what we mean a lot of the time because we try and keep the other person 'sweet'. We bend over backwards to pre-empt confrontation; we soothe ruffled feathers and use our wiles to persuade and seduce, to attend and applaud, to divert and distract.

We like others to be happy and successful (both attributes conferring more power than their opposites) because this reflects back on our role: we are fulfilled by pleasing. We are grateful to be useful, to have a function. We are loyal and possessive. We love getting it right and anticipating others' needs before they voice them because this is what we're good at.

We're also good at *carrying* things: shopping bags, pushchairs, children and a string of invisible responsibilities. Emotionally, we carry adults, mothering grown men as well as our children. On the ideological surface, a husband and wife may both have paid jobs and 'share' the housework but the reality is that women usually do more. In an 'equal' relationship, women find themselves doing the lion's share of domestic chores, the lion's share of bringing up children but all in a very mouse-like manner.

We *expect* to do this. We grumble occasionally but we do it all the same, unasked. Instead of clear negotiation, which accompanies the assumption of equality, we do more than our fair share: it is unlikely that any man is going to complain about this arrangement so it rolls along very merrily for years in this way. Until, that is, resentment bubbles up and the mouse turns into a shrew, impossible to please, and makes her feelings known either in being generally unpleasant or presenting a cold shoulder between the marital sheets.

Lack of direct communication stems from feeling powerless within a system. This promotes the tendency to believe 'A blind eye is preferable to a black eye', so we become adept at covering up. In a loyal and often devoted way, we fudge the issues of responsibility. Sometimes, we do this by stating the party line while knowing that it isn't actually true. We maintain that he is loving, that everything is equal, shared right down the middle, that he is sensitive, attuned and a wonderful father. This, of course, may be true, but it is stoutly maintained many times when it isn't.

We overlook things – actually we don't, because we hardly ever miss a thing – but we pretend to overlook gaps in responsibility or humanity. We ignore lapses in parental effectiveness, emotional or sexual sensitivity, obsession and over-identification with work and absence from the family. We deny the margin between the stated stance and the actual stance; the persistent trail of dirty socks and underwear that never seem to make it to the laundry basket.

We pretend we don't mind about things when in fact we *do*. This need to keep up appearances and avoid direct confrontation can lead us to close our eyes to abusive behaviour towards ourselves and even our children. We hold on to our place and role within the system rather than risk falling outside it completely. Powerlessness, on the ladder, is always relative.

59

Sophie stood on the doorstep of Harwell House as Clare drove away. Helen opened the door, smiled and invited her to come in.

They went into the living room where the yellow walls were particularly bright, reflecting the morning sunshine. Sophie asked about the paintings, said she didn't want anything to drink and sat down in one of the armchairs.

She looked at Helen. There was a scratching noise at the door. Helen excused herself and went to the door, scooped up the dog and disappeared for a minute. Then she returned and sat down again.

'I don't know where to begin,' said Sophie.

'Well, you've come here, which was a decision in itself, and you must have had some reason to do so even if you were uncertain of the outcome.'

'Mum suggested I come and see you because I get quite low and I'm off work more than I should be. Did you talk to her?'

'She told me that she was worried about you because you were depressed and not eating much. That's about all.' Helen paused and then added, 'And that you'd been to the doctor and been given medication that didn't suit you.'

'No, it didn't. I ended up throwing the pills away.'

There was a silence. Helen gazed thoughtfully at Sophie, who was aware of this and looked away.

'It's really hard, isn't it? I don't know what to say,' said Sophie.

'Are you feeling anxious?'

'Not especially. I don't know what I'm feeling, really.'

'Why don't you just tell me a bit about your life. You know, about your family, your schooldays, who was important to you, what you were proud of, what you hated, your first love, anything. It doesn't matter where you start because whatever we need to talk about will emerge of its own accord. Just start somewhere and let it unravel.'

Sophie sighed. 'Well, I have a brother, Daniel, who is two years older than me and the main thing I remember about childhood is my dad dying.' She paused and looked into the middle distance. 'That was really terrible. It was terrible he was dying but I remember the atmosphere in the house that went on for *ages*. It was like living under this dreadful cloud that killed any kind of happiness. I hated it and then felt guilty.'

'Were you close to him?'

'Yes, sort of. I adored him when I was smaller but we ended up being quite distant because he was ill. It was always there and he didn't talk about it much – nobody talked about it. I remember one time Danny and I spoke of the fact that we knew he was going to die and we just sat there not knowing what to do. Each of us went into our own world. Danny got into computers and would spend all his time in his room and Mum would be working. She'd come home from school and be tired and then get the meal and then be up with Dad, trying to do things for him, so she wasn't there much to talk to.' She suddenly looked at Helen.

'I should have mentioned it before,' Helen said, intuiting correctly what had crossed Sophie's mind. 'Confidentiality is important and when I agreed to see you, I discussed this with your mother who is perfectly well aware that anything we talk about will remain between the two of us. If you want to discuss anything, that's your choice, but I won't ever refer to anything.'

Sophie was more reassured than she let on. 'I suppose the big thing for me was losing the baby when I was twenty. It was a little girl. I wasn't that close to the father. I didn't love him or anything but I really loved being pregnant. I don't know why. It really meant a lot to me. I didn't even care if Gary – that's the father – decided to stay around or not. I just wanted to have this baby and have a new life and everything. And then I miscarried. Nobody knew why or they didn't say why. Just a lot of bleeding one night and I went to the hospital in the morning and they examined me and said I'd lost the baby and that they'd have to do a scrape or something to get rid of anything that was left.

'I just felt numb afterwards. I couldn't talk to Gary. I couldn't talk to Mum. I didn't want to eat. I just sat there day after day looking at the table. There was a table with a glass top and I remember sitting looking at this glass top all the time as if the world didn't exist at all.

'I didn't cry, I remember that. I remember thinking to myself: Are you going to cry? but I didn't. I didn't feel depressed or suicidal – nothing so strong as that – just numb. I sat and looked at the table or lay in bed under the covers, trying not to think. I spent days like that, weeks.'

'Was your mother involved at all?'

Sophie shook her head. 'I remember really hating Mum at the time. I don't know why. I could hardly bear to talk to her on the phone and, if she did come round, I would just close off. I was quite nasty to her. I felt as if I blamed her in some way – maybe there was nobody else to blame. Gary moved out because I wasn't talking to him either. I didn't mind really. I didn't mind about anything. After he left, I went out to get some milk or tea or something and that was when I cried. Right in the middle of the shop. It may have been because I saw a kiddie with her mum, I don't know. Just seeing other real people was hard enough. One moment I was standing in the shop handing over some money and then I was in floods of tears. I didn't know what to do, trying to find some money and stop crying. In the end I put the milk down and ran back to the flat.'

'How long did this go on, do you remember?'

'Maybe six weeks or even a couple of months. I had a good friend, Abbie, who'd come round regularly and check up on me and phone my mum and things. She lived quite near. We hadn't been great friends but, for some reason, she was really good to me. She seemed to know not to talk too much and that just being there was a great help. She'd come in and make me a cup of tea and a slice of toast and then stay a while and then go. She always felt easy.'

'Did you eat the toast?'

'I'd have a few bites but I really found it hard to eat, to swallow anything. And that's the thing that's gone on. I got used to it, I suppose.'

'What, not eating?'

'Yes. I liked feeling empty, flat, almost non-existent. I didn't make myself sick – I had a friend who was anorexic – still is, actually – but I wasn't like that. I don't think I wanted to be thin. I just couldn't see the point of eating. It felt too positive a statement, as if you really wanted to be here, and I didn't.'

'Do you think you felt that before your miscarriage?'

'I'm not sure,' Sophie replied, thinking about the question. 'I'm not sure what I felt before.'

'You've seen a counsellor before, haven't you?'

Sophie shifted in the chair. 'Yes. More than one. Pretty useless. Well, they were friendly except for one awful woman.'

'How many have you seen, then?'

'Three – two at the doctor's at different times and one at the hospital after the miscarriage. The last one was only recently. That was hopeless so that's really why I've ended up here.' She looked up at Helen, waiting to know where to go next.

'Can we go back to what was going on in your childhood? I'm trying to get a picture of how you felt. You said what happened while your father was dying but what else was going on? Before he was ill, I mean. Did you have lots of friends or were you a loner? Did you play? Did you have any friends?'

'Did I play? That's a strange question. Yes, I did play. A bit with my brother but mostly on my own. I had a really close friend, Maria: we started at the same primary school together. Then she moved away with her family when I was ten. I missed her *terribly*. She was like me and we could spend hours together without quarrelling much – maybe now and then, a little – but we just got on ever so well and I could tell her all sorts of secrets. She was never nasty to me about my writing.' Sophie stopped. 'Did Mum tell you I had a really hard time at school?'

'No, she didn't.'

'I couldn't write in a straight line. I couldn't finish sentences. Or I'd start one and then never get to the end of it because I'd lose it in the middle. It was awful, like unravelling a very long thread that then becomes unmanageable. Essays were hell. I hated them. Always having to begin somewhere and then proceed through your points to a conclusion. I couldn't do that however hard I tried. I'd be up half the night trying to get an essay written for the next day. I'd write it and rewrite it and then write it again. I was really miserable. I was so cross with myself because I had lots of ideas and I knew I was intelligent – you know, I had it in my head – but I couldn't make it work on paper.'

'You didn't have a sympathetic teacher then?'

'No. Even though Mum was a teacher. I didn't go to her school, of course, but she would go up and see people because she could tell I was intelligent enough. I could do art and sculpture and things really well, but not words.'

'Do you still do any?'

'What?'

'Sculpture or painting?'

'No. I haven't for a long time. Not since I lost the baby.'

'So what happened after school?'

'I went to art college and did quite well except for the written work. I got pregnant in my third year, so I left and didn't finish.'

'And now you work in a museum.'

'Yes, I was very lucky because I have a friend who knew the curator and he put in a word for me and that's how I got in. It's fairly laid-back and they've been good about my time off but I think there'll be problems soon if I don't sort myself out.'

There was a pause. Then Helen asked, 'Who has been really important to you in your life, Sophie?'

Sophie shook her head. 'I don't know. I really admired the art teacher: she was very dedicated and she painted herself, as a living.' She thought for a moment. 'My dad used to be important. Maria, I've told you about.' She looked up at Helen again as she said, 'I guess it was the baby.'

'Did you give her a name?'

Sophie looked startled. 'Yes, I did actually. I didn't tell anyone.'

'Are you willing to tell me?'

Sophie paused and then said very quietly, 'Melanie.'

'So Melanie was the most important person in your life. Tell me, Sophie, did you ever say goodbye to her officially, I mean with a little ceremony or anything?'

'No, I didn't. Never thought about it.'

'It's something you could consider as part of getting yourself better.' Helen took a breath. 'Do you want to know what I think?'

Sophie nodded.

Helen sat forward a little. 'From what you've said, and I'm sure there's more, the theme you seem to describe most is loneliness. A sort of chronic loneliness of the spirit, if you like, as if you've arrived on the earth from another planet and you've found your-self here and wonder at the strangeness of everyone and everything. You're sensitive and gentle and this is hard to be some-times. You found it difficult to fit into the straight lines of school. And then precious individuals you really loved all went away for different reasons.'

Helen seemed to consider something privately then contin-ued. 'So it may be that your sadness when Melanie died was connected to your sadness when you father died and that could also be connected to when Maria left. Losses, all our feelings actually, have a habit of running into each other, like currents of water meeting and reinforcing each other until you've got a strong flow.

'So it seems to me that you could do the following. First, you could create a ritual farewell for Melanie and then perform it. It doesn't matter how long ago it was. These things are very impor-tant to us and we don't do them enough, in my opinion. We can talk more about that if you want to go ahead with it.

'Then there's a second dimension: your other losses that you may need to grieve, the goodbyes you need to say.

'And finally there's the third dimension: your feelings about being here. In this world, I mean. The fact is you *are* here, however much you hate it or wish you weren't. You need to come to terms with this reality, which means finding yourself some solid ground to stand on. By solid ground I mean your own power. This can include your own creativity, sculpture or whatever, but finding some strength in yourself. Being at odds with the world is no good for self-esteem and it may help to affirm who you are. Does that make any sense?'

'Everything except the bit about power.'

'You may find that your own beliefs and convictions – the way you see the world – are not the same as other people's.'

Sophie gave a little snort.

'Does that ring true?'

'It seems funny you saying that about me. Sometimes I really do have the impression of being from another world. It can make me feel so sad being here and so helpless. I think that's one reason I can't eat.'

'I think it is too.'

'When you see so much suffering and corruption and starvation and everything, I mean how can you just go on and eat regardless? It makes me sick . . . I find it really hard.'

'I know,' said Helen. 'It is hard. But you're here, Sophie, and you've got to get out of that bed and put your feet on the ground, if you see what I mean.'

Sophie smiled. 'I don't know how.'

'You need to be seen, to be recognised for who you are. But first you have to recognise yourself.'

Helen sat back. 'Listen, Sophie, what do you want to do about working together? If you want, we could arrange, say, three meetings and work out a plan of action along the lines I've suggested, incorporating anything else we think is important along the way. You can prepare a ritual and, if you like, I'll give you some ideas. If we arrange three more sessions together, we can see how you're doing. It will be a long, probably lifelong, process for you, all of this, but we can get you started. I think that's what you need.'

She looked intently at Sophie, who laughed.

'Why do you laugh?'

'Because you sound so positive about me.'

'Well, I am. Why shouldn't I be?'

They looked at each other for a moment.

'Now, I'd like you to have a think about my suggestions and then let me know.'

'I think I'd like to go ahead.'

'I'd still like you to think it over. It's a big step because it means taking some responsibility for yourself and your "difference".'

'That's what Mum said.'

'What?'

'Responsibility. She said it was time I took some responsibility.'

'Well, there you go. Give me a ring when you're ready,' said Helen, getting up. 'When's your mother coming for you?'

Sophie looked at the clock. 'In about ten minutes.'

'Do you want to wait here?'

'No, I'm happy to sit outside by the gate.'

Helen led Sophie out and opened the door.

'Are you sure you're OK here?'

'Honestly. Thank you very much.' She looked at Helen.

Helen smiled. 'It was lovely to meet you, Sophie. I'll hear from you soon.'

''Bye.'

''Bye.'

Helen closed the door.

Sophie walked down the drive and found a log near the gateway to sit on. She settled herself and sighed. For the first time in a long while, longer than she could remember, she felt hopeful at the possibility of change.

60

The following afternoon, Helen sat on the train travelling home. The outlook through the windows was grey and dreary and she herself was in a foul mood, after a wasted and futile day in town.

The reason for her journey had been to take part in a radio programme – something she usually enjoyed – but from the moment Helen entered the studio, she'd seen from the look on the presenter's face that it was going to be difficult. An unglamorous (she hadn't made a huge effort as it was only radio) middle-aged woman, writing about women's difficulties in the workplace, clearly had zero appeal to a young, male, high-flying presenter. She knew there would be limitations to their interaction but assumed that, as she was an invited guest, there would still be some point of contact.

She was wrong. The other guests were a woman journalist and a man who was a Pilates instructor. It turned out that he was an old crony of the presenter so most of the sixty minutes were taken up with antlers locked in laddish banter and constant namedropping of the 'mega-rich megastars' who were the instructor's clients.

Eventually, the presenter decided he had to ask Helen something, so, introducing her on air, he waved a copy of her book in front of her (holding it upside down), and complained the diagrams were meaningless and confusing.

At this point, she had rallied a little under the welter of his rudeness and asserted that there were many women at work who lacked confidence and that being a woman at work still at times meant being disadvantaged.

The presenter rejected this as complete nonsense and then turned to the journalist: had *she* had ever experienced any difficulty at work because of her gender? She quickly and diplomatically said no, explaining that she was freelance and therefore wouldn't encounter any problems. He then looked back at Helen with a dismissive shrug and changed the subject.

It seemed an eternity until the programme ended. She walked downstairs to get out of the place as quickly as possible but the journalist, Jane, caught up with her, clearly wanting to talk. She told Helen about a book she had recently published. She described how she had been an employee of a national newspaper until she fell pregnant, at which point they had fired her. She stopped suddenly, mid-sentence, and said, 'Oh, I could have mentioned that, couldn't I?' Helen, who was past caring at this stage – she was so angry about the whole thing – managed to nod in agreement.

As they continued towards the exit, Jane went on to explain that one of her assignments had been to cover the systematic process of genocide in Africa. She had been so appalled by the collusion of the West in the whole affair that she'd decided to write a book. She managed to gain access to secret military and political documents and had produced a powerful and incriminating book of which she was really proud.

Such was the power of the book, she told Helen, as they both reached the revolving doors to leave the building, that her husband had advised her to publish it using her initials only. He warned her that nobody would take the book seriously if she used her Christian name, identifying the author as a woman. So this was what she'd done.

She told Helen this without any irony. It was clear to Helen that Jane was completely unaware of the contradiction of her actual experience with her tactful denial twenty minutes earlier on air of *ever* being treated differently because of her gender.

Despite an overwhelming urge to scream, Helen somehow managed to be courteous in wishing Jane well with her book, before turning to look for a taxi to the station.

She now looked through the window at the speeding landscape, still in a lot of turmoil, but thankful to be almost home.

61

Helen was keen to get out for a walk as soon as she got home and was about to leave when the phone rang. It was Sophie.

'I've had a think about everything and I really want to do what you suggested and arrange the three sessions.'

'I'm delighted,' said Helen genuinely. 'Wait a moment while I find my diary.'

She'd enjoyed meeting Sophie. So recognisable as a gentle soul, a moon child as Helen called such individuals. Round at heart and resentful of being squeezed into a relentlessly linear mould.

'So which day would suit you best?'

'Thursday afternoons are good because I stop work early.'

'Well . . . we could start on the sixteenth at three o'clock and then make the other two at the same time with a fortnight in between each session. How would that suit you?'

'Fine.' Sophie hesitated. 'We haven't talked about money, have we?'

'No, I should have mentioned it when you came but I forgot,' said Helen.

'How much do you charge?'

Helen told her. There was a pause. 'Is that all right for you?' asked Helen.

'Well, I'm pushed for money at the moment but I really want

to do this now I've decided. I may be able to borrow the money from Mum. I know it has to be a loan. I want to pay for it myself.'

'I'm relieved to hear it,' Helen responded. 'I think it's essential you pay for it yourself.' She paused. 'Sophie, I have a suggestion. What is important for me in this kind of work is that you value yourself enough to value the work that we do together. Of course I have to earn my living too, but I'm willing to be flexible. How would you feel about not borrowing the money but waiting until you either have some money or until you find something that you can give me in exchange?'

'Like what?' asked Sophie, puzzled.

'I don't know,' said Helen. 'But I'm absolutely sure that when you see it, you will recognise it, as simple as that.'

'Are you sure I will?' asked Sophie, intrigued by now. 'You'll have to trust me, won't you?'

'I will and I do.'

'Are you sure?'

'I promise you, Sophie, that I wouldn't suggest this if I thought there were any games going on, you know. I trust that, at some time in the future, you will find a way of paying me for my part of our work, of fulfilling your part of this contract in a way that you feel is a fair exchange: one thing of value for another.'

'Well, if you're really sure, that's great. Thanks. I'll see you on the sixteenth then.'

'I look forward to it. 'Bye for now.'

''Bye.' Helen put the phone down and left the house.

62

A short while later, she and Rusper were walking slowly among the trees. She stopped by a large oak that was covered from root to almost the crown with ivy. There were two stems of ivy climbing upwards, one of which was particularly thick and gnarled. She took a small saw out of her pocket and proceeded to work her way through the thicker one. Rusper, quite accustomed to these pauses, sat and kept watch. Helen was glad to concentrate on the task in hand, using her whole body behind the movement of the saw.

She was constantly aware of the ivy's presence, even when invisible underneath the summer foliage. She was alarmed at the spread of this parasitic growth on so many trees. Everywhere she looked – from the car, from a train – she saw trees in woodland, bordering playing fields, along minor roads, major roads and in farmland, disfigured and misshapen by ivy.

It was a bit of a campaign and she enjoyed it. Throughout winter and spring, she went out two or three times a week to clear some of the trees in the forest. Not much of an impact, but the best she could do.

After about fifteen minutes, she had made one cut through the thicker root and was embarking on a second cut a few inches lower down. Soon she felt the teeth of the saw strike the outer casing of the ivy. She stopped and wiggled the severed piece, back and forth, until it came cleanly away. One more to go and this particular tree would be freed – for a while anyway.

She loved the physical effort. She felt more peaceful now, no longer engulfed by the aggravation of the day; it had already diminished a little and was beginning to recede into the distance behind her.

63

Adaptation

Women do their best to comply and fit in. As any lower group copies the ways, language and attitudes of the dominant culture so as not to stand out, women too find that imitation is a necessary aspect of survival. This process goes a stage further when we adapt to the system so completely that we make it our own. We embrace the culture and follow suit.

We go to male strip shows because men have been enjoying their version for centuries: why shouldn't we do it too? If you can't beat them ... wearing trousers, smoking, swearing, driving, flying, daring exploits, being the boss ... join them. This is all part of liberation, we cheer, but imitation doesn't stop there: we also absorb the positive and negative dualities of the dominant (monocular) culture.

It is the *approach* that we copy. We could be managers, models, or matrons in a different way but, instead, we copy. When we copy we want to win. We want to be on top. We play for the highest power available to us.

We copy the practice of objectism and join in deriding weakness, failure, emotionality. Aggression appears in our behaviour on the roads, in bars, in the workplace and the bedroom. The 'ladettes' copy 'male' predatory ways and scrutinise prospective partners ('gorgeous bum', 'huge box', 'great pecs') as potential objects of sexual conquest. We seduce, we tease, we reject. We can play the game well. Especially when we get angry.

Powerlessness and protest

Anger is inevitably experienced by any muted or lower group and cannot be ignored. Or, rather, it can be but it doesn't go away. When it erupts, it is almost always in the form of aggression. It is difficult to find an example of a lower group/caste/tribe/class whose anger at being oppressed has not turned into aggression – revenge, punishment, tit for tat – once it has become their turn at the top.

When women feel angry, they copy the aggression. We use aggressive tactics every day of our lives – sometimes loudly, sometimes softly – at home, at work, everywhere. We target other women with snide comments, gossip and envy. We matronise men and treat them like little boys: their egos being alternately too fragile or overwhelming. Correspondingly we either avoid telling the truth because they 'couldn't take it' (convinced they would be unable to brush their teeth without us there to remind them) or deflate them, confiding to other women 'how pathetic they all are,' taking an inverse satisfaction in being the true superiors.

Sometimes anger reaches a pitch of vengeful hatred ('Hell hath no fury . . .') and our revenge becomes extraordinarily imaginative: we know exactly where it will hurt the most. We cut off the trouser legs of the Savile Row suits or empty a hundred bottles of his best claret into the gutter; other women catch themselves smiling in recognition and feeling a vicarious satisfaction.

Occasionally this resentment becomes collectively focused and organised into political or anarchical activity: lobbying, demonstrations, feminist manifestos and radicalism. Hostility to men and a wish to turn the tables (reverse the positions on the ladder) fuel the momentum; it is difficult to keep aggression and revenge completely out of the picture. This means that many of us, as women, are afraid of our own anger because all we see is the possibility of aggression. The possibility of this inversion (women *over* men) frightens us. We are constrained by concern for those we love.

Devotion and dependence

Our love for the others in our lives – especially our husbands, partners, sons, fathers, brothers – is a large part of what binds us to a monocular system. We love these men dearly, but also depend on them, seeing them in a different (higher) place. Meeting others' needs – seeing the successes and achievements and good health of those we love – is the clearest evidence of our self-worth. When love and pleasing become confused, however, devotion is less the outcome of a generous (and equal) heart and more a measure of dependence on others' approval.

Our dependence makes us scared to lose the status quo. Where would we be without it? *Who* would we be without it? If this is the only role we have, it's better to stick to it because we see no alternative.

All our strategies of survival stem from the bonbon effect and the inevitability of our lower status. When girls today form the same gangs as the boys and spit on the old and frail, the young and pathetic, it alleviates the feeling of having no power. But only for a short while. Despite all our strategies for survival, our powerlessness persists. This is because the dominant culture to which we subscribe and to which we have wholeheartedly adapted is inherently and forever *incapable* of seeing both genders as equal.

So what keeps us hooked on a system that ultimately will never change?

64

When Unity is Broken

The bonbon effect, our response to the awareness that we have something missing, is especially pernicious because it relates to an aspect of ourselves that we cannot *alter*. However much we aspire to equality and, even more, however much we strive to imitate, the bottom line is that the body at birth remains the body for life. So right at the core of the bonbon effect is ambivalence about our bodies.

On one hand, our bodies are an essential part of our monocular value. Women's bodies are safe havens, sources of comfort, decoration and pleasure. They are vital vehicles and carriers of reproduction. Our bodies offer softness and curves, a refuge from the angular, linear world.

On the other hand, it is this very flesh, this interior space and female genitalia, that define our position. A woman's body is *at the same time* the cause of her 'lower position' (i.e. she's not a man) and potentially her best asset in terms of status and survival within it. From this paradox arises an ambivalence. This ambivalence and uncertainty about our bodies lie at the heart of our powerlessness and keep us trapped.

Every aspect of the female body defines a woman as non-linear. We bleed. Our bodies are round and soft and fleshy. They are unpredictable, curved, messy, chaotic, susceptible to rhythmic changes. Many of us experience obvious emotions that can't be understood logically and seem to operate according to a system that isn't linear or straightforward or controllable.

Straightening naturally curly hair or lightening naturally dark skin are examples of efforts to emulate the physical characteristics of a dominant (white) group. Women's differences from men similarly become downgraded to faults that we try hard to eliminate. This ranges from hiding menstruation to morbid obsession with eradicating smell – perfumed tampons during our periods, perfumed mini-pads in between, perfumed douches daily just in case – to removing any natural body evidence of reality: wrinkles, cellulite, hair, smell, roll or roundness. We look at other women's bodies through the same critical eyes of distaste for fat and round – 'Good grief! Did you see her thighs?'

Early in life, our bodies cease to belong to us. Women become aware of the cultural pressure to be attractive and to present themselves in a certain way; we learn the overriding importance of external image. How we look becomes more significant than who we are. This sows the seed of a burgeoning and lifelong self-consciousness. From this moment, we begin to compare and compete with other girls for the right to be considered an attractive object.

The unity and integrity of body, mind and spirit is at this point broken. Our physical identity and selfhood are split: who we are versus how we need to be seen. Pregnancy and the early months of a child's life are times when many women feel reconnected with their bodies. However, this is only temporary. Living this divide lasts for life and robs us for ever of the wonder of our being.

The disadvantage of being female may be obvious within the family unit or at school or it may only become evident later through sexual encounters or when a woman enters employment: whether she's selling sandwiches in the local deli or managing an insurance company, she'll soon spot the inequities.

Whether we put all our efforts into endorsing our feminine role or rebel against it, this process affects every one of us.

As young girls, some of us become tomboys; some of us develop anorexia to try and put off developing physically into womanhood. Many of us put our efforts from an early age into being as feminine and as attractive as possible. The catch is that those who are adored for their bodies as they *naturally* occur are a fortunate minority. We eradicate, for example, hair from legs, arms, underarms and face. And waxing the bikini line is a must for those who intend to reveal this part of their anatomy in public or even in private. For most of us, having a woman's body entails a lifelong struggle to suppress the natural in favour of an imposed and artificial ideal.

Current trends to 'sexualise' little girls before puberty, turning them into self-conscious objects at an increasingly younger age, mean that even those few precious years of bodily integrity – when there is no division between mind and body – are ever dwindling. Self-consciousness starts earlier and, with the aid of medication or surgery, the struggle with nature now lasts longer.

We are therefore trapped, physically and psychologically, in *denial*. This is why we monitor, compensate, cover up and imitate. We become inured to the objectism, in general and in particular, of our bodies. We learn to be pleasing in body and behaviour. After a while, external persuasion isn't necessary. We don't need it any more because it's internalised. Our bodies are transformed permanently into objects in our *own* monocular perception.

Ultimately our bodies disappoint us because they will not conform. Our bodies betray us. They are objects of betrayal.

The trap is now securely in place. The loss of bodily integrity robs us of personal power. We have no option but to perform our duties well. We endorse the dominant god of image, often sacrificing our own integrity on its altars.

The bonbon effect renders us powerless on the *inside*: this is why we uphold what is on the outside.

65

The content of the morning's work left Clare very thoughtful as she went downstairs to join Helen for their break, and she looked forward to having the time to read it later on.

'Why don't we take the coffee outside?' suggested Helen.

As they settled themselves, Clare asked about her trip the day before.

'It was dreadful,' replied Helen with feeling. 'An absolute waste of time . . . and effort.'

'What happened?'

Helen told her about the presenter and then the interaction with the journalist.

'Isn't that strange?' said Clare. 'Why do you think she didn't say anything at the time? Do you think she was just nervous?'

'I think it's more than that. Women often come up to me after an event and confide they can really identify with what I've been saying but they always tell me in private, you know, that they wholeheartedly agree with me but never say anything at the time. You're right that people can be anxious about speaking in public gatherings but I think it's also fear about being seen as a feminist or a troublemaker. It's a bit like belonging to a secret society — except that instead of banding together through a mutual regard or esteem, we belong to this society by default; somehow it's the "reject" club so we're not that keen to acknowledge our membership. Do you know what I'm talking about?'

'I think I do,' replied Clare. 'If we don't really want to belong to the club but *have* to, we're not going to feel proud of the fact.'

'Exactly. We disown the other members. We stop supporting them in public. We stop trusting each other and we even stop speaking truthfully until we're out of earshot of the "other" club; then we make a gesture of recognition, but it's all terribly guarded.'

Clare sighed. 'I've thought about what you said about feminism being about love, not anger.'

'Well, there's anger too, but yes, as part of the love which is central. That's connected to the secret society again. Feminism always seems to make women defensive, even hostile. I can't tell you the number of times, in ordinary social situations, that women make a point of telling me, because I have a "feminist" label (Helen outlined a big square across her chest), how their husbands are "ever so good in the kitchen" and how lucky they are to be married to such sensitive men. And, of course, the men are also primed so they approach me really sheepishly or wind me up with comments like: "Well, I can tell you who wears the trousers in *our* house." That sort of thing. It drives me mad.'

Clare burst out laughing at the expression on Helen's face.

'It does drive me mad, I promise you,' said Helen, laughing now as well. After a pause, she looked at Clare. 'You know, it's very good to be able to laugh about it. I felt awful yesterday.' Her face became quite sad.

Clare waited, aware that Helen's tone had changed and become suddenly more personal.

'What I hated afterwards was how easily I got into self-recrimination. On the train on the way back, I kept trying to stop myself but it was the same old thing. The presenter had been rude and arrogant and unprofessional too but I could not stop blaming myself: what I *could* have said, *should* have said, how I *might* have handled him differently to avoid being treated badly. It's always the same twist: when others treat us badly, we find fault inside ourselves. It took all my effort to try and regain a little compassion, you know, just to be gentle to myself at the same time. I did go out for a walk when I got back and eventually managed to put it aside. But it was really hard.'

Clare nodded, profoundly aware of the echoes of Angie's response to her work colleague not so very long ago. 'I do admire your commitment, Helen. You make me think a lot. I'm not sure what feminism is any more except that what we usually think misses the point as far as you're concerned.'

'Yes.' Helen sighed. 'For some reason, I've always believed that women were the route to real change in the world. I believe somehow that women can be vehicles of the new, of a gentle power that *could* transform the system.'

'Are you sure it's only women? There are men – a few men anyway – who are keen to change the system as well.'

'There are *words* of change, yes, but I've never personally found a man genuinely willing to entertain the idea of a new kind of power. They may be out there but I haven't met them. Men tend to halt at the first hurdle: seeing themselves as losers within a monocular culture brings up a lot of fear which few men want to even acknowledge, let alone feel.'

Clare wasn't sure.

'You see,' Helen continued, 'I don't believe it's ultimately a men v. women conflict. I'd like everyone to see beyond that but in terms of *initiating*, I think it is only those who are the "under" group of any dominant system who can promote change: anger's always more energetic than fear.' Helen looked at the clock and moved her chair back in order to stand up.

'Feminism, for me, isn't about women's rights or personal power for its own sake . . . or even about individual female autonomy.' She looked intently at Clare. 'When I look at our world, I see it ruled by aggression and aggression stunts our human capacity for loving. Do you see that?' She didn't wait for Clare's response. 'I believe we're faced with a radical challenge to stop the slow, relentless destruction of the vulnerable.'

Helen smiled. 'I know that sounds grand but I think it affects us all and I think it's women who have to move first, to show the way, if you like.' She stood up. 'But first, we have to see beyond the male/female debate to the whole picture. We have to recognise how much everything has fallen out of balance . . . and then see if we care about it!'

As they climbed the stairs, in silence, to start work again, Clare was aware of feeling moved by their talk downstairs. She wasn't exactly sure why but it had something to do with a moment of seeing that Helen's forcefulness and her fragility were inseparable parts of the same being.

66

The Political is Personal

What do we see in our world today? It is clear that the cultures of the majority of the world's nations operate along the paths prescribed by monocular (exclusively right-eye) culture. Objectism is rife.

Our media wouldn't exist without turning people into objects of interest. We refer to stars becoming public property: lack of respect for boundaries or privacy is an aspect of making others into objects. Young men and women are bought by enterprising companies and turned into celebrities in the world of sport or pop music.

We often subscribe to objectism without thinking about it. On holiday, for example, we make curious and colourful strangers into objects when we photograph them without giving them a choice by asking them first. It's very easy when they speak a different language. Once you see someone else in the round, once you see them through the left eye, the foreigner can no longer remain an object. The one-dimensional – 'what an interesting face' – 'what a lovely family scene' – 'what a funny shot' – evaporates. You see someone fleshed out, with thoughts and feelings and sensibilities; suddenly, and with no great effort, there is the recognition of a real live fellow human being.

Which, of course, is the *last* thing you want if you're waging a war. When soldiers are trained for military violence they are systematically brainwashed to see those they have to destroy as the enemy, not as vulnerable human beings like themselves. They are trained to see everyone of a particular race, nation or tribe, of whatever age or circumstance, as an object. It helps to use words like 'gooks' or 'rats' or 'Hun' or 'terrorist': labels always help maintain object status. Men who have fought on the ground in any of the past bloody wars talk of seeing the other side, not as fellow human beings, but as 'the enemy', as objects to be destroyed.

The aim of objectism is always to distance yourself from

feeling. For purposes of combat, measures to eradicate emotion can be extreme. Behavioural psychology 'techniques' are employed to 'desensitise', by repeatedly exposing human beings to images until their physiologically measured responses register zero: they stop feeling. If you want an efficient army, you have to eliminate any feelings (softness) because hesitation loses wars. Does anyone ever consider the cost to the human being behind the label of soldier?

No. The right eye looks only at strategy. It is known that humans respond with aggression to aggression. The only way to relieve some of the pain and anger of being personally treated (in the past or present) as an object is to mete out the same treatment.

This little gem of human psychology is not lost on those who want to train an effective army or police force. The use of young men as objects being sent to their death (as 'cannon fodder', as kamikaze pilots or into battles that were entirely strategic, conducted by those on the higher echelons like a game of chess) is well documented. There are countless examples of men led to slaughter, of men left to starve or freeze to death by the 'powers' of the very nation for whom they were fighting. Brutality breeds brutality.

For many soldiers object status doesn't end when a war is over. Black American soldiers who fought alongside white Americans in the Second World War returned home to be treated once again as segregated 'niggers' and objects of hatred. British soldiers, once vital to the wars in the Falklands or the Gulf, afterwards found themselves unable to get compensation for injuries and illness sustained as a result of their involvement.

There are other kinds of war that touch the lives of each and every one of us: corporate war. Men in the uniform of corporate armies fight a global war against their rivals for the prize of being the biggest and most powerful. The men heading the multi-million-pound corporations who make the decisions to prioritise the need to save money or save face are ordinary, not psycho-pathic, human beings: they believe *whatever* they do is justified by the god-goal of profit.

Aggression is only ever self-serving. The left eye closes. Any concerns that might jeopardise the certainty of reaching the goal are minimised in the monocular mindset, a process similar to clicking an icon on a computer screen. These concerns can then remain on the periphery or we 'disappear' them altogether. We stop seeing people – casualties in military war or ordinary investors whose pensions or livelihoods are ruined – as human beings.

Corporate war, like military war, uses labels as part of the practice of objectism. One example is *workforce*. The vast majority of the world's workforce is poor and desperate and therefore vulnerable. Hierarchically, these people are seen and labelled as substandard objects – brown, uneducated, illiterate as well as poor – and this makes it much easier to turn a blind (left) eye to maltreatment.

A cheap workforce plus cheap products means high profits: a simple equation. Exploitative working conditions – ignoring employees' rights, low wages, long hours, inhuman conditions, under-age workers – become possible because you can justify anything by ensuring the outcome of the equation.

Who will provide the profits in this equation? Human beings are now labelled *consumers*: passengers, clients, patients, customers, the market. We can be categorised and counted. As soon as you can reduce human beings to numbers, objectism is given carte blanche: you can't take risks with human beings but you can with numbers.

As a result, consumers are exposed to inadequate safety on trains; contaminated blood supplies; contaminated food; unhealthy air in planes; dangerous side-effects of drugs; chemically poisoned land, water or air supplies; unsafe cars; dangerous roads; the loss of hard-earned pensions or savings; unnecessary high death tolls of the poorest people housed in inadequate buildings; miserable conditions in old people's homes and the suffering of those at the mercy of inadequate hospital facilities.

This is not done out of hatred or malice aforethought, it is the result of the virulent disease of indifference that looks at others as objects, cases and statistics. These decisions are actually discussed, debated and agreed upon by human, sometimes intelligent and possibly caring, individuals. Yet, because the monocular vision of the right eye keeps its aim steadily on profit power, any risk to other human beings, if noted, is underplayed or ignored.

Occasionally, a commercial enterprise is genuinely caught out by an unforeseen outcome but the need to appear infallible and to avoid responsibility (i.e. to avoid the costs of compensation and losing power) lead to denial or fudging. Numbers help decision-makers first deny or later suppress any possibility of real concern for other human beings: 'the risk is negligible' or 'the amount of radiation in the food/emitted into the atmosphere/ that anyone might be exposed to is well below permitted levels'.

We are so used to these practices in the world that we take them for granted. This is how aggression becomes the norm.

A free-floating energy

Aggression is a free-floating energy in all our lives. Accustomed as we are to splitting everything into categories of two, we define generally acceptable and unacceptable forms of aggression. The arenas of competition, sport, commerce and national conflict employ acceptable (even if occasionally 'regrettable') aggression. Less acceptable is the deliberate destruction of human life or property. Then we begin to have reservations because it is no longer controlled.

When aggression is whipped up in a group context, where individual responsibility becomes diffused, it gathers its own wild and devastating momentum enhanced by alcohol or drugs ... looking for objects on which to vent its destructiveness. Every now and then, a lone individual, himself an object within the system, goes on a killing spree crazed with vengeance and seeking random targets.

Because these events are newsworthy, we are less aware of more sinister and persistent forms of aggression that occur when it becomes institutionalised. Wearing uniforms of all kinds takes away personal identity, and so suppression of 'others' becomes completely devoid of emotion: no hate or anger, simply cold and mechanical control or eradication of undesired objects. A very tough self-defensive skin develops in the perpetrator, to a point of complete detachment. Institutional settings of all kinds ensure that objects can be imprisoned, lobotomised, sterilised, bought or sold without causing much of a fuss.

For objectism to continue, the left eye must stay closed. It is certain, for example, that policemen in uniform, who are themselves fathers, must close off the personal and human part of themselves so that they can *see* children who live rough on the streets of Brazil as objects like stray dogs ... in order to shoot them.

Examples of those two old cronies – objectism and denial – appear in every newspaper every day. If we move beyond categories of acceptable and unacceptable, we see an entirely interconnected web. We see this web connecting the atrocities of genocide in Africa with the sterilisation of half a million Indians in Peru; the disposal of girl babies in China with the abduction and murder of two little girls in England; the sexual abuse of children in Irish schools with the sale of children into prostitution in Thailand; through the entire world, we see a connecting thread of domestic violence against women. All of it, all of it, is part of the same aggression that fuels corporate enterprise. What connects the threads, and therefore affects us all, is the unchallenged practice of making other human beings into objects.

These connections spread. People are connected. Events are connected. Through an understanding of objectism, we see connections between the conventions of ordinary sexual attraction and the extremes of pornography. Poverty of the many is connected through a system of ladders to the wealth of the few. We see emotion as a crucial connection to the health of mind and body.

This is binocular vision: beyond the denial and rationalisation; beyond the convenience of 'them' and 'us'; beyond an exclusively up/down focus on self-interest. It looks beyond indifference. It gives us the opportunity to see, to know and to feel.

67

Clare arrived home after work and picked up her post from the mat. There was an airmail envelope written in a vaguely familiar hand but she couldn't quite recognise it. She was about to close her door when Ellen opened hers.

'Hello, Ellen, how are you? I haven't seen you for a few days.'

'I'm not too bad,' Ellen replied. 'Have you got time for a cup of tea?'

Clare hesitated, then said she'd love one, so she followed Ellen into her kitchen.

Everything was very tidy and ordered. Ellen switched on the kettle and, as she did, Clare noticed that Ellen felt with her fingers up the back of the kettle to find the switch. She thought for a moment and then asked Ellen if she had heard from her family recently. She knew Ellen had a married son living abroad. She replied that she'd had a birthday card but hadn't spoken to him for a while.

'It was your birthday, was it?' exclaimed Clare. 'You should have said. We could have had a celebration cake or a glass of wine, or something.'

'I know, we did that once, didn't we? Everyone was very kind. Anyway, when you get to my age, there's not a lot to celebrate.'

'How old are you now, Ellen?' said Clare.

'Seventy-nine now. I think it was two years ago, wasn't it, when we had that little party?'

Clare nodded, remembering, and thought, but didn't say, that things were different now.

'Things are still bad between Moira and Mr Allinson, I think,' ventured Ellen, echoing Clare own thoughts. 'I heard them exchanging heated words the other day. Have you spoken to Moira recently?'

'Only briefly. She was on her way out. She hinted that she was looking for somewhere else to live but she didn't stop for a chat.'

'She really had a go at me the other day.'

'Who, Moira?'

'No, Mrs Allinson.'

'What happened?'

'Well, the dustmen must have moved the dustbins around so I put out my bag in the one on the corner where it usually is but I didn't see the number on it. Apparently I put it in *their* bin and she rang my bell and really told me off. It was my fault, I know, but she was really most unpleasant. I felt awful.'

'That's terrible,' said Clare. 'She had no right to treat you like that!'

'Now don't say anything, Clare, *please*. Tell me you won't. I don't want any more trouble.' Clare looked at Ellen and was touched to think that Ellen saw her as a person who would champion someone else's cause.

'I promise not to say anything.' Clare thought how much she was beginning to hate this kind of climate in the house, not only for Ellen but just as a presence to live with. She had a mental image of a cloud of poison gas hovering over the entrance.

Ellen reached up for some cups. 'Let me get them for you,' said Clare. She reached up into the cupboard and took down two cups and saucers. She put them on the table and could see they were really quite dirty. The rims and the handles were very stained. She didn't say anything but it unsettled her, and when Ellen opened a tin to get out some cake, Clare realised with alarm that Ellen couldn't see the mould on it. She started to cut a slice.

'Ellen, I think that the cake might have a little mould on it.'

'It can't have,' said Ellen, 'I only bought it last week.'

'Well, these things don't last well sometimes, you know.'

Ellen peered at it. 'It's not very bad, is it?'

'I think it would probably be better not to eat it.'

'Oh, dear, that's a pity. I haven't got anything else.'

'Let's just have the tea, that will be fine.'

'I've got some biscuits,' Ellen remembered, and opened a cupboard door to look. She peered in and found a packet, which she opened, and put some on a plate.

They chatted while they had tea – the biscuits were fine – and Clare found herself wondering how long Ellen would stay here.

Halfway through her second cup of tea, Clare went to the bathroom. As she washed her hands, she saw the basin was striped with little dribbles of toothpaste, half-congealed on to the enamel. She looked for something to clean with and found a sponge underneath the basin. She rubbed the marks, finding them quite hard to remove, but eventually she managed and swilled round the basin.

She then found herself inspecting the rest of the bathroom, seeing heavy stains in the bath and a layer of thick dirt along the outside edge. She had a go at these with the same sponge, feeling at the same time compelled to do this and also silly. After all, what difference would it make to Ellen, who couldn't see it anyway? What mattered, Clare realised, was that she knew it would matter to Ellen if she *could* see because she would be mortified. She was so dignified and proper.

She suddenly leapt ahead in her mind, seeing in Ellen her own plight in twenty, thirty years' time. Would it make any difference having a daughter? She would hardly expect Sophie to take care of her. How vulnerable we all are, she thought. Living alone in little units, at the mercy of neighbours who bully you. You really were at the bottom of the pile, when you were old.

Was it so different in other cultures? Clare didn't know. She only knew that there was little love, little inclusion, little value – that's what it was, no value for age. Was it because you were vulnerable then? she wondered. A bit incompetent. A bit incontinent. Powerless. Ellen was intelligent and could still think. She had apparently been a very respected headmistress. She had a function then, on the ladder, I suppose, thought Clare, but now, what on earth was there?

Clare made a good enough job of removing the stains, although it needed some proper cleaner and more time. Then she went back to finish her tea. She knew that the whole issue of Ellen's welfare was serious and she didn't know what to say or do, so she kept quiet. It wasn't her place, after all, but who else would say anything? Should she? If she did, Ellen would be very upset. It all settled in her uncomfortably when she returned eventually to her own flat.

68

She decided to put her feet up and spend half an hour catching up with her reading to see if she could take her mind off things, but she suddenly remembered the letter. She got up again and found it in her bag. The envelope showed it was from Toronto, from her sister. She was astonished. She'd never had a letter from her sister in her entire life. They had got into the habit of exchanging Christmas cards, with an annual update of family news, but a letter was most extraordinary. She opened it and resettled herself to read it.

Dear Clare,

I don't really know where to start. You must be amazed to get a letter from me! I don't know exactly why I am writing to you but I need to be able to write to someone and my friends here are part of everything so I need to talk to someone completely outside life here. Basically, things are very bad between David and me. And the whole thing has been going on for a few months. We've been married twenty-seven years, you know, and I just don't know what to do. Having had the business together, as well as bringing up the children, I can't believe he wants out.

I didn't know anything about it until a month ago when he was shouting at me for something and I just felt he was really angry about something else, you know; he'd been really moody for a while. So I asked what was really going on, and because the kids were around we went out to the park. He told me he'd met, by chance, a woman he'd known years ago when they were both students, and that the old spark had been rekindled. In a nutshell. She's already divorced because her marriage went wrong as well.

At the time, I didn't feel much except total shock. Like a bad dream. We talked about it again after a couple of days and I felt so angry with him. I really had believed in our partnership, you know, we did everything together, split down the line. We've had a real struggle these past few years. It makes me so mad now when I think how I just stood by and worked alongside.

I'd like to talk to you but I wanted to write first to give you a chance to take this in before I phoned. I can't really face my friends at the moment. I've one or two fairly close ones, who know, but I can't bring myself to talk to them because I feel so embarrassed, almost ashamed in a way, as if I've failed. I've put so much of my energy into David and everything we've done together. I can't bear to think they are feeling sorry for me or even worse. It's silly, I know, but that's why I thought I'd contact you. I know we're not that close but it doesn't seem to matter. It helps that you're outside of everything here.

I'm giving this letter two weeks to get to you and then I'll phone.

Love, Ruth

69

As Clare got to the end of the letter, she found her heart was beating faster than usual. It was odd to be shocked because it happened all the time, but in some way getting a letter from her own sister, despite their lack of closeness, really affected her. She could somehow feel what Ruth must be feeling, an empathic turmoil through their shared genes. She stayed on the sofa, completely still for a few minutes, letting the news sink in.

Should she phone Ruth? No, she needed time to think a bit. Would Ruth really come over? And stay with her? She'd never considered the idea of having Ruth to stay before. It was all so bizarre.

She jumped as the phone rang suddenly. It can't be her now, thought Clare in a panic, not feeling ready to talk to her yet and aware of her relief when she recognised Sophie's voice.

'Oh, hello, Soph,' she said, with a huge sigh.

'Hi, Mum, are you all right?'

'Yes ... yes, I'm fine. It's just that I've been reading a letter from Ruth, you know, my sister?'

'From Canada?'

'Yes. She sent me a letter I got today and I'd just finished reading it when you phoned.'

'I didn't think you were in contact much.'

'We're not. That's why I'm surprised. Anyway, she's written because she's in trouble. Her husband is leaving, or thinking of leaving.'

'Oh dear,' said Sophie.

'Yes, oh dear,' echoed Clare. 'She may want to come over and visit.'

'How do you feel about that?'

'I'm not quite sure,' said Clare, smiling at her daughter's directness. 'I don't mind if it isn't for too long.'

'Well, if she does come, I'd like to see her.'

'Course you can meet her if she comes. Anyway, how are you doing?'

'I'm fine. I'm having my first session with your boss soon and thought it would be good to read something she'd written.'

'Really? I'm impressed.'

'Why?'

'Well, you were so doubtful about going and now you want to do some homework.'

'Yes, I thought I would. I want to make this work, you know.'

'I don't suppose I should ask, but are you all right for money?'

'No, I don't think you should ask, but as you have, I can tell you that I asked her about it and we've agreed that I can wait until I either have the money or see something I can give her in exchange.'

'What do you mean, in exchange?'

'I don't know what yet, but something to say thank you or to show I have appreciated everything.'

'Are you sure that's OK?'

'Well, when she explained it, she sounded very clear about it and said she trusted me. I rather liked it, actually, because I don't have the money now because of having to pay the rent and I didn't want to ask you to lend it to me.'

'You could have, you know, but that's fine. I'm pleased you've sorted it out,' said Clare. She had supposed Helen would be far too formal somehow for such a flexible arrangement. 'Do you want me to give you the names of her books, or would you like me to send them to you? I've got a couple here.'

'That would be great, Mum, if you could. Will you do it first class and I'll repay you?'

Clare felt a twinge of sadness, but replied, 'Yes, I'll post them tomorrow.'

'Or we could meet instead. I won't read anything till the weekend and we could meet on Friday if you like. Should we do that?'

The sadness converted into a small burst of happiness.

'I'd love that, Soph. Do you want to see that exhibition you mentioned? I'd like to see it myself. I'll bring the books with me.'

'Great. We'll meet at six. By the statue in the main entrance.'

'OK. Thanks for ringing.'

'Good luck with Ruth. 'Bye.'

Clare put the phone down and noticed how much lighter she felt. She decided she would call Ruth. What was the time difference? She looked at the clock and decided she'd phone in two hours' time. Meanwhile she'd read the last chapter.

70

A Different Power

This book is about a gentle revolution.

No evangelising. No converting. No rejection or imposition. It starts small, and essentially from within. Not in the head alone.

It doesn't even necessitate words. It is an attitude, an approach to yourself, to others and to the world around you. It is rooted in personal power, a quality that shines through the way you take responsibility for any other power you may be granted temporarily in this world.

Time to detach a little, take stock and consider how we move from here if we want to. When we open both eyes, we have more choice of response. We may feel perfectly happy within the confines of perpendicular vision. We may wish to diverge on occasion or not at all.

We may feel much more at home with left-eye vision, even without having a name for it and wondering whether or not it really existed. Perhaps simply reading some of these pages will be enough of a prompt to consider that if we already do see things differently, we are not mad, hysterical or deluded: our thoughts and impressions and senses are not wrong.

If perpendicular power is to be balanced, we need to access a different form of power. We need to access it, to speak and act from it. In this way it becomes manifest. There are three key aspects to consider – the ABC of gentle power – and these can always act as a reference: acknowledgement, balance and connection.

Acknowledgement

Acknowledgement is vital if we are to break through the stronghold of denial. We deny because we fear reality will be far worse, but, in truth, reality, when seen and acknowledged, is not nearly so exhausting and dispiriting as continuing to keep the door shut against what we imagine.

As soon as we stop pushing against the truth – what we are really feeling, what is really going on, what is the real state of play – something clicks into place. We become at one, instead of at loggerheads, with ourselves. When we see what is there and acknowledge it, something changes inside and strengthens us, even if we cannot actually change that reality, now or ever. We can engage more honestly with it.

Balance

Balance helps us to understand that one-eyed vision is only one half of the story, and therefore we have to explore and uncover the other half. Just the simple seeing of another reality has a profound and lasting effect and remains in awareness. It remains alongside everything else. Not one thing or the other, not rich or poor, but two realities at once. This is an example of binocular vision. It allows a different, more rounded and, above all, *deeper* perception. This is seeing in the round.

Balance keeps us flexible. We respond to an inner fulcrum, moving to remedy whatever has fallen out of balance: when compactness leans into rigidity, we move towards openness; when flexibility leans into flabbiness, we move towards establishing a clear limit.

We can learn when to shift gear, when to open and love, when to close up and set limits. We know when to push our bodies and when to rest. When to take in and when to give out. We know when to use intellect and when to trust our intuition. When to speak out. When to keep silent. When to laugh and when to fight. We arrive at the possibility of loving without compulsion, confronting without blaming, acknowledging reality while forgiving.

Connection

Connection helps us to knit the fragments into a whole again and is an antidote to the splitting of perpendicular mentality. Through combining all aspects of our being – what we do is what we think is what we feel is who we are – at any given moment, we arrive at a point of integrity and coherence. We understand what it means to be fully within our skin.

Connections establish a deeper understanding of equality that sees through differences. As soon as we respond to connections, we are able to move towards others without aggression. This gentle power is offered in the service of love. It combines the openness of vulnerability with the force of conviction. It allows for the creative energy within us to unfold. It demands fulfilment not as an end in itself but as surrender, ultimately, to a greater whole.

There is a huge task before us and it is time now to act. The world needs a different strength, not imitation or absence.

Acknowledgement, balance and connection are the essence of an alternative vision, a means of establishing an alternative power. If we have the courage to apply these principles to our lives – our emotions, our body image, our sexuality, our responsibilities and all our relationships to others – we can make an alternative power visible.

This power depends on a wealth that is given out, not hoarded. It is not driven by disappointment but by pride. Like a moonquake, it is time for a different power to come forth, to bear witness and be heard. It is an invitation to show and tell.

71

Later that evening, Clare sat thinking about everything. She'd just had a long talk with Ruth. Ruth had sounded thrilled when Clare called. After a few minutes, Ruth had said she wanted to pay for the call so she had rung back. Ruth had talked while Clare had mainly listened, aware of the contradictions.

On one hand, Ruth lamented the end of this 'perfect' partnership, with everything split exactly down the middle for twenty-seven years, that he was now intent on throwing away. On the other hand, there were clear indications that things hadn't been perfect. They'd run a successful soft furnishing business until five years ago when David had decided he wanted to expand and take over a rival company. Despite Ruth's misgivings and against the advice of his financial adviser he'd gone ahead and they almost went bankrupt.

When the business was in difficulties Ruth had apparently stayed at home to be there for the day-to-day needs of their three children.

Clare found it odd that Ruth hadn't told the children. David had asked her not to until he was sure. Then he'd gone away for the weekend with this other woman while Ruth sat and waited. Apparently he'd came back in tears, saying he couldn't decide what to do. So Ruth had told him to take as long as he wanted to make up his mind. No wonder she'd told Clare she felt numb! Clare had been exasperated listening to Ruth at the time but, now, she recognised that she'd probably have done the same. She understood how it was possible to just sit and wait for everything to pass over, one way or the other, without having the strength to alter the course of events. Numbness she knew about.

Anyway, Ruth had already found out about the flights and fare deals and was only waiting to check with Clare about dates and whether it would be OK for her to visit before booking. Clare had agreed, though she wasn't sure how it was going to help the situation.

She went into the kitchen to make herself some tea and turned on the radio. A teacher was being interviewed about a project at her school. Two years previously, teachers and parents had organised a visit to a Bangladeshi village so that the Bangladeshi pupils, born and brought up in England, could become acquainted with their roots. They were about to make a follow-up visit to see how the funding raised by the school and the community had actually helped the villagers.

What caught Clare's attention was the way the teacher described her apprehension at the prospect of this return visit because now, she said, she *knew* what she was going to see. She explained that the first time she had seen such indescribable poverty had had a devastating effect on her. She had found it very painful and described how, afterwards, she could never entirely forget about what she'd seen as she continued back in her ordinary life. It certainly moved her to action, thought Clare, smiling to herself as she thought how often now she was reminded about Helen's words.

She sat down at the table and wondered what it would be like having Ruth to stay. Ruth hadn't been over since their mother had died . . . how long ago now? It must be sixteen years. Two years after Len had died, their mother had been diagnosed with cancer of the womb. By the time they found the cancer it had spread too far for surgery and she had died within six weeks. In less than a year, their father had remarried and moved to Florida.

Clare and Ruth had never been very close even as young children. She hardly knew Tommy, Ruth's youngest son, who was fourteen now, Ruth had reminded her, and she hadn't seen Jack and Anna (now twenty and seventeen) since they were young children. It was funny having a sister to whom you were connected because of family ties but for whom you didn't feel any real depth of affection. Sometimes she'd read of siblings meeting again after decades of separation and finding their closeness with one another totally undiminished by the intervening years. She couldn't understand this. Yet she remembered that she had responded quite emotionally to Ruth's letter – as if there really was more between them than she thought.

72

A week later, Clare sat in the arrivals hall. It was busy and there were very few seats; she scanned the area for somewhere to sit. When she saw someone get up she moved quickly to grab the vacated seat and sat down with relief. Clare looked at the clock. The Toronto flight was already an hour late and still thirty minutes remained to wait. There was a buzz of tension everywhere, like a visible presence throughout the airport: people worried about missing someone, employees trying their best to look preoccupied so as to avoid having to answer anxious or frustrated queries.

Clare found her own anxiety rising as well. She wondered what it would be like to see Ruth again. Her family – apart from her own children of course – had become quite distant.

Clare exchanged Christmas cards with her father but had no contact. She had never managed to get close to Sylvia, his new wife – well, she was hardly 'new' any more, Clare reminded herself. She didn't know if it was still a lingering bias because of her mother but she hadn't warmed to Sylvia at all and, as she hadn't felt very close to their father, she'd drifted away from him in his new set-up. She wondered whether Ruth had felt the same about Sylvia, whether she kept in touch more with Dad?

So many things she didn't know or had rarely thought of, about her family. How had her mother felt about her life? About being a woman? There hadn't been any overt sexism in the house but she supposed it had always been there in the form of who did what and that sort of thing.

Her mum hadn't worked outside the house. Her father had been a tax inspector. Her mother did all the chores and her father came home to his dinner every evening. His shirts were ironed and his trousers pressed. Her mother did the gardening, except mowing the lawn and the annual pruning of the roses: these were Clare's father's 'duties'. Her mother also did a lot of the painting and decorating, Clare remembered.

The doors slid open letting through several people pushing loaded trolleys. Squeals of delight rose from a small crowd of waiting members of the family. Clare was touched as she watched all the embraces and smiles, a few tears and the more formal hugs of the greeting scene. She couldn't imagine how she'd feel when Ruth appeared.

She thought of Sophie. She'd been so happy to see her last week. They'd had a good evening. The exhibition was disappointing, with too much to say and too little on show, but Sophie had agreed to have supper afterwards. This was a major breakthrough and they chose a nice-looking Indian restaurant. Although Sophie didn't eat much, Clare was pleased they'd been able to share a meal and talk together. She'd been longing to know how it had gone with Helen, but asked nothing. Sophie volunteered something that Helen had said about her belonging to a different way of thinking and looking at the world, but Clare hadn't wanted to press her for more.

Clare had been strongly aware of a lessening of the tension between the two of them. They still had a long way to go, she thought, but something had shifted.

She glanced up again at the board: the expected time of arrival hadn't changed, so she decided to catch up with some reading before the plane landed.

73

The Rhythm of Life

Our feelings are triggered by the dynamic of relationship. Whom we meet, how we meet them, when or where we meet them: the entire cycle of short- and long-term encounters in our lives will affect our needs and therefore contribute to our emotional lives.

When we talk about the importance of managing emotions, we're mainly describing the interpersonal layer of emotion: interpersonal meaning between people, arising through contact between individuals. Most of the time, emotional concerns are connected with this interpersonal layer because of our preoccupation with relationship to others. From birth (probably from conception) until death, we are constantly subject to interaction with other human beings.

We are affected by all those people with whom we come into contact as we attempt to meet our emotional needs and follow our own rhythms. Remember our needs for closeness and separateness, engagement and containment, safety and risk. These will be fulfilled at times, neglected at other times, and, in response to what happens, we feel all sorts of emotions, to a greater or lesser intensity, throughout our lives.

Emotion is generated by our personal reaction to all the others in our lives. This includes the literal others, the actual individuals who become part of our lives, but also all those people, whether they are real or exist only in fiction, who influence us for better or worse along the way. It includes all the significant people who play a part in our lives.

Our feelings are triggered by the dynamic of relationship. Whom we meet, how we meet them, when and where we meet them, the entire cycle of short- and long-term encounters will affect our needs and therefore contribute to our emotional lives. This is an inescapable aspect of human experience.

74

Feeling the Difference

You do not compromise emotionally because you know that, if you do, you will deny something in you that is part of the beauty of who you are.

Emotional attunement means familiarity, awareness and management of our own emotions. It means understanding the language of the heart and being sufficiently conversant in it to be able to communicate with others. Emotional attunement requires familiarity, ease and a sense of companionship with one's emotions.

Acknowledgement of the importance and relevance of feelings is clearly counter-cultural. Whereas we worry, even get alarmed, when our memories fail or we become irrationally muddled, we don't become remotely concerned when we fail to register feelings: on the contrary, we're immensely relieved.

Emotional management includes taking responsibility for what we feel ourselves instead of taking care of everyone else's feelings. It requires balance: redefining love and balancing it with anger, seeing the place for both in a relationship. Anger without care or respect will automatically become aggression and we know what that entails and where it leads. So for both love and anger to operate genuinely, they need to balance one another.

We can learn to distinguish between authentic and learned fear. Women often experience anxiety at the outer edges of anger. We have learned to be afraid because of our conditioning, and sometimes, just as men respond to fear with knee-jerk aggression, women respond to anger with automatic anxiety. The symptoms and sensations are very similar physiologically, so it is easy to understand why this happens.

It is helpful, therefore, to catch yourself sometimes when you're anxious and ask yourself if that is what you're really feeling. Sometimes, of course, it will be genuine anxiety, but perhaps you'll discover something else that is harder to acknowledge, lying just underneath.

When you're anxious about someone not arriving home on time, is it possible that you're also annoyed that you've been left in the dark and that nobody let you know what was happening? When you register anxiety about putting your views across in a meeting at work, is it possible to acknowledge that you're secretly angry about the number of previous occasions when you've been ignored? When you're anxious hearing someone walking behind you down a dark street, is it possible that alongside that fear, you feel furious about always having to be careful as a woman in this society?

When you're anxious about which clothes to wear to make the right impression, could it be that you're also sick to death of the emphasis on appearance when you know you are extremely competent at your job? When you're nervous about confronting someone who's superior to you or criticising a colleague whose job you've been doing for months, ask yourself if, deep down, you're actually angry at being intimidated or frustrated with carrying the extra load?

None of these is an excuse for launching in with aggression but it is a very worthwhile exercise for us, as women, to check inside what is really going on and acknowledge the truth.

The seesaw is familiar: pretending to ourselves that we are only anxious is like adopting a favourite posture of submission, guaranteed (we hope) to placate and stave off aggression from anyone else. In time, we'll find a way of giving others a hard time and hitting below the belt. Recognising the clean clear power of anger is an act of empowerment. We can bring anger into our vocabulary without aggression, if we take the time and make the effort to learn the difference.

75

Clare was driving back from the airport with Ruth sitting next to her. Their meeting in the arrivals hall had been emotional: a surprise for them both. Ruth leaned her head back on the headrest and surveyed the urban landscape passing swiftly before her eyes. She was high on jet lag, nervous energy and general pent-up everything.

'I can't believe I'm here! It's strange – it changes and yet doesn't change. Everywhere is like everywhere else, isn't it?'

'I haven't seen much of anywhere else,' replied Clare.

'Isn't Danny in America?'

'Yes. I'm actually going to see him in a few months.'

'Will you go and see Dad?'

Clare smiled. 'Do you know, I was thinking about Dad while I was waiting for you. I'm hardly in contact these days. He doesn't show much interest in the children. He doesn't phone. I write at Christmas but I think he's more involved with Sylvia's family now to tell you the truth.'

'I'm sure you're right. They came over to visit about four years ago. I told you, didn't I?'

Clare shook her head. 'Don't think so. I can't remember.'

'Anyway, they stayed a week on their way somewhere else but it wasn't easy. Sylvia's very difficult somehow. Quite critical and you get the feeling that whatever you do, it's not quite right. She seemed to want him to go out all the time and do things with her rather than spend time with his own grandchildren. I lost my patience with her after a bit – which soured the atmosphere – and I got cross with Dad too because he just did what she said. He never once contradicted her.'

'It's funny, isn't it? You really wonder, or rather, I really wonder what this family bond is all about.'

'Mum would have been very involved with her grandchildren if she'd still been alive.'

'I know. She would,' Clare agreed.

They drove in silence for a while.

'Who's looking after Tommy?'

'Jack's around because his studies are over and he's got to get a job. Anna's away. But Tommy's fourteen now so he can take care of himself.'

'And David?'

'In principle, David has agreed to be around while I'm away.'

'How did he react when you said you were coming?'

'He was a bit surprised. Said he didn't think we were that close. Didn't I have anyone nearer I could talk to?'

'Didn't you?'

'Well, not really. It's not just a question of talking to someone. I needed to get away. From everything. Just for a bit. I'm really good at keeping the whole day-to-day machine going – you know, the domestic stuff, the conversations, the routines, everybody's needs and rhythms – but once you know that the central mechanism's broken, it becomes too much. I'm lucky that the kids are old enough now for me to go away. I feel totally up in the air about everything so there was something about coming back to my roots that appealed to me . . .' Ruth gazed out of the window. When she spoke again, she asked about Sophie. Clare's reply, which also brought Helen into the picture, took up the rest of the journey home.

76

'What do you want to do while you're here?' asked Clare as they sat in the kitchen with a cup of tea.

'I don't know really.' Ruth considered. 'I'd like to see Sophie, find out a bit about what you're doing with your life. Maybe I could meet this woman you work for?'

'Helen? I don't see how. We don't have a social relationship.'

'I mean a professional meeting. Don't you think I should go and see her too?'

'What, just like that?'

'Just a thought. I mean, if it's her line of business, then I could do with a professional opinion. It helps sometimes. I'd pay her, of course.'

'Well, I don't know,' said Clare, a little flustered at Ruth's proposition, without knowing exactly why. She hadn't told Ruth about her own personal experience of Helen; only a bit about what she was writing and that Sophie had started to see her on a professional basis. 'Surely you could see someone back home?'

'It would be different there. I don't want to get involved in regular therapy or anything. I just need to talk, that's all, and sort things out a bit in my head. I can't see your objection, if it's her job anyway.'

'It feels a bit sudden, that's all. You've only just walked in and now you want to set up some therapy.'

There was an inexplicable tension between them. They looked at each other. Ruth sighed and shook her head. 'I'm sorry. I suppose I'm being pushy. I know how desperate I am and I can't expect you to listen to me all the time.'

'I'm happy to listen but you can't get everything sorted by the time you leave,' said Clare quietly. 'You've had quite a shock. It will take time.'

'You sound like the big sister now,' Ruth commented with a smile.

'I know. It *is* a shock. You find out that what you've been thinking all along is completely wrong. Do you know what he said, when I told him he was throwing so much love away? He looked really surprised. He said: "I didn't think you loved me," as if all these years had been some kind of mirage. I mean, how could he say that?' Ruth stopped and shook her head.

Clare didn't know what to say.

'Anyway, we don't have to talk about it now.'

'Ruth, I don't mind listening – it's just that I can't be of much help. I suppose that's why you want to see Helen . . .'

'We'll see. I don't have long: I go back on the twenty-third. It would be good to arrange something with Sophie anyway.'

'You can phone her later. Do you want to sleep?'

'No, I think I'd rather hang on till bedtime and then try to get a good night.' Ruth paused and looked out of the window. 'The only other thought I had was to visit Mum's grave,' she said.

'I haven't been there for ages. I don't mind doing that with you. I never seem to get around to it myself.'

'You don't have to but, if you'd like to, we can go together. You mustn't think you've got to do everything for me while I'm here. I'm just really pleased to be away and have time to think. I'd also like to get to know you a bit better,' she added, with a slightly embarrassed smile. 'I hardly know you at all. I was thinking that on the plane. We don't have to be anything we're not. I don't want to pretend we were a close-knit family but I would like, at least, to know a bit about who my sister is. Is that OK?'

Clare looked at Ruth, smiled and simply nodded in reply. She was uncertain about what that might involve but felt open to it anyway.

77

The Body Politic

The power of gentle resides deep within. It shows in your relationship with the miraculous system called your body. You understand that your body is not a thing you make the most of or do battle with. You recognise that it is neither burden nor asset but indivisible from who you are: what you think and know and feel. You regard your body as an outer self that bears the visible and invisible details of your entire physiological and psychological history.

One of the hardest tasks for any woman in this world is to reclaim her body, seen for so long as an object, and transform it into a dimension of herself that she cherishes.

The kernel of the bonbon effect, remember, is the key absence in a woman's body. It's not that every parent wants a son or that little girls are unloved: it's simply that being in a female body has very different implications for self-esteem within a sexual, social, professional and emotional context. A woman's body is defined as incomplete and powerless. Women of all ages and all classes and all nationalities – in monocular cultures, the vast majority of women – find fault with their bodies. We do not like our bodies – as they are.

If we could count the minutes, hours, days, months spent in consideration of our appearance and critique of different parts of our body and their concealment, eradication, disguise, removal, enhancement or reduction, we would find a colossal amount of woman-energy consumed. Without our commitment, of course, several huge and dependent industries would collapse.

The preoccupation with making good an inherent flaw has been around for a very long time. So, in some ways, we take this effort for granted. Fashions change: our feet are not bound any more or our waists squeezed into breath-constricting corsets. Modern women feel liberated from such restraints and point in horror to the barbaric practices of clitoridectomy yet, at the same time, we remain undisturbed and increasingly tolerant of the growing 'normality' of cosmetic surgery, undertaken by many women as lightly as altering the curtains or getting a new kitchen.

Surgical intervention in the cause of cosmetic improvement is no longer the prerogative of a few film stars. Money is all you need – a lot of money – whether you're sixteen in South America, wanting a boob job to increase your chances of marriage, thirty-six in North America, seeking a designer vagina, or fifty-six in Europe, desperate to remove bodily indications of middle age. We don't need encouragement or coercion from an individual partner. We have internalised our object status so well and for so long that we blithely say there is no harm in it, just fun, and who doesn't want to look good?

If it were harmless fun, like applying make-up or dyeing our hair, we would still retain an awareness that, at some point, we can and do remove it. But cosmetic surgery cannot be reversed or taken away – in fact, procedures have to be repeated again and again over time to maintain the desired effect.

More sinister and potentially more harmful than the actual experience is denial. The wolf is hidden behind the face of the lamb: the mechanics of surgery – cutting, slicing, bruising and breaking – reappear disguised in the soothing, euphemistic terms of 'lifting', 'augmenting', 'shaping' and 'realigning'.

Denial expands to the insistence that cosmetic surgery is part of women's right to choose. It is promoted as an aspect of liberation because access to breast enlargement, facelifts, liposuction and bottom reduction means we now don't have to be lumbered with a natural woman's body.

Acknowledgement confronts us with a different perspective: the reality of having a body that has become an object, in others' eyes, yes, but, far more importantly, in our own. With age, many objects become dispensable. It's easy to see why we vent our frustration on our own bodies. Much of this kind of 'fixing' is due to the bonbon effect and our frustration at such inequalities as the difference in social attitudes towards ageing men and women. Acknowledgement gives us an option not to take out this anger on ourselves (our bodies) as the cause of our predicament. We accept that hair grows, discharges happen, rolls of flesh appear, tummies are round and skin wrinkles with age.

It really isn't easy to convert our perspective. We have images of ugliness so deeply etched into the right eye that it is no small task to genuinely make our peace with fat and flab, varicose veins, cellulite, pimples, pendulous boobs or hairy legs! Clearly change takes time but it helps to remember that we don't have to exchange one view for the other: all we need to do is aim for the balance of binocular vision.

If we open the left eye, our relationship to our bodies – what we put in them, put on them and how we treat them – changes. This enables us to cherish our bodies more. We can accept the natural shape and proclivity of our bodies and become not so ready to alter, change or hide what was there simply because it would make it a potentially more desirable object for someone else.

Balance is essential because we cannot avoid the reality that our bodies are under constant external assessment. It doesn't alter the outside trends but it gives us a choice as to how to respond.

Somewhere between letting it all hang out and the extremes of objectism is the game of managing our appearance. Some cosmetic activities can be enjoyed from a core of self-esteem. Changes and fluctuations in shape can be viewed with less horror and more care: am I putting on weight because it is part of getting older? Is it a time in my life when I need a protective layer or a sign that I am eating unhealthily? Is my body telling me that I am eating instead of acknowledging feelings? Do I need to take better care of my body with more exercise?

Again, it means seeing connections. It means seeing that we are all of a piece, that what happens in one place affects another. What happens emotionally affects us physically and vice versa.

With binocular vision, for example, you see that if your breasts are too large to carry round without damaging your spine, you have to make a decision that concerns the health of your entire body. Since a removal from the body is a loss, breast reduction may bring sadness in its wake. You can take care of the physical and the emotional aspect of your body as well.

Similarly, if you are considering cosmetic surgery, you could, through binocular vision, consider the effect on your whole body. Is it just going to perpetuate an already faulty relationship with your body? Will it be worth it in reality or in fantasy only? From a place of personal rather than perpendicular power, there is a connection between cosmetic surgery and self-mutilation. Is prospective surgery a gesture of love or hate?

Think of someone – any age – a child, a partner, a friend, a sister, an animal whom you love dearly, whom you love fiercely and protectively, whom you love as they are, because they are who or what they are. Would you put them through excruciating pain in order to alter their appearance for a while? Would you allow anyone to perform surgery on them, not because their lives were threatened in any way – but simply because you wanted them to look different? If your answer is no, then why not?

Love cancels out the vision of the other as object. As soon as you stop relating to a body, whether someone else's or your own, as an object, you see and feel differently. Lose the ladder and you see individual beauty. This is not beauty defined by cultural desirability. This is beauty beyond attractiveness, beyond individual preferences and external affirmation. It is the beauty of integrity.

78

'Are you sure I can't help?' shouted Clare in the direction of the kitchen. Ruth was making supper, having insisted Clare relax and put her feet up when she came back from work. They'd had an afternoon session for once because Helen had had to go to some meeting in the morning.

'No. I'm fine. Do you want more tea?'

'No, thanks.'

She was enjoying Ruth being here; it had all been much easier than she had expected. She wasn't quite sure what she'd expected but she was surprised anyway. Ruth was here another four days. She settled back to continue reading, relishing the thought of being cooked for.

79

Reuniting Lust and Love

You know that your sexuality is a constant part of you – waxing, waning, fluctuating and changing – but always present. You celebrate your needs for sensual pleasure, for lust, for conception or closeness while insisting that those who touch or enter you can be trusted to see you and care.

Reclaiming our bodies means sharing and negotiating sexual encounters in a different way, while acknowledging the inevitable impact of the up/down model. As well as the mechanics of sexual activity, and the emphasis on performance, we can integrate the emotional and the spiritual dimensions of the left eye.

Through the left eye, sexual activity is both the same and different every time. We may want to ring the changes or refresh a dull routine but this is not the same as compulsion. As well as lust, there is a place for an exchange of sexual *and* heart energy. This redresses the imbalance, making it a different experience.

Then, of course, we would have to recognise our need to trust. Being at one with our bodies is potentially the most direct way to an out-of-the-body experience. This doesn't have to be dramatic but can occur every time we lose ourselves, every time we disappear into our bodies, yielding to sensation – emotional or physical. Given the conditioned split between mind and body, it's one of the hardest aspects of experience to reclaim. And we need to be safe to do so.

We need to trust first ourselves and any other who might be present. Unbrokenness is the key: a seamlessness between sensation and you. This cannot be a permanent state and is not the same as oblivion induced by an ingested substance. But we can yield temporarily before returning to our rational and conscious selves. Pretending we can trust when we can't is counterproductive and will only push us more into the need to perform.

As soon as we observe, we judge. As soon as we judge, we

perform. As soon as we perform, we are self-conscious and aiming for a goal. Anxiety intervenes. We do this when we willingly participate in sexual activity although our bodies tell us we don't want to. As soon as we get into the activity for its own sake, it is split from your heart or soul. Fragmentation infiltrates everywhere. It is one way we give away our personal power by colluding with the status of object.

If we make a commitment not to use others as objects, how can we guarantee sexual arousal? Habits of sexual arousal are so ingrained that it takes time to find new paths in the mind/body. It helps to remind ourselves of the connection with care. It may mean a time of reassessing your sexual relationships to find out exactly what quality of relationships you do want in your life. Whether in a long-term context or a one-night stand, the principle of connection means we consider whether this is chosen and fun or compulsive and dependent.

With the left eye open, we see the force of monocultural influence. It leaves us with no easy escape routes of denial: sexual attraction and experience becomes less of a one-way no-option excursion and more of a joint enterprise, negotiable at each step of the way. This can only happen once we see that our sexuality is an ever-present aspect of our autonomy and when the connection between body, mind and spirit has been re-established.

80

Clare put down the pages and could hear that Ruth was on the phone, talking to Tommy. She stayed where she was, thinking over the past few days.

They'd been up to the cemetery together to see their mother's grave. It was purpose-built, in a park setting, well maintained but with an air of impersonality about everything. Here was no romantic church setting with evocative fragments of prayers engraved on higgledy-piggledy headstones, just line after straight line of un-remarkable slabs.

Inevitably, they'd talked about their mother on the way home. They shared a sense of not having really *known* her, as a person or as a woman. Her personality hadn't made a deep impression on them because they'd only ever known her as a mother. Maybe she would have come out of her role more as they had got older, but there hadn't been time. They had loved her though: she'd been a caring and constant figure in their childhood.

It was Ruth who'd said first that she'd never seen Mum laugh. As Clare thought about this, she had to agree. She'd smiled but never actually really deep-down laughed. 'Perhaps she did when we weren't there,' Ruth had said, but they'd both been doubtful.

Clare had later recalled an occasion when an aunt had visited from overseas somewhere. She had been staying with them and Clare recalled an image of the two of them giggling like little girls and laughing quite unselfconsciously at something or other. It stood out in a whole sequence of memories as an occasion when her mother had come out of role, so to speak, because of her sister's presence. For a brief moment, there had been a glimpse of another and real person. Ruth could remember it as well, although neither had attached any significance to it until that moment.

There was a silence. Ruth must have finished. Clare got up and went into the kitchen. Ruth appeared tense and flustered but said nothing.

'Everything OK at home?' enquired Clare.

'Seems so. Tommy's fine – the others are about. David apparently was there last night but went off again today saying he had to go to a meeting.'

'Do the children really not know anything?'

'No. I told you David said he didn't want them to know before he'd made up his mind.'

'Even though you've come over here? They must have picked up something.'

'Well, they didn't mention anything,' said Ruth, beginning to sound defensive.

'Didn't you find it hard, not being able to say anything to them?' asked Clare.

'Yes, I suppose I did. I just had to keep it all inside.' Ruth paused. 'Do you think I'm doing the right thing, going tomorrow?' she asked, looking up at Clare.

'You mean to see Helen?'

'Course that's what I mean,' said Ruth impatiently.

'Well, you said at the time that you really wanted to see someone to talk to.'

'I know I said that but maybe I was wrong.'

'Why are you thinking that now? You'd better phone her if you're not going,' said Clare, reluctant to be caught in the middle of this. Ruth had made the appointment herself but somehow she felt implicated in the whole thing.

'Do you know anything about her?' asked Ruth. 'I mean, is she married? Has she got children? What's her life history?'

'I'm not sure. We haven't talked about much. She hasn't any children and she's never mentioned a husband. She doesn't talk much about herself.'

'Is she gay, do you think?'

'I don't *know*,' said Clare.

'But you must have thought about it,' said Ruth. 'You can't work for someone all this time and not think about their lives and who they are. Especially when nothing is obvious. Aren't you interested?'

'I suppose I am, but there's been too much going on. I've wondered occasionally but I've never felt the need actually to have all the information. Why is it so important all of a sudden?'

'Because I can't see how she's going to be able to help me. I mean I've got to sort it all out when I go back, haven't I? God knows what David's doing. I should be there sorting everything out. It was silly to even think about coming here—'

'Ruth!' Clare interrupted her. 'Just hang on a minute. What has happened? What happened on the phone?'

Ruth's eyes filled with tears and her cheeks turned quite pink.

'Oh, Ruth,' said Clare, gently. 'Just sit down, for heaven's sake.'

Ruth sat down a little heavily on the chair and swallowed hard. Clare sat down opposite her. 'Don't stop yourself crying,' she said, surprising herself with the authority in her voice. 'It'll do you good.'

Ruth put her elbows on the table and her face in her hands and sobbed. Clare tentatively touched the sleeve of Ruth's cardigan and then let her hand stay there, neither too absent nor too present, but somewhere in between. After a few minutes Ruth reached into her pocket.

'Here,' said Clare, reaching for the kitchen roll. 'Use this. It's not too rough,' and handed her a couple of sheets.

Ruth blew her nose. 'It upset me talking to Tommy because it brought home how awful it is going to be for all of us if David goes,' she said quietly.

'I know, love. Must be really heartbreaking.'

'You know, Clare,' said Ruth with a big sigh, 'I'm so angry with him. It's so unfair. It's all so un-fair,' she repeated more emphatically, enunciating each syllable in turn. She looked down into her lap. 'You know, I keep thinking, if only I hadn't been nasty to him when the business failed. If only I'd wanted more scx . . . we had some problems a few years ago. I didn't feel like sex and he did and although I wanted to go and see someone to try and sort it out with him, he didn't want to. So we never did anything. Things improved a bit but not much. I guess that was why he found this other woman so attractive. I keep thinking I could have avoided all this somehow.'

Clare didn't say anything.

Ruth continued. 'I daren't even think about the future. I mean, what man is going to look at me now? I've never even thought about anyone else, do you know that, never even *thought* about another man, other than fancying someone on television or something. I've never considered being unfaithful. I just couldn't bear it if he really did go. After everything.'

Still Clare said nothing. But she listened.

After a few moments, Ruth looked up at Clare. 'Did you ever think about marrying again, or at least another relationship?'

'I've thought about it but it took me ages to even bother to go out and meet anyone again in that sort of way. It was Angie who sort of bullied me into it.'

'But you didn't find anyone?'

'No. I haven't exactly tried hard, I have to say. I guess it will happen if it's going to happen. At the moment, it doesn't seem to matter much.'

'Still, it was different for you, though, wasn't it?'

'What do you mean?'

'Well, Len didn't exactly leave you, did he? I know he did go, but it wasn't the same as being discarded or rejected. You still had your dignity left. Nobody thought you were a failure.'

'You're not a failure, Ruth. These things happen, that's all.'

'Yes, but they're meant to happen to other people,' Ruth said, with a wan smile. 'Clare, what am I going to do?' she asked in a weak little voice.

'Come on,' said Clare, deciding it was time to get back practicalities. 'When's supper going to be ready? Should we open the wine you bought?'

Ruth nodded and got up to find it.

'Hang on a minute,' said Clare. 'You'd better make up your mind about tomorrow. Don't you think you should decide what you're doing before we get into drinking?'

'Oh, I'll go,' said Ruth, nodding slowly. 'What the hell,' she added to herself with a shrug.

81

The next day, Clare waited in the road outside Harwell House. Ruth was due out at four, but didn't appear until half past.

'Did you start late?' she asked as Ruth got into the car.

'No. It just went on a long time.'

They drove in silence and although Clare was longing to know how it had gone, she exercised great self-discipline and kept quiet.

Ruth still hadn't said anything when they got into town so Clare ventured, 'Are you all right to do the shopping?'

Ruth looked surprised. 'Course I am. Sorry, I don't know what to say really.'

'It doesn't matter. You don't have to say anything.'

'No, I'd like to tell you about it but everything is going round in my head. She's quite unusual, isn't she?'

'In what way?'

'Well, she really pays attention, doesn't she? She seems to see right into you.'

Clare smiled. 'I know what you mean.'

'There was so much that she said that struck so many chords. It made so much sense that I don't want to forget it. I need to write it down before it all goes away.'

'Right now or can it wait till after the supermarket? We have to go because of dinner tomorrow.'

'I know. I can wait until we get home but I won't talk about it until I've written things down.'

'Fine. So let's talk about what we're going to cook.'

82

Later that evening, Clare cleared the kitchen. They'd decided on a moussaka, vegetarian because of Sophie, although she probably wouldn't eat much, and Ruth planned a pavlova. The meringue was on a very low heat in the oven and everything was basically done. They had worked well together, not really talking much, more in companionable silence. Clare was looking forward to seeing Angie again – it had been quite a while – and Sophie, of course. It promised to be a good evening and she was relieved, in a way, that Geoff was away so that Angie was coming on her own. She'd asked Sophie if she wanted to bring Phil but she'd been adamant that she didn't. So it was just the four of them.

When she'd finished in the kitchen, Clare sat down on the sofa and put her feet up with a sigh. Tomorrow was one of her working mornings. Ruth was busy finishing the notes she'd started when they'd got back from shopping so she turned on the television for the news. As the pictures came on the screen, she wondered whether everyone's stomach sank in the same way when they watched the news. It wasn't just that the news contained so much awful violence and suffering; it was the mechanical way in which everything was presented, and all the lies.

'Is there any connection between the millions of dollars given by the oil companies to the presidential campaign and the president's decision to give the go-ahead to drill for oil in the Red Desert?' an interviewer was asking.

'None at all,' replied the senator, speaking for the president.

Clare sighed. It was all too ridiculous. And yet, it did matter, didn't it? she thought. But what on earth could you do?

She continued to watch, passively, waiting for it to be over and yet unable to muster the will to switch off. Then Ruth appeared in the doorway. 'Are you watching something or would you like to know what I've written down?'

'I'd love to know,' said Clare eagerly. She switched off the set, sat back and looked at Ruth in anticipation.

'Well,' said Ruth, sitting down in the chair. 'It seems to be in three sections. That's what Helen said herself, that there were three levels of looking at my "situation", as she called it.' She paused. 'Shall I just read what I've written?' she asked.

'Whatever you like,' said Clare.

Ruth took a breath. 'The first bit is about being honest. She didn't actually say anything, you know, for nearly an hour. Then the first thing I remember she said, because she said it again later, was that as long as I kidded myself about things, I would keep feeling numb. Do you remember I told you about feeling numb?'

Clare nodded.

'She said that numbness wasn't really numb at all but too many feelings all jumbled up together – anger, loss, betrayal, fear about the future. She said that from the picture I'd given her, there had clearly been lots of good things, lots of love as well as lots of compromise, and perhaps this was the problem because I had compromised too much.

'She pointed out that while I talked about everything being split down the line equally, I also complained that I was doing most of the chores. She asked me which was the truth and when I said that I did more than David did, she asked me what I'd done about it and I said, "Nothing." I couldn't say why. I think it was a mixture of believing that, deep down, it was somehow my responsibility and that's why I didn't say anything. Or when I did, I'd have a real go at him and make snide comments. And things didn't change. But I had to admit that I wasn't ever clear, you know, I never actually asked him outright to do more.

'She asked me what role I thought I was fulfilling when I did all the housework and looking after the children. I said a parent. She asked me what role I was fulfilling with David. I couldn't answer at first. She asked if it was a wife's role. I said yes first but then I thought about it, and it was more than that . . . I think it started off as a wife but then I think it became something else. I started to take care of him too, more like a mother. So where did the equality go, she asked, and I couldn't answer. All I could say was that I thought I had to do it all, really, that somehow everything had to be kept going and that the children had all sorts of needs and David had too.

'We talked about whether this was connected to me going off sex. She helped me see that I was angry towards David but unable to express it. One of the things we do when we're angry, apparently, is turn it in on ourselves, so that's what I did. I kept working harder and harder. Do you know, I actually remembered, when I was writing this down just now, that David would say sometimes, "Leave the housework, let's go out and do something," and I would be the one refusing to go, saying I had too much to do. A real martyr!

'Then Helen said something really interesting about how sexual problems can occur when women started being too motherly because the attraction wanes. It is hard to maintain a sexual relationship to someone while mothering them at the same time, because there isn't any equality. I wondered what effect this had on men: show me a man who lusted after his mother, she said. I'd never thought about it like that before but I can see it now.

'The truth about the past twenty-seven years is that it wasn't perfect. Nor was it all bad. Something in between. But unless I face up to my part in the whole thing, I can't come out of this with any self-esteem at all. I started to blame myself when I was there but Helen was very fierce and basically said, None of that. She wasn't pushy, in fact she was extraordinary really because she was incredibly forceful but always gentle at the same time. Difficult to describe.

'So that's the first bit,' Ruth said, looking down at her notes. 'Be honest with myself, and see it for what it was and don't blame myself.

'Then we talked about my actual feelings and whether I was able to express them. She thought it was a good idea to release things as they came up, to find the time and space to air them. She said if I felt like a good shout, I should do so – in the car, for example. Anywhere that gave some privacy. You never think about these things on your own, do you?' Ruth paused.

'I've written down something that I still don't quite under-stand. Helen said women often don't challenge a situation they're unhappy with because they don't feel they have the right to. Something about being less important and valuable. She asked me what model my mother – our mother – had shown in terms of being a wife and mother. Funny, having gone to see her grave so recently. I told her that Mum was always very submissive and that Dad made the decisions: Mum went along with everything he said. Would you agree?'

Clare nodded.

'Helen said that part of my behaviour would be related to my impression of their relationship. That I would copy it or rebel against it. I suppose I copied it a bit, certainly in terms of going along with David's decisions. It's interesting because I did disagree with him about the business idea but I could have said more. I relied more on the adviser persuading him, but he didn't. I can see some of Mum in the way I gave in quite easily. Very easily, in fact, when you think that it concerned me and the children and it affected all of us so directly. I could have been a lot more forthright than I was.' She looked at Clare. 'Do you want me to stop or shall I go on?'

'Go on,' said Clare. 'I'm really interested.'

'Well, then there's the third layer, as Helen called it, which was more to do with being a woman, she said. Not just me personally. It was hard to be proud of yourself when your mother hadn't shown you how to be proud of yourself as a woman. She said this caused a lot of sadness in us even though we were not conscious of it. She asked about Anna and my relationship with her. I said it was fine but it wasn't close. We have quite a bit of distance between us.' Clare smiled. Ruth saw her smile and added, 'That's right. Like you were saying about Sophie.

'Anyway, the main thing Helen said to address was boundaries. She talked about this a lot. To stop feeling numb, she said, you'll have to set limits and deal with your feelings differently. So first, stop lying to yourself about the past. See it for what it is, without blame – either towards David or yourself. Then she went on to ways of setting limits. Instead of waiting for David to make up his mind, she suggested saying what *I* wanted. Did I want him to move out? Could I give him a deadline to make up his mind? What did I want? I said all I wanted was for nothing to have happened.

'Helen looked at me without saying anything. I said I knew it was stupid but it just came out. No, it didn't, she said, it didn't "just" come out. You're still hoping, deep down, that this will all go away like a bad dream from which you'll be woken by the kiss of a charming prince. I had to laugh then.

'Like you, she said it wasn't good for the children or me to keep silent. I realised, talking to her, that I was scared that David would be furious with me if I told them without discussing it with him first. Helen told me to work out whether I was too scared to take any initiative or whether I was genuinely concerned about being fair to him. Good question. I think, now, I was just too scared to upset him because I don't want to make things worse.

'She asked me how long I was prepared to walk on eggshells in the belief that he would renounce this other woman if only I could prove myself the "sweeter" of the two of us. The prince's kiss again. As long as I kept silent, I'd risk continuing to play the maternal role, keeping the whole show on the road for everyone else and yet, personally, being crushed under the weight. I hadn't thought of it like that. But she's right.

'I can now see that it's easier to keep going on automatic than face his rejection. I don't have to wait, do I, for David to make up his mind: perhaps I'll feel better if I make some decisions for myself.

'Helen reminded me I was vulnerable and not the "impregnable matriarch" that I was pretending to be. I'll have to remember that one!'

Ruth looked down at her notes again. '"Think about finding your own power first because whatever happens with David, nothing can go on as it was before. Nothing." She said that maybe I'll have to be alone first.' Ruth's voice faltered. 'Obviously she couldn't predict the future, but whatever happened, she was very clear that I had to find some time to stand alone from everything and see who I am.

'"Get the measure of yourself and stand on your own feet. If you can learn to separate emotionally, you can understand what it is like to be equal. You can't be *given* equal status by anyone else. It has to start within you. Then you can share with someone else on equal terms."'

Ruth sounded quite strong as she said this. She looked at Clare. 'You know, she really seemed to care, Clare. She said it was a lot to take in. I have to decide whether to look at things differently or not. I felt that it was possible, somehow, when she spoke to me. She's quite inspiring, isn't she?' Ruth paused and looked into the distance for a few moments before continuing.

'I don't know if I'll be able to do everything. But that's why I wanted to write everything down so that I could go over it again. It's quite a lot to take on board, isn't it? A whole lifetime. But I don't feel hopeless,' she said emphatically. 'And what I don't feel any more is a failure. I've made lots of mistakes, I'm beginning to realise, but this is the first time since the whole thing blew up that I haven't felt a failure. I feel more real in a way. Do you know what I mean?'

After this great outpouring she looked up at Clare, who couldn't help but go and put her arms around her sister's shoulders and give her a hug. 'You've done so well, Ruth.'

Ruth replied, halfway between laughing and crying, 'I haven't done anything really. It was Helen.'

'No, it wasn't,' said Clare. 'I mean, yes it was, but it takes two. She'd be the first to say that, you know. You have to be brave just to be able to open your eyes and you've done that. You really have.'

83

Love Is All You Need

The power of gentle glows in the quality of your loving. You know that love needs air around it if those you care for are to flourish. Love can be fierce and protective; it can also be dispassionate. You see when to allow others time to be alone even if you feel helpless for a while. You know you are, like anyone else, a vehicle for love: that the effort of loving lies not so much in what you do, but in a commitment to staying clear and open.

The principles of acknowledgement, balance and connections apply also to this most personal area of our lives: who we love, how much we love and in what ways we love will be affected by whether or not we start off from a place of personal power. Opening the left eye reveals that love is not always what it appears: that self-interest, dependence and even objectism appear in love's fair guise.

Loving others is not always straightforward. Our natural human urge to love gets entangled with other needs, for example, for security or validity. If the role of caretaker is important to our sense of identity, then love will be caught up with a need to be appreciated. If you've ever felt disappointed or hurt because adequate gratitude or reciprocation has not been forthcoming in response to your loving efforts, it will be because of this kind of tangle.

It's important to acknowledge how much we are influenced by the right eye. Love often becomes *lurve*, that *lurve* of romantic popular songs of past and present, of the stories of Mills & Boon, the *lurve* promoted by commercial interests in wedding gear, Valentine cards, diamond rings and so on. Much of the time, romantic love is based on a felt or unaware need for 'the other half' or a completion of the self. We are all susceptible to this: few of us escape the persuasion that being part of a couple will present a proper image to the outside. Few of us avoid the sense of loneliness or the preferred status of the 'partnered' when we're 'solo'.

Through the right eye, love gets caught up with competition and comparison. If we are lucky enough to encounter *lurve*, we start comparing it with an invisible ideal: why isn't it more sexual? Isn't it time he made a commitment? Why can't she be more grown-up? Through the right eye, love seems insufficient at times: not what I want, when I want it, in exactly the right manner. Why couldn't you be more imaginative? Why haven't you done what you promised?

It's easy to be critical when we've been led to believe that one of the highest prizes of this system is meeting the right man or woman, the One who is waiting to fulfil our dreams. Of course, there are partnerships that are vital, flourishing relationships but many that are not. And the partners who flourish with each other know that this is less to do with the blessing of Cupid's arrow than a constant and good amount of hard work together, needing, equally, closeness and separateness, intimacy and boundaries.

As women, we often think secretly that we're the experts at loving. We sometimes look askance at men and complain that, as fathers or husbands, they don't have our sensitivity or capacity for endurance. There is also a danger that we become possessive, our love revolving around the presence of the 'object(s)' of our affections. Because of our dependency on others for our self-esteem, it is a real challenge to draw back a little and sort out choice from compulsion. Acknowledging that our boundaries do, in fact, get blurred is important. Balancing love for others and love for self requires us to rethink loving from a personal place to an impersonal place. We can do this by discovering the wisdom of compassion.

The challenge of compassion

The word compassion is so often used glibly that we think it is easy to feel compassion, but it is actually a real challenge for most of us. It is at the heart of inner power and belongs completely to the left-eye vision. Unlike pity, compassion has absolutely no possibility of existing in an up/down context.

Remember that love and grief are at the heart of the first polarity of emotion connecting the complementary human needs for closeness and separateness. Opening the left eye offers another dimension to love: neither better nor worse, simply different. It is evoked less by one individual person and more in response to love as an energy that passes through us, a potential which can be realised through all kinds of relationships and doesn't depend on familiarity or control. This kind of love cannot be possessive.

It is a love which is there, all the time, allowing us to risk reaching out to others without the guarantee of being loved in return; it is a love that is dependent on *being*.

We recognise balance and connection. Intimate love is exclusively for those who we believe belong to us, for those we call 'mine'. It is a love reserved for the known and familiar. This can coexist with a different love that is immeasurable and not confined to one's nearest and dearest. This is compassion.

It is an immense energy that connects us to everyone else. It includes rather than excludes, it embraces rather than conquers, expands to accommodate rather than rejecting. This love is based in equality and has no relation to an up/down model of who gives/loves/contributes more or less. It is not a love which needs to see the other as an object of one's love or as a recipient of one's loving efforts.

With the left eye, it is not a question of loving too much while secretly hoping, planning or expecting that this love will one day be returned with interest, that one's own turn will come. This is a love that simply *is*.

There is no question of loving others at the expense of self-love. Balance is achieved by reciprocity, each nourishing the other. Compassion is the best antidote to the poison of aggression because it immediately transforms the vision from the perpendicular to the round. Differences still exist but compassion allows the heart to open in a way that sees through the external trappings of an object, to the person residing within. Compassion is felt when both our eyes are open. It is not the same as infinite love, which is actually pretty hard for a mere human being. Compassion doesn't require an advanced spiritual state.

It is simply the care of an equal, for an equal. It is not self-sacrificing. Because it is based in equality, it respects boundaries.

The need for boundaries

As soon as you feel genuine compassion towards another human being, you also become aware of genuine boundaries. Objectism breeds best in relationships of too much or too little distance.

Perhaps as compensatory behaviour for the stereotypical 'emotional distance' of men, many women find it difficult to observe the need for distance. Close becomes too close. For all sorts of the very best intentions (and sometimes distorted personal needs), we overstep others' emotional boundaries. We take on board their anxieties, their resentments; we sometimes assume we have caused them and can therefore undo them and make them happier.

Others' feelings act as a magnet that draws us in, often where we should not go, because all of us need a measure of separateness to survive. Through the left eye, therefore, we encounter another paradox. Compassion, being based in the care of an equal for an equal, also has limits: to be compassionate, we also need to learn to be dispassionate.

When to say no

If compassion is difficult to understand, dispassion is an awful lot harder. Just as compassion is misrepresented as soppy sentimentalism, so dispassion has long been confused with cold indifference, which describes shutting our eyes to another's needs. Dispassion requires us to enter a new emotional zone and experience keeping both eyes open. We can learn to care and see a limit to that care *at the same time*.

What gets in the way? First, our own investment in changing other people's lives. We want so much to make things better that accepting and acknowledging our own powerlessness is nothing short of agony for most of us. Genuinely accepting that someone else prefers to stay feeling self-pitying or confused or in pain is tough going when we are habitually devoted to monitoring, compensating, helping and making others feel happy!

The action of keeping your heart open and acknowledging your powerlessness exercises muscles in your heart you'll be surprised you have. It is tempting to close off completely, of course: closing a door in the heart (and the left eye) is less of an emotional effort.

We see the person in need and respond with concern: we also know we can (for whatever reason) do nothing about it at that moment. This applies to any relationship – a friend who refuses to acknowledge an addiction, a client who won't take a risk, a child who won't listen, a partner who refuses to take responsibility for his health, a colleague who persistently rejects any advice – and always entails acknowledging love and, at the same time, love's limits. This is when we discover the balance between compassion and dispassion. Close enough to see and far enough away to let the other choose their own way. We learn to loosen our grip on our need to help, to make better, to repair, to mend, to heal.

It is easier when there is a professional boundary because the hour finishes, the person leaves, the group ends and there is an in-built sense of ending and separation. But building this skill into interpersonal relationships is the key to a different kind of love.

There is a surprise to love if we allow it. Once we stop dictating its forms and place and relative importance along the ladder, we can be surprised by its emergence in the most unexpected of places. Similarly, when we let go control of our need to effect change, something remarkable can occur. Instead of the other person feeling rejected or ignored (interpreted as an indication of our own inadequacy), we find a hidden benefit. When another person actually feels *seen* – as they are – it constitutes possibly the greatest gift we can give another human being. Being seen without the need to do or be anything other than we are, to be loved as we are right now, is surely the greatest of all joys. Something shifts at a very deep level: compassion and dispassion in equal measure form a powerful catalyst.

Acknowledging love and its limits is bound to be painful at times. Compassion enables us to see a common vulnerability. Friendship most easily describes this kind of mutual regard and this quality can be present in intimate partnership, in parent-child bonds, in interaction at work or with strangers. It works with, not instead of, other dimensions of intimacy and closeness.

Without friendship, there is no equality. Equality shines through circumstantial differences leaving no room for pity, awe, obsession or fear. When we open our hearts, and look through binocular vision, we see our differences against a background of a connected whole.

84

The next evening, Clare was aware of how much she was enjoying the atmosphere in the kitchen. Everyone seemed relaxed. Angie had mainly been catching up with Clare, and Sophie with Ruth. They had enjoyed their food and were pausing before dessert.

'Well, Sophie, how are you doing, love?' asked Angie.

'I'm fine,' Sophie replied.

Angie half closed her eyes in a mock scrutiny of Sophie's face and said, 'Are you sure?'

'Yes, I am sure. What's Mum been telling you?'

'Oh, nothing except she was worried about you not eating.'

'Well, look at my empty plate. There's honestly nothing to worry about.'

There was an edge of something approaching defensiveness to Sophie's voice that Angie noticed so she changed the subject. 'How's work going?'

'Much the same,' replied Sophie. 'I don't know how much longer I'll stay there.'

'What will you do instead?' asked Ruth.

'I don't know,' said Sophie. 'I really don't know.'

There was a pause and a silence. Why was this happening? wondered Clare. What was the tension about suddenly? It hadn't been there before.

It was Ruth who broke the silence. Looking at nobody in particular she said, 'It's strange, isn't it, how we all change?'

'What do you mean?' asked Angie.

'Well, I'm about to go back to Canada in a couple of days. I've been there twenty-seven years: my children are there and my husband – or soon-to-be ex-husband, who knows – but it doesn't feel as if I'm going home any more. Things have changed in the few days I've been here.'

'Like what?' asked Sophie.

'Did your mum tell you I went to see Helen, this woman she works for? I went yesterday.'

'My God, Mum, are you sending everyone to see her?' said Sophie and then flushed. She knew she'd been too accusing.

'Ruth decided she wanted to go; it was nothing to do with me,' retorted Clare.

'Why are you cross?' Angie asked Sophie.

There was another silence. Clare felt embarrassed because she'd told Ruth about Sophie. She couldn't now remember if she'd told Angie or not. Not that it would have mattered.

Sophie felt put on the spot. 'I've started to go and see Helen too – for a set number of sessions.'

'Oh,' said Angie, 'she's kind of in the family then.'

'Do you know her?' Ruth asked Angie.

'I know *of* her but I haven't met her.'

'Well, I have to say, she was extraordinary.' Ruth then went on to present to Angie and Sophie a very much shorter version of what she had shared with Clare the night before.

Clare wondered how Sophie would respond to all this; whether it would break something. She didn't know quite what, but she thought that privacy was important in these matters. She noticed that she was quite tense and consciously tried to relax her shoulders and breathe more deeply. Why on earth was she so wound up?

Angie listened intently to Ruth. Clare wondered if Angie was listening with her 'counsellor hat' on and worried she would be bored because it was more work. She began to wish Ruth would stop but Ruth was into her stride, intent on conveying how much it had meant to her because she didn't feel a failure any more. She was quite unselfconscious about it all, quite open in her praise of Helen and her gratitude for being able to learn so much in such a short space of time.

Then Clare found herself feeling protective towards her sister. She wondered if Angie was feeling superior, or if not exactly superior, perhaps blasé about these things. Angie would never go and see anyone, unless maybe as part of training but that was hardly the same: once you were training you were already halfway to doing it for 'work' purposes so you weren't nearly so vulnerable. Also you had some idea who you'd be getting, not like some ordinary punter off the street who didn't know anything and was completely vulnerable, like Ruth or Sophie.

Clare tried to breathe again, aware that she was caught between feeling protective and embarrassed for Ruth, regretting that Angie was having to listen and be bored, and then worrying about the effect of all of this on Sophie, who'd only just managed to go and get some help . . .

'I can't stand the tension any more,' she heard a voice say and then, seeing all three faces turn to look towards her, she realised the voice must have been hers.

They looked at her and waited for her to explain.

'I'm sorry,' Clare said. 'I don't know quite what I mean. It's just that I am sitting here feeling really wound up because Ruth is talking and I don't know if it's boring Angie – no, I don't know,' seeing Angie's frown of puzzlement, 'and then I'm wondering about Sophie feeling that her privacy is being invaded in some way.'

'I'm sorry,' said Ruth. 'I'll shut up. I was just—'

'No, don't,' the others said in chorus.

'I didn't mean that, Ruth,' said Clare. 'It's good that you are talking about it.'

'I don't have to,' said Ruth. 'I don't know why I started. I guess it's on my mind, that's all.'

'No, I think it's generous of you,' said Sophie. 'I couldn't begin to talk in the same way. You're very honest and I admire that. I don't want you to stop because of me, anyway.'

'It's OK,' said Ruth. She gave a sigh. 'Are we ready for dessert yet?'

Her question hovered in the air, unanswered.

Clare looked at Sophie. 'How are you feeling, Soph?'

Ruth stood up but stayed to listen to Sophie's reply.

'It's strange. When it first came up, I felt furious with you. I don't know why. Like something really personal was being revealed. Which is silly, because nobody here is going to judge me badly, but it was something about another part of me being brought into the conversation. I wasn't ready to talk about it, like you' (she looked up at Ruth) 'because ... I just couldn't. It's a process I can't describe. I know something happens, that's all. But as I listened to you,' she said, now looking directly at Ruth, 'I felt a huge surge of love, I really did.

'It sounds silly, but I felt something go right through me as I listened to you. You looked lovely as you spoke, because you were real. So honest, I suppose, not making any impression, just being vulnerable and open. And that became more important than my irritation. It was much bigger than that.'

Ruth smiled at her. She didn't know what to say so said nothing and sat down again. 'Should I get the dessert or not yet?'

'I don't know. How are we doing?' Clare addressed everyone. Angie was looking resolutely at the floor. Sophie, who was sitting closest to Angie, put her hand on her arm. Angie looked up at her. 'Are you OK?' asked Sophie.

Angie gave a weary smile. 'I don't know ... too many things going on.' She moved her chair back. Looking at Ruth, she said, 'Can we delay dessert a bit? I'd like to go and sit next door and stretch out. What I could really do with is a cigarette so I'm going outside to have another glass of wine.' She looked at everyone. 'Is that all right?'

'Course it is,' said Clare, relieved that Angie had finally spoken. 'Good idea to move.' They stood up. Clare put on the coffee machine and cleared away the plates. When she went into the sitting room a few minutes later, Ruth had settled on the sofa and Sophie on the floor. Clare sat beside Ruth. She noticed they were all waiting for Angie to return. Angie came back and sat in the armchair.

'It looks as if I'm about to make a major speech to you all from here,' she said with a smile.

'Are you?' asked Sophie.

'Well, I can tell you what was going on. Listening to you, Ruth,' she said, looking at her, 'made me feel so desperate. You know I spend my days listening to and helping others. I mean they're all students so they're much younger and they've got different concerns from me, but I also end up listening to my colleagues . . . I guess I'm more depressed about my own life than I realised.'

Clare was very surprised. Angie had always been defiantly undepressed about everything.

'You know how I come across, Clare,' said Angie, as if reading her mind, 'always coping exceptionally well. And I do most of the time. But, right now, I'm in a relationship that's going nowhere. Nothing particularly wrong. Nothing particularly right. Not much love,' she said, looking at Sophie. 'And I wonder about love a lot at the moment. I don't think I love much, personally or profession-ally. I just don't seem to feel it any more. And I'm getting older.' She paused.

'Do you think it's because things are stale?' asked Sophie.

'That's a good word,' Angie replied. 'I don't know. I just feel a great emptiness in the middle and it makes me very, very sad.' Her voice broke a little. Clare had never seen Angie like this.

'Do you know why?' asked Ruth.

'It may have something to do with grief from long ago, but I don't know, more than that, a loss of something much deeper. I sound like a bad pop song, don't I?' she said, laughing.

The others smiled and said nothing.

Angie continued. 'I really envied you your openness too, Ruth. The way you could describe what happened and what you had learned was so simple and unpretentious. I envy you that ability to be free of cleverness, in a way. I don't mean you're stupid but you don't try and make an impression. You were just able to trust. That's what it is,' she said emphatically. 'It's trust. I don't think I trust anybody. I mean I trust you, Clare. To talk to. But I don't trust myself. I don't trust Geoff. I don't trust. I don't feel safe. And I'm tired of hiding and making an effort and keeping things going and pretending I feel safe and confident when I don't. I would love to trust. I really would.'

She stopped. 'Anyway, that's what I was thinking. There are bits of me all over the place, with none of them fitting into each other. And that makes me insecure . . . I think it's time I stopped rambling!' After a moment or two, Sophie said to her, 'I know what you mean by being in little bits and hiding, always watching out and trying not to do the wrong thing. That's why I was so struck by the feeling of love just now in the kitchen. If I felt that more, it wouldn't matter so much.'

Clare spoke then too. 'It amazes me that you have all said what you've said. There was I, imagining all sorts of other things, and getting knotted up with anxiety, and it turns out I was completely wrong. And I thought I was quite good at knowing what was going on in people!'

Sophie smiled at Clare. 'Shall I go and get the coffee, Mum?'

'Yes,' said Angie. 'Good idea.'

'I'll get it, you stay there. I'm going to get our dessert, anyway,' said Ruth. As she left the room, she felt delighted at the prospect of presenting what she knew would be a stunning treat for everyone. Somehow it really suited the occasion.

As she passed the front door, the bell sounded. She opened it to find an elderly woman, in a smart dressing gown, holding one hand wrapped in the crook of her other arm. She looked very pale.

'Hello,' said Ruth.

'Is Clare there?' said Ellen.

Clare appeared at the door. 'Ellen! What's the matter?'

'I'm sorry to trouble you, Clare, but I've hurt my hand on the oven and I can't see to it myself.'

'Come in, come in. Ellen, this is Ruth, my sister.'

The two women smiled at each other as Ellen came in and Clare closed the door. 'Come into the kitchen and we'll have a look.'

As Ellen walked in, she saw the plates. 'I'm so sorry. Have I interrupted your dinner?'

'Not at all. We finished ages ago,' said Clare. She reached up to the top cupboard where she found her first-aid tin. She cleared a space on the table and put it down. 'Now then, let's have a look.'

Ruth peered over as Clare unwrapped Ellen's hand. There was a vivid red burn mark stretching from her wrist to her knuckle.

'Dear!' exclaimed Clare as Ruth winced and said, 'That looks nasty. What did you do?'

'I was very silly. I must have forgotten to turn off the oven when

I'd cooked my dinner and so I went back just now and opened it to put the tray back and put my hand inside. I just didn't think.'

'Sit down a minute,' said Clare. 'Then I can have a better look.' She saw the wound was beginning to blister. 'When did you do this, Ellen?'

'I don't know.'

'It must have been a while ago,' said Clare. 'Why didn't you come earlier?'

'I was looking in the bathroom for some lint and the scissors and tried to cut it with my other hand but couldn't do it.'

Clare rummaged in the box for some ointment. 'I don't know if it will stop the blistering now but it will help heal it.'

Clare covered the burn mark gently with the ointment. She then cut a strip of lint and placed it over, fixing plaster to keep it in place. 'You'll have to try not to get it wet,' she told Ellen. 'Perhaps tomorrow, you can let the air get to it for a while because that would be good for it. Come over tomorrow and I'll fix it for you.'

Sophie put her head round the kitchen door to see what was going on.

'You've met my daughter, Sophie, haven't you, Ellen?'

'Yes. Hello, dear. Your mother's coming to the rescue here.'

'What happened?' asked Sophie.

'Oh, I've just been very silly.'

'She burned herself on her oven,' said Clare. She looked up and saw Ruth mouthing something at her and alternating her eyes between the coffee pot and Ellen. She smiled and said, 'Ellen, do stay and have a cup of coffee with us. Ruth has made a wonderful pavlova and we'd love you to join us.'

'Oh, I couldn't interrupt,' faltered Ellen.

'Yes, you could,' said Sophie. 'Come on. I'll introduce you to Angie. Or have you met her before?'

Ellen took Sophie's proffered arm and went into the sitting room, saying, 'You really are having a proper party, aren't you, with so many people. It's very kind of you to invite me to join you. And look at me in my dressing gown!'

85

Angie had gone, giving Sophie a lift home; Ellen had been put safely to bed; Clare and Ruth had cleared up and they now sat having a final cup of tea before they too ended the day. They agreed it had been a very special evening.

'It somehow made things complete, did you notice, when Ellen joined us,' asked Ruth.

Clare nodded. 'What do you think it was?' she asked.

Ruth thought for a moment and shook her head. 'I don't know. All those things she was talking about – the past values and how they've gone – seemed to touch on what we'd been talking about earlier.'

'Mm. It makes you think how awful it must be for so many old people now, you know, in their eighties and nineties, who have seen so much change. They really have been left behind.'

'She's almost the same age as Mum would have been, isn't she?'

'Yes. And unfortunately her son doesn't seem to have much to do with her. He lives abroad.' Clare told Ruth about the state of the bathroom and the cups and her dilemma about what to do about Ellen.

'You can't really write to the son, can you?'

'No. It wouldn't be right.'

'She's a real sweetie, I thought.'

'She is. You know, some of what she was talking about reminded me of what Helen writes. Ellen mentioned a sense of community that she grew up with, people looking out for each other, helping when someone lost a member of the family or had a bad harvest or met with some kind of misfortune through no fault of their own. And I remember it being safe to wander as a child, don't you? We would cycle off on our own. Nobody would ever worry.'

'I'm not sure it was entirely safe. I remember being flashed at on my way back from school once and I was absolutely terrified.'

'When? You never said anything.'

'No. I didn't say anything for ages. It was one afternoon on the train and I was alone in a carriage and the man in front had a coat or something folded over his lap and, as the train pulled out from one of the stations, he moved his coat aside and there he was, masturbating – well, I know that's the word now but I didn't then – and all I could see was this huge thing and his knuckles. He had LOVE tattooed on one set of knuckles and HATE on the other. I was mesmerised . . . and terrified.

'I can still see his face looking at me all the time – round face, very dark hair and a small moustache. I looked at the train door, one of those with a window that you could pull down, and I watched everything rushing past the window, thinking is it going too fast for me to jump out. I didn't know what to do. The train finally came into the station and I remember jumping out before it had come to a stop. I ran and ran, all the way home.'

'Why didn't you tell me?'

'I don't know. I guess because you were younger and I didn't want to frighten you. I did tell Mum a couple of weeks later and she said it was probably too late to do anything about it by then. So that was it. I wonder why I'm remembering that now?'

'I think because we were talking about being safe as a child.'

'Yes, we were.'

'How old were you?'

'I must have been about ten. Definitely before secondary school. Did anything ever happen to you?' asked Ruth.

'Only the odd flasher exposing himself in the park when I was a student.'

'Do you know if Sophie's ever had anything like that?'

'She's never said.'

'Neither's Anna. I wonder.' She stopped for a moment. 'Do you think Ellen's values have really gone?'

'Yes,' replied Clare, nodding as she spoke. 'I mean, there have always been people who were violent but now it's all so commonplace.'

'I do sympathise with Ellen when she says that everything has got so fast. No waiting for anything. No acceptance of anything you can't do. If you couldn't have children, you accepted it. If you had an illness, you accepted it. Now it's always a fight to prove that you are better than what life hands you.'

'Do you really think we care less for others?'

'Yes, I do,' said Ruth adamantly. 'I can't imagine a suffragette movement now, can you, or even an anti-slavery movement. It wouldn't happen. People don't care enough.' Ruth shook her head.

'Just listen to us criticising the uncaring masses. What about us? I sometimes wonder if *I* care enough?'

'What do you mean?'

'Well, I don't do anything myself to change things. It's all very well talking now, but my normal life is spent looking after the family, working all day and every day just to survive. I've never even thought about global capitalism let alone protested about it!'

Clare smiled. 'I know. I wonder what it would be like to be more revolutionary.'

'We could be subversive and stop shopping,' said Ruth.

'And where would you get food,' asked Clare, 'if you didn't have supermarkets?'

'I don't know. Grow my own! They have markets in other countries even if they don't here. But there have to be ways of organising things if you're really committed.'

'Why would you bother?'

'Are you playing devil's advocate or something?' asked Ruth.

'Not really. I suppose I'm asking myself the same thing.'

'I think I'd bother if I really wanted to do something to change the world and make a stand. I couldn't get into all this fighting on the streets. I'd need to be much more subversive.'

Clare laughed. 'I never knew you were such an anarchist at heart.'

'A closet anarchist, more like.'

'Come on, I'm exhausted. It's time for bed.'

'OK, but I'll just say one last thing: if I knew there were other closet anarchists around, then who knows . . . maybe I'd be willing to join forces!'

Now that Ruth was finding her voice for the first time, she was pleased, on this occasion, to have the final word.

86

Getting Back on Your Feet

Personal power shows in the way you handle others as equals, neither looking up at them nor pitying them. It shows in the way you do not subjugate yourself to others, giving your personal power away.

How do we know when we've lost our personal power and what can we do about it in the short term? There are clues and it is possible to detect them, once we know what we're looking for.

Numbness
When we are feeling 'nothing', when sensation disappears and we find ourselves in a fog of uncertainty and confusion, learn to recognise this as a sign that you are actually feeling a great deal, so much so that you have shut down against it. Even the simple acknowledgement, to yourself, that you are feeling a lot will act as a catalyst: something, somewhere will shift.

Invisibility
You seem to vanish as a person – your opinions, your feelings, your authority, your competence, your words – everything seems to disappear. This can last for a few moments or extend into weeks and even months. You feel as if you don't exist. This may include literally shrinking against the wall when someone passes by or psychologically shrinking when in the company of someone else. Even if you're normally talkative, you find that you let others speak, hold the floor, take over the discussion.

Preoccupation
Notice if you are preoccupied with someone else's response to what you are thinking of saying or doing, because this is another clue. Obviously this is normal to some extent but when you find yourself practising over and over in your mind a rehearsal of what

will happen, you can assume you have lost your personal power. If you're an adult and notice you're afraid of someone being cross with you or dread losing their approval, your power has definitely gone. Gone doesn't mean that it has necessarily been taken away: we hand it over most of the time, on a plate.

Pretence

Pretending always makes us powerless. This includes pretending you're not feeling what you are feeling or vice versa, pretending you agree, pretending you don't mind, pretending you're not intelligent and especially pretending you're not powerful. Concealment is part of this. When you hide your successes, strengths or mistakes, you are giving away your power. Learn to recognise denial as an early warning signal of problems you may be storing up ahead.

Waiting

This can be a necessary part of being and for those of us who are naturally impatient with life, waiting is a very good discipline. However, waiting can often be another clue to powerlessness. It can degenerate into a sluggish torpor, a state of psychological lassitude masking a lot of anxiety and powerlessness. It is a way of pretending we don't have a choice in the situation.

If we really don't have a choice, this is a true indicator of powerlessness. There is much in the world that we are truly powerless to change – the inevitability of death, the suffering of a loved one, endings, natural disasters – but the tendency to keep repeating 'There's nothing I can do about it', as a kind of mantra, only reinforces internal powerlessness. Sometimes we have to dare.

Being treated like an object

There are many occasions when others see and treat us as objects. This approach, as we've seen, triggers a corresponding passivity or state of 'objecthood'. We cannot stop this tendency but we can stop playing along with it. We are quite capable of acting to counteract the assumption that we exist only as an object through the lens of someone else's monocular sight.

The best way of doing this is not to resort to blame because the other person is, like you, part of the system that encourages such treatment. More likely than not, they are completely unaware of their assumptions.

When stung, hit, prodded or knocked by something, our automatic response to pain is 'ouch'. This shows that you are alive and responsive. Remember that the most basic assumption is that an object doesn't have feelings: the most immediate way of challenging objectism (and powerlessness) therefore is to communicate an 'ouch'.

Start by saying this in your head, just to remind yourself you are a living human being, even if it's escaped other people's notice. Then, depending on the situation, you can express your feelings about your treatment. In doing so you show that you *feel* something.

When you say 'ouch', it often comes as a huge surprise to the other person because up till then they may have assumed you – as an object – couldn't feel anything at all. The fact that you say 'ouch' indicates you don't like this, you're hurt or annoyed or whatever, but one thing is clear: you are not an impassive object.

Emotion is the key to remedying the harm done to us through objectism, by putting us back in touch with our bodies. When we say 'I feel', we regain our status as a person, whatever the role we have in the other person's landscape. Communication in this way is often enough to make the other person think twice about their behaviour towards us, especially if we manage to communicate without blame – which an 'ouch' is. Then we don't invoke any unnecessary hostility as a consequence. Simple but effective.

87

Clare drove to Helen's house straight from the airport. She'd arranged with Helen to start later so she could get Ruth to her flight. Ruth had been adamant that Clare should not wait with her: she wanted to have the time to herself to adjust to the idea of going back.

Clare had felt surprisingly sad saying goodbye. She knew she was going to miss Ruth now and wondered if they'd keep in touch or whether this newfound closeness would evaporate. Obviously there would be lots to sort out with David. They'd talked about the possibility of her stopping in Toronto when she flew back from her trip to visit Danny in California, but she wanted to wait and see what transpired at home for Ruth before getting too excited about it.

'How are you feeling now your sister's gone?' asked Helen on the way upstairs to start work.

'I feel quite sad, actually. It's strange because we were never really close, you know, but somehow this visit has been a meeting point. I guess she's at a time in her life when everything is up for grabs so she's more open – and I'm more open too, I suppose.'

'More open to what?' asked Helen.

'I don't really know. More open to seeing each other as real people, perhaps. We've never spent time together without a family framework defining our interaction – our own family, then our combined families. This is the first time we've spoken to each other as individuals, even though we have a shared history. It was fun and I hadn't expected that at all.'

'Excellent,' said Helen. 'I'm delighted.'

'She found her session with you extremely helpful. I'm sure she wouldn't mind me telling you that.'

Helen smiled. 'She wrote to me . . . a little card came yesterday. Sweet of her.'

Clare was surprised, because she assumed Ruth would have asked her for the address or told her she was going to write. These things really are private, aren't they, she thought.

As she sat down, she noticed a small piece of twisted driftwood on top of the desk, with the word WOMB carved into it. No, not carved, she saw as she looked more closely, but burned. She had to move it aside to get to the keyboard.

As Helen saw her do this, she came over. 'I'm sorry. I'll take that out of your way.' She picked it up and laid it along a lower shelf of the huge bookcase. She sat down in her usual place on the floor and started arranging her papers. As ever, her dog was lying very close by. Clare sat waiting, wondering about the piece of wood.

'Does the word stand for anything?' asked Clare tentatively.

'What word?'

'WOMB. Does it mean "womb" as in womb or something else? I know I'm being nosy but you've got me intrigued.'

Helen was amused. 'Well, it's not only the word, although that's part of the story. The letters on the wood there stand for Wonder Of My Being. It comes originally from the New Testament. St John, I think. The wood was found and prepared by a woman who was part of a special healing ritual, so it has a lot of meaning for me.'

Helen seemed to close the conversation so, left with several more questions unanswered, Clare turned back to the desk. She really doesn't give much away, thought Clare, as she stared at the screen in the ensuing silence. She waited.

'I was looking at it this morning because of what I want to write this afternoon,' Helen suddenly continued. Clare turned back round in surprise.

'It's odd but that simple phrase – the wonder of my being – encompasses everything I want to say about women and their spirituality. The word "wonder" is so powerful. It suggests awe and reverence and cherishing, doesn't it? A complete contradiction to every way we negate ourselves.

'And then the word "being" has such a sense of continuity and depth, something untouched by self-consciousness and judgement. Do you understand what I'm talking about?'

'I think so.'

'I find it hard to put into words. For me, the phrase suggests a place within ourselves that's been buried under everything else. An embodiment with everything true and just as it is.'

For a moment, Helen looked so sad that Clare felt a rush of tenderness towards her.

'I understand a bit of it,' said Clare, who wasn't simply trying to be helpful. She did understand some of it. She could feel it. She had a sensation of something like a very fine silk scarf floating down slowly and gently settling in her somewhere, in her 'being', she supposed. No good trying to force her mind to pursue this, she knew that much by now. This kind of understanding had to be approached from another direction.

'You can't go out and search for what you're describing, can you? Are you saying we have to be open to it so that it can come to earth in a different place? Is that what you mean?'

'Yes,' said Helen, slowly, 'I think that is what I mean.'

Clare thought she could see tears in Helen's eyes. Helen didn't say any more but looked at her with a warm smile before turning away to find where she wanted to begin.

88

When they finished work later that afternoon, Clare followed Helen downstairs. As she put on her coat, Clare turned to Helen.

'I don't know how to put this, Helen, but I wondered if, at some point, you'd like to come to supper or something. It's just that I realised when Ruth was here that I know so little about you. All I know is that you're writing a book that means an awful lot to you but I don't know anything about you . . . personally.'

'I'm not sure how relevant it is to working together,' said Helen slowly, looking and feeling quite awkward.

'I may be speaking out of turn,' continued Clare, 'but you know a lot about me now and you're important to my daughter and to my sister and . . . I'd just like to know a bit about you.'

'To make it more equal, you mean?'

They both smiled.

'I hadn't thought of it like that, but I guess so,' replied Clare.

'Well, I don't know about supper but if you want a cup of tea before you go, I'll endeavour to fill you in a bit.'

'Fine,' said Clare, taking her coat off again.

'There really isn't anything very interesting to tell,' said Helen as they went into the kitchen. Helen switched on the kettle and Clare sat down at the table. 'So what do you want to know?'

'You make it sound like an interrogation. I don't have a list, really, just . . .' Clare shrugged. 'How did you come to write this book? Do you have any children? Have you been married? Anything about your own life, really. I'm curious to know something about how you've come to these things that are so important to you.'

Helen took a deep breath and considered Clare's questions silently. 'Oh dear,' she said. 'There's not much to say. I grew up in a fairly dysfunctional family. I have a brother who lives abroad, with whom I have little contact. I've never been married. I would have liked children but can't have them . . . I had an abortion a long time ago that went wrong.' Helen paused and sat down. Clare thought about the piece of wood and the healing ritual but didn't feel she could probe too far.

'It always depresses me, this kind of exposition,' said Helen. 'In the eyes of the rest of the world, as we know it, I really am not very interesting. I haven't got any status of any kind.'

'I'm not asking about status,' protested Clare.

'But you are, you know. You want some sign of credibility.'

'All I wanted to know was a bit about you, that's all,' insisted Clare, 'because . . . '

'Because you want to fit me in somewhere. Into something you understand.'

'I didn't know it would upset you so much.'

The kettle boiled. Helen got up to make the tea.

'How did I find out about you, Clare? Things emerged as they emerged, didn't they? Apart from your interview to establish certain relevant details, which we *exchanged*, as far as I remember.'

'Why is this making you so cross?'

Helen was quiet. Then she said, 'I'm sorry. I am getting defensive, I know. I just hate all this business of putting people into categories to assess credibility.'

'I didn't mean to do that. I was just interested.'

Helen sat down again. 'Tell me something, Clare. Tell me what you have perceived about me, anything you may have gleaned from working with me for these past few months.' She looked evenly across the table at Clare. 'What do you know about me without my having given you any details?'

Clare thought for a moment. 'Well. I'd say you were passionate and committed, that you mean what you say, that you can be moody. You're intense and emotional. I imagine that you are a bit of a loner but that you care a great deal about others. You are quite a powerful person, a bit intimidating at times, but you are also vulnerable.' She looked directly at Helen now, getting into her stride. 'I imagine you could be quite difficult to be close to . . . and I'm not sure how easily you trust other people. I've also seen a lot of humour in you, although we've always been working on serious things.' She stopped. 'Are any of those close?'

'I wouldn't disagree with any of them and that's what I mean. You have taken in some important things about me without any *facts*.'

'Facts are part of the story too.'

'They are, yes, I agree, but a lot of external details are incidental to the human being in front of you. They can also be misleading, you know, when we assume too much from a given label. I mean it when I say that I have little street cred. I have no professional pedigree, no social status – husband, family, wealth, glamour – or even inverse status, like coming from a minority background. I am an ordinary woman in a middle-aged body, yes, like you,' seeing Clare's grimace, 'doing her best to say what she sees. And if what she says means anything to anybody else, then it won't be because of who she *is*, but what she's saying.'

'Perhaps I should add "self-opinionated" to the list,' said Clare with a smile. The two women regarded each other with affectionate amusement.

Helen poured out the tea.

89

A Spirituality in the Round

The power of gentle is the power of paradox. You can feel your own boundaries as well as threads of connection to others. You are aware enough of the past and you have one eye on the future; but you are in the present. Upright. Neither concave nor convex. From your centre, you see with compassion and dispassion, knowing you are significant and insignificant at the same time.

As long as we remain entangled in the limited ideas and perceptions of monocular thinking – our heads muddled, our bodies fragmented, and our hearts overloaded – what happens to our souls?

Many religions reflect the perpendicular power systems and values of the culture at large. We have long been alert to the implicit sexism of most formal doctrines. We can close our eyes to this, as many of us do. We become staunch followers of Judaism and Islam even though women are not allowed into the holy spaces in a synagogue or mosque. We commit ourselves to Catholicism despite the relentless bastions of male hierarchy. Sometimes we pretend not to notice or we assume the given male, hierarchical order is there for a very good reason. The bonbon effect influences our beliefs about religion as with every other aspect of culture.

Spiritual practices of prayer and meditation are vital for many of us as a means of disengaging from over-attachment to the material concerns of life: the quest for money, possessions or romantic love. The creeds of Buddhism or Hinduism or Taoism are popular with individuals from nations that have been overrun by monocular culture and who yearn for an alternative. Certainly these offer an alternative to the dominance of the bonbon hierarchy but are not always specifically pro-equality, affecting a more neutral stance, so sexism appears irrelevant against the wider background of human salvation.

One common denominator in most religions is their approach to emotion. It is constructed around the need not to manage emotion but to *suppress* it. Embedded within a cultural and historical context, emotion is viewed as bad, unwelcome and *anti*-spiritual because it is powerful, dehumanising and, above all, associated with the uncontrollability of the flesh. The divide between the airy, clean and divine space of the spirit and the damp, suspect and unwholesome quagmire of emotion retains its stronghold on our imagination. This split is easily recognisable as a duality of right-eye vision.

A left-eye approach embraces Goddess worship and the elemental nature of Wiccan ritual as well as all animist beliefs. But while our body image in real life is so fragmented and negative, we cannot truly celebrate womanhood. What use evoking forces of unknown elemental powers on high if, on the ground, we continue to compare and compete with other women or still find ourselves at the bottom of the work ladder? Even the vital teachings of feminist theology are reluctant to admit a real and practical acceptance of vulnerability, of the mute, of chaos and emotional release.

A different starting place

When religious doctrines preach the necessity to divest ourselves of the 'ego', they fail to observe, because the preachers are not women, that women often have no real sense of ego. When all we know of ourselves is learned in relation to the 'dominant' gender, it isn't surprising that, for many women, a sense of self is elusive. We gain a sense of identity by comparison with men, through our function and our personal or professional roles; we gain a sense of ourselves as objects, but not easily do we find a sense of our own person.

We may have an adapted identity, dependent on everyone else around us, and we certainly learned to be egotistic, but rarely do we have a solid self-affirming sense of self. The boundaries are simply not well enough defined. We are starting from a lower position on the ladder.

You cannot give up or divest yourself of an ego that you don't have. For women, it would be wiser, first, to find and establish an ego, a sense of self, and then learn through compassion and dispassion to put this aside when appropriate.

Our starting point needs to be different: a base of personal power has to be established first. Find your self first, live into it, explore your boundaries, test its limits: discover and know who you are with all your weaknesses and blind spots and virtues and strengths. Then, and only then, you can transcend this self – its needs, wishes, demands and obsessions – not to escape the (lower) status of personal, social and professional nonentity, but as a spiritual commitment and choice.

Spirituality based in personal power again recognises the importance of acknowledgement, balance and connection. There are many examples of binocular vision in action as women continue to work within a church, in a religious order or in the ministry, functioning and seeing through both eyes at once. They acknowledge the monocular structure while making a commitment to their faith and serving others through their vocations. Many women in these circumstances hold both realities with great roundness of power and by necessity, great integrity and courage.

Coherence is especially important if we are to find a spiritual dimension to empowerment. All those aspects of the external world that inspire us, move us, evoke awe, humility and joy have one common feature: integrity.

This means that who you are is who you are wherever you are. It means a sense of continuity and connection. For integrity to exist, women must affirm themselves not only intellectually but emotionally, sexually and physically through their spirituality. Obviously we have different roles at different times but there needs to be a thread of continuity. If you love yourself, you love your body. If you love your body, you treat it as a whole.

Inner power is always diminished by imbalance. This is what happens if you 'think' feminist at work because you're passed over for promotion while also having your face lifted; if you 'think' compassion while at the same time turning your back on your next-door neighbour. You cannot 'think' equality while refusing to be honest with a man because his ego is too fragile for the truth. With the left eye open, we have to establish coherence between the different aspects of our lives if we are to find a spirituality with any real integrity and meaning.

Coherence comes through seeing our connection to others. A binocular approach to spirituality helps us see beyond ourselves, our personal lives and problems, to the wider reality. This means sharing responsibility for collusion (or change) within a system of monocular values. It makes us question, for example, how we maintain the system: how we tolerate the incoherence of our commitment to any doctrine that upholds and values a perpendicular view of the world.

An integrated spirituality speaks of passion, compassion and dispassion but not indifference. This is not a spirituality of the exclusive, of the up/down power system. It is inclusive; it is coherent; it is wise; it is open to change.

An integrated spirituality challenges the conventional understanding that the term spiritual has become in most contexts, a defence *against* the emotional aspects of life. It has come to be associated more with the attic spaces to which we retreat as we hastily seek refuge from the rising tides in the basement.

The left eye indicates the possibility of evolving a spirituality *through* the emotions, not as a defence against them. Our ability to be open to emotional energies, to manage, express, release and move through them can allow us to use emotion as a medium of transformation, to become more fully who we are, both individually and collectively. If women seek a spirituality that conforms to a roundness of power, affirming womanhood, not above or below, but as *equal*, then emotion has to be an integral part.

Finding a form of spiritual expression that emanates from within is a particular challenge. To discover this for ourselves, we need courage. We also need wisdom, another intrinsic feature of personal power. Wisdom arises from inside and is different from knowledge acquired from outside sources. It is not necessarily a quality of age and experience: many children show wisdom alongside their worldly naivety. It is a source of seeing that comes from an unbroken connection to the inside so, for most of us, this entails a good deal of inner repair.

90

Re-evaluation

Reclaiming integrity is a repair we have to do for ourselves. Nobody can do it for us. We can start by acknowledging the oppressive nature of what we've learned. Nothing can alter the current dominance of cultural beliefs but allowing ourselves to see the bigger picture gives us the chance to counteract the bonbon effect and to perceive ourselves as different and *equal*.

Reviewing the bigger picture

We can re-evaluate some well-known assumptions. Alongside our individuality, there are certain common features of women's behaviour that are often considered to be in need of alteration. Being passive, dependent, indecisive, weak, changeable or emotional, for example, are traditionally inferior to being active, independent, decisive, strong, stable and rational.

Re-evaluation beyond the ladders means that indecision, for example, could be seen as indicative of a roundness of perception, seeing from different angles at once, taking into consideration the needs of someone other than yourself. That 'unfortunate' condition of dependence could be seen as part of interdependence, an aspect of connection with others, a perception that acknowledges the impact of each part of the whole on another. Seeing dependence as an aspect of mutuality gives it quite a different value.

Similarly, changeable could be seen as sensitive to the present and an aspect of flexibility. Emotional could be seen as an essential aspect of relationship, not just an embarrassing tendency. Passive – currently synonymous with underdog – can also mean allowing, accommodating and yielding.

What we often dislike about ourselves are only faults through the right eye: they can equally be seen as attributes. Through the mindset of the right eye, they've become labelled too quickly as negative. They can certainly develop into unhelpful characteristics in our behaviour but this is when these qualities become distorted and excessive. Indecisiveness extends from being aware of many possibilities to being over-concerned about making the right decision. Passivity becomes unbalanced and excessive so that when we need to set limits, we don't. Our changeability becomes a nuisance to others and a chronic habit: we don't take responsibility for feelings or decisions and play helpless instead. Once again, it is balance that is needed.

Equality is impossible while internal doubts make us excessively dependent on outside approval. We can only move outwards as equals from a reference point *inside* ourselves.

91

The Wonder of my Being

Even though you are subject to constant persuasion that outside image is all, you can remember that this is a mere deflection for what you hold true: inside is what matters.

This aspect of repair is less conscious. The importance of interiority, once understood, balances the external objectism of the body with one's own body, the only body that each of us is given for this lifetime.

Having all our sexual and reproductive organs inside makes

a difference to our relationship to our bodies. So many physical events in a woman's life – sexual arousal, orgasm, menstruation, conception, pregnancy – occur in secret, in the interior. We carry within us an awareness of invisible cycles over which we do not always have total control. Our response to this interior life will be influenced by how we perceive it: whether inhabiting a woman's body is a cause for delight or dismay. We carry within us the potential for pride or shame that will have the greatest bearing on how we value ourselves.

Habitual self-consciousness has damaged our real connection to our bodies. As long as we deny the connection between our bodies and our feelings, we cannot repair this damage. Emotion is one normal possibility of repair that each of us has access to.

Emotional detox

Understanding our physical relationship to emotion is, for women, especially important. The mind-body experience affords us an opportunity to be at one with our bodies instead of fighting against them.

This means more than just talking: it means, at times, going beyond words. We need to taste the texture of release of emotion – to understand from within how tears are released, how anger is released, how fear is released. This is how we learn to feel the difference between manipulative tears and self-pitying tears or tears which spring up as a cover for anger.

We learn the physical difference between irritation and hurt, between chronic anxiety and genuine suspicion, to identify emotional changes and register them. Sometimes we need the space to shout and scream and roar – in private – without hurting or blaming anyone else, as part of physical, emotional, mental health. Allowing your body the physical experience of release (in a safe setting) is one of the most extraordinarily empowering experiences in life.

Analysis of emotional connections and cognitive perception

alone will not offer an opportunity to experience emotional surrender to your own body as a measure of self-trust. If we only ever talk about feelings, we will stay remote from our bodies. We won't ever experience the pulse, the heartbeat, the sweat, the pounding, the roar, the pain, the yell, the moan, the shiver, the wet, the dry, the hot, the cold, the judder, the tremble, the scream, the chaos, the mess, the power of our bodies.

Some women experience this rawness in the process of childbirth, others through sexual expression. All of us can learn to experience, every now and then, this kind of vulnerability and discover an inner trust by going into it and through it, not under or over. We find an autonomy that strengthens and clarifies but only if we can reconnect the emotional split between body and mind.

Emotional experience is part of who we are. It is part of our singularity and aloneness. It offers the possibility of an intimacy with ourselves that helps us to relate and love and work with others while simultaneously keeping our autonomy, our own power, intact. It provides a centre to which we can return, time after time, a centre characterised not by absence but by presence.

Through the bonbon effect, our bodies have become objects of betrayal. Becoming more aware of what is inside – emotional, intuitive, powerful, changeable and fluctuating, mysterious, painful, pleasurable – gives us an awareness of interiority. This is the antithesis of object status. Living inside a body that we know is different but *whole* allows us to experience the beauty of interiority: connecting our emotionality, our sexuality, our spirituality and forming our real power.

92

Clare stopped reading and put the pages on her lap. She lay on her sofa, letting ideas and images float through her mind. She thought of Danny, and wondered what kind of man he had become now. He'd always been a gentle soul, like his father. What would she think of BJ? She'd have to get her ticket organised, so she decided to ring him soon.

The sound of the phone surprised her. It was Sophie.

'I was ringing to thank you for the other night, Mum. It was a really nice evening. How's Ellen?'

'She seems a bit better. At least, her hand is healing but I still don't know what to do about her.'

'What do you mean?'

Clare remembered it was Ruth she had spoken to about her concerns. 'Well, I'm worried because she's losing her sight and I don't know how long she'll be able to look after herself. And basically, it's not my business.'

'Doesn't she have any family?'

'Yes, a son, but he lives abroad and doesn't seem to bother much.'

'Have you talked to her? She seemed pretty much on the ball.'

'No, I haven't yet. I don't know if I should or how I should go about it.'

'Just be truthful. What's wrong with that?'

'Nothing,' replied Clare, intrigued at Sophie's forthrightness. 'Maybe I will say something,' she added, 'when I'm a bit clearer.'

'You could wait for ever then, Mum. Try saying something and see what happens.'

'That could be highly irresponsible.'

'I don't mean that. You could tell her you're worried and take it from there. You don't have to have all the answers before you start.'

'Since when have you become the wise one then?' asked Clare, half joking and half serious. She was unaccustomed to Sophie being in the guiding role.

'I'm only trying to be helpful, Mum. I'll shut up if you prefer.'

'No, don't,' said Clare quickly. 'I'm listening, really I am. What you said is very sensible.'

'I don't know about sensible but I can't see the point of waiting.'

'Sometimes you have to, Sophie,' said Clare, with a touch of exasperation. Is this what equality meant? she wondered. 'Anyway, how are you?'

'No, I haven't finished with you yet. I want to know if you're missing Ruth. How did all of that go?'

'It went fine, thank you,' said Clare a little tersely, and then, hearing herself, softened. 'It really did go well, actually. I'd never expected to feel so close to her. It was a real surprise and I do miss having her around the house. We grew up together without really knowing each other, and now finally we are getting acquainted.'

'That's good,' said Sophie. 'I'm really pleased.'

'Am I allowed to ask how you are now?'

'Yes, you can. I'm fine really. Things are beginning to shape up a bit. I've been crying a lot.'

'Why?' asked Clare, alarmed.

'Nothing to worry about. It's all good stuff. It's just been good to let go. Once I started, I thought I'd never stop. Then eventually I *would* stop and up would come another wave a couple of hours later. I thought I'd never reach the end but I did. Strange, all that stuff inside and you never know it's there. You don't think about it because you can't actually see it.'

Clare was happy to listen, touched by Sophie sharing these things with her; she didn't want to push by asking questions. There was a silence.

'Are you there, Mum?'

'Yes, course I am. I was just listening to you. I didn't want to interrupt.'

'Do you want to know what the crying has been about?'

'If you want to tell me.'

'But are you interested?'

'Of course I'm interested, Sophie, but I'm well aware that these things are private. If you'd rather not say any more, that's fine. If you want to tell me, I'd love to hear. I mean it.' Clare immediately felt anxious that she'd been too abrupt but Sophie continued.

'Actually, when I'm crying, it's a muddle, or rather it isn't a muddle – it's a mixture. I remember Dad dying and I remember being terribly lonely at school and hating the silence at home and then, of course, I remember Melanie.'

'Who's Melanie?'

Clare heard Sophie's sudden intake of breath at the end of the phone.

'She . . . that's the name of the baby I lost.'

'Oh,' said Clare, her heart giving a lurch inside her chest. 'I didn't know you'd given her a name.' Clare hadn't even known it was a girl until this moment. Her heart was pounding now. 'It's good for you, feeling these things, isn't it, Soph?' continued Clare, trying to be detached, in spite of her own swirling emotions.

Sophie sighed. 'Yes, I think it is. I mean I know it is.'

There was a small silence.

'Have you read the books yet?' asked Clare, thinking she had to change the subject.

'Yes, I've almost read one of them. You know how long it takes me to read. But I really wanted to, so I kept going. I find it very powerful, actually. I can feel some of what she says in me as well. She's said to me more than once that if I can empty out some of the past, then I can make room for something new. And I can sense that inside sometimes, like stirrings of something. Like I've been thinking, I'd like to go back to college and maybe take up sculpture again. I've never had the confidence before but I think I'm almost there now. And things are better with Phil.'

'How does Phil cope with all this?'

'With all what?'

'With your crying and everything.'

'I tend to cry when he's out. I don't think he'd mind. I don't know. But this isn't really anything to do with him.'

'Well, it's to do with you.'

'I know, but it's to do with me before I met him.'

'Does it make a difference to your relationship?' asked Clare, secretly wishing that Sophie would move on to someone else.

'Yes. I can be more myself with him. It's better. I'm not sure, but what's really beginning to matter is the art, I think.'

'I'm so glad,' said Clare. 'I really am.' This news was far more important than her doubts about Phil.

'Mum, before I go, I want to ask you something.'

'What?'

'Well, it's something that I'm doing with Helen. She suggested doing a ritual, you know, a kind of ceremony for Melanie.'

Clare felt apprehensive. 'What kind of ritual?'

'I don't know quite yet. It's going to be me who makes it up. I'm going to design it with Helen's help. And,' she hesitated, 'God, Mum, I feel really terrified saying this to you, but I wondered if you'd like to come.'

Clare simply didn't know what to say in response. 'Well, I don't know . . . course I'll come, if you'd like me to.'

'You don't have to, Mum. I've really thought about this and to be honest, when Helen and I first talked about it, I didn't want you to be there. But I've been thinking and I suppose things have changed a bit between us. So I decided that if you'd like to be part of it, then I'd like you to be there.'

'I'm not sure I'll know what to do,' said Clare, trying to work out what she was feeling about it all, other than completely flummoxed.

'It doesn't matter about that. I don't know either, yet. I just wanted to know if you'd like to be there.'

Something in Sophie's voice triggered an unequivocal urge in Clare to accept. 'Yes, I would,' she said emphatically. 'I would certainly like to come.'

'Are you sure? Do you want to think about it?'

'No, love, I don't want time,' said Clare, feeling a little more resolute. 'I'm sorry if I hesitated. It was my own anxiety and I'm quite sure. Really. I'm very touched you asked me.'

'Are you?' said Sophie in a very small voice.

'Absolutely.'

'That's great. God, these things are difficult, aren't they?' Sophie said with a laugh.

'They are,' agreed Clare.

'OK, Mum. I'd better go now. I'll let you know where and when later. I don't know the details yet.'

'That's fine.'

'Take care.'

'You too, love. Thanks for ringing.'

''Bye.'

Clare flopped back down on the sofa, shaking her head, in disbelief. How things are changing, she thought. So much change. Hardly visible, everything looking the same on the surface but down below, everything was different. Who'd have imagined that, first, she'd feel so close to her sister after all these years and, now, her own daughter was inviting her to share a really intimate part of her life.

She felt exhausted and invigorated in equal measure. She felt she had a choice and no choice at the same time, and no idea what would happen; but it didn't seem to matter. As she settled back to continue reading, she knew that, in her own life, there could be no going back.

93

Roots and Branches

The layer of emotion we've been concerned with has been the interpersonal – feelings arising through relationship with other people. But there are two other layers which we can understand by evoking an image of a tree: if the interpersonal is represented by the trunk of the tree, then two other layers are connected: the roots below and the branches above.

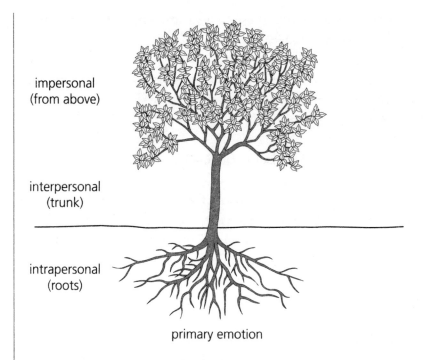

impersonal
(from above)

interpersonal
(trunk)

intrapersonal
(roots)

primary emotion

Roots and branches

Roots

The deepest layer of emotion is the intrapersonal (intra means within) which incorporates the animal aspect of our biological history. We are connected to the animal part of our being through this basic level of emotion.

Like the others, it is possible to understand in three distinct but overlapping strands, each representing a basic need, from which our own, human, emotional needs develop. Basic instinctual needs work together to ensure survival. The determining impulse is to continue life in face of the threat of death: the need for food, the need to establish territory and the need for safety. Food is obviously necessary for maintenance; territory and safety from harm are also essential for survival.

Each need promotes the acquisition of appropriate skills. First, animals need to know what to eat and where to find it: they need to keep close to the supply of *sustenance* and signal hunger when young. Second, they need to learn *boundaries* because, in this way, a creature acquires the skill of distinguishing self from others. It also learns rules of hierarchy within the family group. It learns when to submit or attack and how to respond in a way that will offer the best chance of survival.

The third skill is *communication* through a rudimentary language – the recognition and imitation of a range of complex signals, smells, sounds, movements, gestures – that help a creature to recognise its own kind and to distinguish friend from foe.

All three needs are interdependent: the more food there is, the fitter an animal will be to defend itself; the more effectively it can communicate, the greater the possibility of obtaining food and protecting its young. When left in conditions that are natural for that species, an animal will bond with a parent or others of its own kind and will learn the whole communication system necessary to maintain the entire cycle of generation and regeneration.

When these basic needs are not met or are blocked in some way, a physiological response is evoked in the animal that corresponds to a primitive emotion: loss, anger or fear. We know and recognise this in the more intelligent animals: dogs, horses, whales, elephants, dolphins and many more.

Primitive love and grief, fear and anger, delight and trust are all evident in many of our fellow creatures. These crude emotions are the raw material of human emotions. Our own are more sophisticated but essentially connected to these primary ones. They are often labelled primitive, but the word 'primary' speaks more of the connections between animal and human and avoids the inevitable assumption of human superiority over all other living creatures.

Primary emotions of love inform and form the fabric of our own family bonds, of intimate companionship, of our human awareness of skin hunger: that deep and wordless ache for the closeness of someone else's skin. Primary emotion is found in our loving and in our loss. When a mother loses a child, especially if the death is sudden and violent, you can hear in her wild and so-called 'crazed' grief strange and 'non-human' sounds of pain, echoing the cries of animals when they, too, have lost their young.

The instinct, for example, to nurture, that comes from this primary source, is vital to us. We move to nurture and bond as part of being human and so inevitably we will at some point experience loss. If we didn't experience love, we would not experience sorrow.

The instinct to play and for hostile display (to put off the enemy) are the raw material of our own human emotions of joy and anger which we experience when our boundaries are honoured or invaded. The animal instincts of fear and trust are the raw material of our own gut instinct that 'tells' us of possible danger.

Even though their influence is shaped and refined through human development, these emotional roots still appear in our own behaviour. They are recognisable as the feeling in your gut when you find yourself outraged that someone has planted a tree on your side of the boundary, touched your things, invaded your space on the road, slept with your partner. In pack activity, we can see the roots of gang warfare and crowd violence of all kinds. Any immediate threat to survival can act as a trigger: under the influence of extreme fear, sophisticated humans stampede like cattle. Sometimes we become paralysed by intense fear, in a similar way to our animal companions.

This intrapersonal layer is the raw material of emotion in every one of us – an indissoluble link with other creatures – and an intrinsic part of our humanity. This raw material is there inside all of us. How it is developed and shaped will depend on individual learning and experience but primary emotion is a source of energy inside us from birth till death.

Root impulse

Our animal roots, in the depths of our humanness, generate a source of energy. Just as a healthy seed is imbued with the energy of growth, so we are imbued with three potential life energies – to create, to exert our will and to explore.

Creativity

This is seen in patterns of mating, reproducing and building in animal behaviour. As humans, we develop this into creative thinking, action and imagination. Creativity means the potential to breathe life into matter, to create with a variety of components or ingredients: fabric, food, ideas, rhythm, sound, seeds, metals, clay, colours, movement. This potential is what we channel into initiating, growing, setting in motion, generation, ordering, making a new shape or form. We enjoy this as an individual enterprise or a process of creative fusion with one other or with a group: singing in a choir, conceiving and carrying out the sewing of a quilt, starting a team project, parenthood, planning a new home together.

Challenge

This describes our fundamental urge to impose our will on our environment. We seek to change, to overcome an obstacle, subvert a restriction. The energy required to build a beaver's dam is echoed in our human desire to harness the elements of earth, water and fire to suit our own purposes, to adapt them to our needs and surroundings.

Curiosity

Curiosity is a timeless part of our biological inheritance: the impulse to sniff out, to unearth, to negotiate unknown territory. We want to find out how things work, to take things to pieces, to analyse and find explanations. We have a profound and universal desire to understand. Our quest for knowledge has led to achievement, both ordinary – tying your own shoelaces, taking a watch to pieces, looking up the meaning of a word – and extraordinary. Any compendium of flora and fauna or repertory of homeopathic remedies bears testament to our curiosity, as does the discovery of DNA and the splitting of the atom.

These energies are all part of a celebration of human potential and our rooted connections with other forms of life: not so much 'lower' as different.

Branches

There is one final ingredient in emotional experience that affects us regardless of personal circumstance, rather as the overall climate and air quality can affect the growth and development of a single tree. This layer is called impersonal, because it isn't concerned with us personally: it is an additional circumstance completely beyond our control.

All sorts of things just *happen* to us. Indiscriminately. We feel emotion in response to impersonal catalysts: earthquakes, floods, plane crashes, random violence, the discovery of oil or gold, avalanches, stock market collapse, the effects of a civil war or the technological revolution. As well as these often sudden and dramatic events, we are exposed to profound longer-term influences of social and political change, climatic and geographical change that affect us on a global more than an individual basis. Few of us are directly involved; all of us are affected.

These then are the three layers, each offering a different aspect of emotional experience. The primary layer is raw, animal and powerful and experienced in times of extreme distress. We are put back in touch with our origins, our roots, with what we share with other forms of life.

The interpersonal layer teaches us about our own personal feelings and those in our immediate circle. It teaches us about the emotions involved in human relationship.

The impersonal layer illustrates a more universal emotional connection in life. It engenders a level of emotional experience beyond our individual selves. Events, stimuli and outside phenomena affect and move us en masse, and put us in touch with participation in a greater whole, reminding us of our existence as one tiny fragment in a vast collective process.

94

Sophie felt awkward: she wasn't finding it easy to communicate.

'Did you invite your mother to the ritual?' asked Helen.

'Yes, I did,' Sophie replied. She looked at her watch and saw she'd only been there twenty minutes. It seemed ages.

'What's going on then?' asked Helen. Sophie shook her head.

'What are you feeling?'

'Nothing much,' mumbled Sophie. There was a pause.

'What was your mother's reply?'

'She said yes.'

'How did you feel?'

'Nothing much.'

Helen smiled. 'Sophie, you invite your mother to a hugely important ritual – a big decision for you – and she says yes and you're telling me you don't have any feelings about it?'

Sophie looked back at Helen. 'I just don't know.' She shook her head and looked into the distance.

'Do you really not feel anything at all?' asked Helen.

Sophie thought for a while. Eventually she spoke.

'I don't know what it is, or was. I came off the phone to her feeling very shaky. I was pleased that I'd asked her but as time went on I started feeling really heavy. By the time I went to bed, I didn't want to do the ritual at all – decided it was a complete waste of time – and woke up feeling depressed. I don't want to know any more. It seemed a good idea when we talked about it, here I mean, and it seemed a good idea to phone and ask Mum, but now I'm not so sure.'

There was another silence between them.

'Sometimes, Sophie, when we make a big move like this, you know, when we begin to look at things directly, like you've been doing, unexpected feelings are stirred up.'

'Like what?' asked Sophie defensively.

'I don't know what's in you, Sophie, but it would seem a good idea to find out.' Helen indicated the empty armchair nearby.

'Will you try something different, Sophie?'

Sophie looked uncertain.

'I'd like you to imagine your mum sitting there, now. Imagine what you might want to say to her about all this.'

'Why?'

'Because it sometimes helps to imagine someone you can speak to directly instead of a dialogue going on in your head. Why don't you try it and see what happens?'

Sophie half-heartedly turned towards the empty chair, looking at it in silence for a couple of minutes.

'I can't do this,' she said.

'You can. Just speak as if you are speaking to her.'

Sophie shrugged her shoulders.

'Start with "Mum".'

'Mum?' Sophie repeated, looking sceptically at Helen.

'Don't look at me,' said Helen with a mischievous smile. 'Look at "Mum",' she added, nodding in the direction of the chair.

Sophie moved round and faced the chair. 'Mum,' she started mechanically. 'Mum, Mum, Mum, Mum,' she repeated, getting louder each time. 'I don't know what I'm supposed to feel,' said Sophie, turning to Helen.

'You're not "supposed" to feel anything. See what's there. Be honest with yourself.'

'I just feel so cross with her,' Sophie wailed, dropping her head down in front of her.

'Cross,' repeated Helen.

'Yes,' said Sophie, her head still down. 'I don't know why but I feel cross and . . .'

'Cross and what?' prompted Helen.

'I don't know,' said Sophie pathetically.

'I'm going to make another suggestion, Sophie.' Sophie looked up and waited while Helen got up and placed a large cushion on the armchair. 'I'd like you to do something very simple, even if you don't understand it. I want you to repeat the word "cross" and every time you say it, hit the cushion. Allow yourself to say it and get louder, really use your voice and your arms too, to build up a bit of momentum. We don't know where it will take you but you can trust me and trust yourself and trust whatever happens. Will you have a go?'

Sophie didn't say anything but obligingly knelt down in front of the chair and started to hit the cushion and repeat the word 'cross'. She shouted the word a few times and then felt something very hot inside. She immediately sat back on her knees and stopped.

'Do it again,' urged Helen, 'and allow yourself to go through that sensation.'

Sophie carried on; she felt the heat again and then felt something she didn't understand but suddenly found herself shouting, really yelling the word 'Mum'. It had somehow changed from 'cross' and she didn't know why she was shouting but she felt so full of . . . something. She stood up and continued to hit the cushion. Dust rose in little clouds from where she punched it.

'Make a sound,' urged Helen. 'Keep your throat loose and a sound coming through.'

Sophie uttered a kind of groan, then it became a surprising sound, from deep within her, a vast overwhelming noise, like a dragon trying to get out of her. Sophie found tears streaming down her face and realised she was crying. She started to sob.

'Trust it, Sophie,' murmured Helen, who was by now standing very close.

'Mum,' yelled Sophie. 'MUM!' she yelled again, half sobbing, half shouting. She saw an image of her mother in the kitchen, a fleeting picture of them in their old house. She paused. When was it? She was quite young. Helen asked her what she was thinking and she described the scene of them in the kitchen together. When Dad had been ill. And she had wanted her mum to hold her because she'd felt so alone. Sophie started crying again.

'I was so unhappy at school,' she said, 'and I remember those teachers . . . telling me I was too slow and I couldn't explain to them . . .'

'How did you feel towards the teachers?' asked Helen.

'I *hated* them, hated the other kids. I hated everyone.'

'Just say that now, to them, imagine they're all there.'

Sophie giggled at the idea of it.

'Go on,' said Helen. 'Have a go.'

'I hate you, I hate you, I hate you,' Sophie yelled, then found herself crying again.

'Try saying "no",' she heard Helen say.

'No,' Sophie cried. 'No, no, no . . .' And then she heard herself screaming 'no', and realised she was jumping up and down on the floor, in time with the word, as if her body couldn't contain the energy without the movement. She simply *had* to move. She felt elated. She jumped higher, enjoying it, and found herself shouting with glee more than anything else, up and down, up and down, relishing the freedom of the action.

Suddenly, unbidden, her jaw trembled. She started shivering, so much that she couldn't control her teeth clattering together; she started shaking, including her whole spine. She looked at Helen, alarmed. Helen touched her gently on the shoulder.

'It's all right, Sophie. Trust your body,' she reassured her. Sophie noticed the print on the curtains and saw the flowers were huge poppies. Meanwhile her body continued to shiver. She felt cold and sweaty now and aware she was part child and part adult. She stood there feeling Helen's touch and looking at the poppies and feeling her body's trembles becoming less acute, as if they were slowing down in urgency.

She gave a spontaneous, deep shuddering sigh, like a small child does after a big cry, then looked up at Helen, who was gazing at her with the most extraordinary warmth. Sophie's eyes filled with tears again. She turned towards Helen, who gently put both arms around her shoulders and simply held her. They stood there together. She put her head on Helen's shoulder and wept. Images of all kinds swam through her mind. She stayed there until her tears seemed to exhaust themselves. Something eased. She felt tired but somehow lighter and clearer in her body. She looked up and gave Helen a weak smile.

'I'll get you some more tissues,' said Helen, noticing the box on the floor was almost empty. She left the room and returned with another box which she handed to Sophie, who was sitting on her chair again. Sophie blew her nose and cleared her throat.

'Will I have a sore throat?' Sophie asked, with a little smile.

'Maybe a little,' said Helen. 'It takes us a while to learn to relax and open the throat to shout without forcing the muscles. But it won't do you any permanent harm. Would you like a glass of water?'

Sophie nodded.

Helen went out again. Sophie sat there looking at everything in the room as if emerging from a dream. The colours seemed very vivid. She saw the little dog take advantage of the open door to come in and join whatever was happening.

Helen returned and handed Sophie the glass of water. 'You're not allowed in here yet,' she said, addressing her dog, and bent down to pick him up.

'He can stay, I don't mind.'

Helen sighed and looked at him. 'OK then, stay quietly.' Somehow aware of this unexpected privilege, he lay down immediately and 'froze' into position.

'How are you doing?' enquired Helen, after a while.

'Surprisingly, I'm fine,' said Sophie with a low chuckle.

'You said you'd been allowing yourself to cry at home, didn't you?'

'Yes, but never like that. I'd never experienced letting go like that. It's another world, isn't it?'

'Yes, it is another world. A bit like an underwater world. Which is why we need different equipment to survive there. It is a different medium, emotion. Did you notice pictures at all?'

'Yes, lots of images. There was one—'

'No, don't talk about it now,' Helen interrupted. 'If you start talking, you'll start going back into things while you're still very open and, at this point, you need to come out so you can face the real world.'

'But we feel things about the real world, don't we?'

'Yes, we feel things in response to the real world all the time. The problem is that what we see and how we feel as a result gets very muddled and twisted. We have such an accumulation of emotions to do with all sorts of things in our lives that our feelings get distorted by time and by accumulation itself. Do you know what I mean?'

'Not really.'

'I think it's better not to talk too much now, Sophie. You've had an intensive experience and need to come back into your body properly. You need to close up again.' Helen looked at her watch. 'We must stop soon,' she said.

'What's the time?' asked Sophie. When Helen told her, Sophie gasped: 'I'm way over time!'

'Don't worry,' said Helen. 'I'm just not sure what to do now.' She thought for a moment. 'How are you getting back? Is your mother coming?'

'No, not today. I was going to walk or wait for the bus.'

'The bus?' exclaimed Helen. 'You could be waiting till next week!'

'No, I did some research and there is one that goes every hour or so.'

'Well, I'm wondering ... we both need to stop and have a break. I have to write a couple of letters and then I'm going into town, so I could give you a lift.'

'Well, if you're sure, that would be great. I thought I'd go and see Mum anyway.'

'You can rest or make yourself a cup of something. Will that be all right?'

'Sure. Can I do something in the garden?'

'Like what?' asked Helen in astonishment.

'Well, I did notice a few weeds in the front,' said Sophie. 'I quite like weeding. I could do with some activity like that now.'

'OK then,' said Helen. Sophie stood up and Helen led her into the garden, followed by Rusper. 'You'll find what you need in the way of tools in the shed. I'll leave you to it then, shall I?'

'Yes, I'll be fine.'

95

An hour or so later, Helen came downstairs to find Sophie and Rusper in the garden next to a big pile of weeds and clippings in the wheelbarrow.

'Gosh, you've been busy,' said Helen.

'I'm really enjoying myself.' Sophie beamed, flushed with exertion as she reached up towards the top of the climbing roses.

'Do you want a drink?' asked Helen.

'I'd love a juice, or just water would do.'

Helen went inside. It had been right to have a break, she thought. She returned to the garden carrying a cup of tea and a glass of apple juice and sat down.

Sophie strolled over to join her after a few minutes.

'I'm delighted with what you've done, Sophie,' said Helen. 'Thank you very much.'

'I enjoyed it. It was good to do, after everything else.' Sophie sipped her drink, then turned to Helen. 'Do you mind if I ask you another question or are we not allowed to talk about it any more?' she asked with a grin.

'It depends,' said Helen.

'Well, one thing I've been thinking is, how do you know it's real? I mean, if you described what happened to somebody else, they'd think you were mad, or something.'

'They probably would. The line between sane and mad isn't as black and white as the world out there would have us believe. There is at least a little craziness in all of us. But it doesn't have to harm anyone. You have to remember that inside our bodies is our whole personal history. Everything that's ever happened to us is remembered in the body/mind memory.

'When we feel things as children but don't express or release them, those feelings stay there. Then, as we go through life, all sorts of other experiences occur, some stirring up old feelings so we get old mixed with new. Then we have more experiences and these too get mixed up, old, new and in between. We end up with quite an emotional jumble so what happens when we start releasing feelings is unpredictable. You can't decide "I'm going *here*" and aim for it because emotion doesn't travel in a straight line.'

'Is that why I ended somewhere very different from where I'd started?' asked Sophie.

'Exactly. But, in time, you'll see a connection. And when you make the connection in your head, you've completed the link from head into body back to head again.'

'What link?'

'Each link is personal. You'll find out yours for yourself. You'll have some insight when you're ready.'

'It's a strange experience, the whole thing, isn't it?'

'Strange in the sense it's unfamiliar. It's like the impact of an underwater world to those who are used to living on dry land: full of weird creatures and bizarre forms and hidden nooks and crannies.'

'It's not frightening.'

'No. We can travel between the two worlds without harm but they are separate and different worlds even though they function together.'

'How do you mean?'

'Well, you have a real relationship with your mother, for example, as two adults. Now any relationship can be either nourished or distorted by feelings. If there are feelings around from the past that haven't been processed, your perception of each other can change because unacknowledged feelings get in the way – a bit like peering through a smudged and dirty windscreen – and your vision gets distorted. This is often a two-way thing so you end up with two people not seeing clearly. As you release emotion, physically, like you have been doing, you shed some of the pile of stuff inside and the distortion clears: you literally *see* differently.'

'Will I see Mum differently?'

'I believe you will. It's the best way that I know of cleaning up the messes we all get into in relationships. Once you can see clearly, you can decide how you really feel in the light of new information.'

'Like seeing she was stuck in an awful place as well at the time. I thought of that while I was weeding.'

'Precisely. We see what we couldn't see as children. We see from an adult point of view but only once we've cleared up enough of the backlog.'

'How long does it take?'

'There is no finite time. It's more of an ongoing process. Once I know my perception is getting blocked again – it's a bit like an overload of static – I know I need to clear my feelings a bit.'

'You do it yourself?' asked Sophie.

'Of course. Otherwise I wouldn't be able to make it safe for you or anyone else. I would be too scared and confused by the physical process.'

'I still don't quite understand why you said not to talk about it. I was wondering whether to say anything to Mum.'

'Let it settle in you first and, from the whole process, some connection will be made. Wait until you get clearer. Emotional work of this kind needs to be in a safe context with very clear boundaries, because the content is, as I've said, often distorted.

'That's why you can say or express things that you wouldn't or shouldn't do in the real world. The mere fact of having been kept in and festering for so long means that some of what emerges will be rubbish. We get things wrong. I don't mean that we imagine everything but even when we experience trauma, from a child's perspective, things look a lot different. So it's important to release some of those feelings to be able to make more adult sense and to move on. Old feelings keep us stuck in the past and unable to be fully in the present. Some insights can be helpfully communicated and applied to present relationships; lots of stuff can be left behind.'

'It's strange how your body almost takes over,' said Sophie, remembering.

'Exactly. This is why talking and analysing afterwards misses the point. You are trying to rationalise what isn't rational. It belongs to another sphere. Like getting a fish to live outside its medium of water, it won't work. That's why rushing to communicate things that haven't become clear enough is unwise because, in the other world, they'll be given a label and significance and a power that they shouldn't have because they belong inside you.'

'Maybe I won't say anything, then,' said Sophie with a big sigh.

'Wait and see. You'll probably find that when you speak to your mother, something will have shifted. You often find that you can respond more fully to the other person, whether this means more lovingly or more angrily: either way, the heart is open and not clogged up with blame or reproach. So communication can be a lot cleaner and clearer.'

'One more question,' said Sophie. 'I cried a lot when I was on my own but I didn't do anything like what we did today. Was that because I was only feeling it today?'

'You can only do so much on your own, Sophie. The feelings that scare us most are the deeper, more painful ones and it is impossible to touch those without the safety and support of another person, on dry land, so to speak.

'It's also safer with someone else because we can get stuck. We get drawn into places from which it's very hard to extricate ourselves. I have only ever known it possible to work effectively – going in *and* coming out – with someone else there.'

'Someone who can help?'

'Someone who can take the role of what I call a "loving witness", which involves a fine balance between doing and non-doing. It means being fully there for the other person but also apart, not embroiled in what's happening. This gives safety while allowing the process of catharsis – that's what release is called – to occur. It is one of the most loving roles we can offer to take for anybody.'

'I had a friend, Abbie, like that; I told you about her, I think, do you remember?'

'I do,' said Helen. 'I think you liked the way she was unobtrusive and yet caring at the same time. It's a bit like that but more so. It's more formal than being a friend. When we do this kind of emotional work, we have to have the safety to sift through whatever we find. So the other person marks the boundary, if you like, between what is your own time to be yourself – all your selves – messy, crazy, angry whatever – and the "real" world in which you have to behave appropriately and attend to your responsibilities.'

'It's a lot to take in,' said Sophie. 'But I'm learning.'

Helen looked at her watch. 'We need to go very soon,' she said.

A little while later they were driving along the country roads, both content to enjoy the welcome and peaceful lull that follows intense interaction. As they neared the town, Sophie asked, 'Can you drop me in the High Street? I want to go to the shops for something before I go and see Mum.'

As they turned into the centre of town, she said, 'I realise we haven't had time to look at the ritual plans. I don't suppose I could have thought very clearly about anything today, could I?'

'I think you're right. We had to do what we had to do.'

'Can I arrange another time, then, so that we can do some planning?'

'Yes. How about the same time next week, instead of two weeks?'

'That's fine. Thanks a lot,' said Sophie as Helen drew up alongside the kerb. 'See you next week,' she added, getting out of the car. ''Bye.'

96

Clare was thinking about Ellen. She looked at the time. Three o'clock. She thought of phoning her to see if she could call round. But that felt too formal so she decided to follow Sophie's suggestion: take a risk and see what happens.

She knocked on Ellen's door and heard a lot of shuffling going on before the door opened.

'Oh, hello, Clare. I'm sorry. I'm in the middle of trying to hoover the hall here and I knocked the plant over, so there's a bit of a mess, I'm afraid.'

'Don't worry. Ellen, I wondered if I could come in for a chat?' What a stupid expression, Clare thought.

'Course you can. Come in.'

Clare went in and walked behind Ellen carefully through the spilt earth. 'Can I give you a hand to clear it up?' she asked.

'No, don't you bother about that. Come into the kitchen and we can sit there.'

They sat down and Ellen said, 'Was it anything in particular you wanted to talk about?'

'Not really,' started Clare. That's not true, she told herself. 'Well, actually, yes,' she said. I should have planned before I came, she thought. What exactly am I going to say? 'Ellen, this is really none of my business,' she began, 'but I am getting concerned about you. You know, the accident you had the other evening and well . . . I'm worried about your eyesight.'

'There's nothing wrong with my eyesight, dear, but it's very sweet of you to be so concerned.'

'Are you sure there's nothing wrong?'

'Well, I wear my spectacles for reading, of course, and I sent off for a magnifying glass, which helps. I had an eye test a few months ago, I think.'

'Really? What did they say?'

'They said my sight was deteriorating but it's bound to, isn't it, at my age? They didn't say anything out of the ordinary.'

'When was that?'

'I don't exactly remember. The card is in the bureau drawer. Would you like me to get it?' asked Ellen, as if she were simply indulging Clare's curiosity.

'No, it doesn't matter at the moment.' Clare took a breath. 'Ellen, I'm not doing this very well. It's really hard to talk about these things, especially when I'm not your family. It's just that I really do think your sight is perhaps worse than you believe it is and I am worried about you having another accident. I wondered whether your son should know about this.'

Ellen looked sharply at Clare. 'I don't think so. He wouldn't want to be bothered, I'm sure.'

'Is that really true, Ellen? I'm sure if you phoned him, he could arrange something.'

'No,' said Ellen, with surprising vehemence. A little pink patch appeared on either cheek. 'You really don't understand, Clare.'

'No, I don't,' Clare sighed. 'Families are families and I know things happen. I'm not asking you to tell me but I'm worried because I see you not managing very well . . .' She winced at the clumsiness in her words.

'What do you mean, not managing very well?' asked Ellen, by now very defensive. 'What am I doing wrong?'

'You're not doing anything wrong,' Clare said. 'It's just that sometimes your cups and things, you know, aren't that clean . . .'

'What do you mean? That everything is dirty?' Ellen's frame stiffened. She was visibly upset.

'Oh, dear. I'm making a complete mess of this,' said Clare.

'Of what? What do you mean? I don't understand what this is all about.'

'I'm just worried about you being able to take care of yourself, properly, that's all,' Clare desperately.

'I am fine,' said Ellen, pronouncing each word with precision. She stood up, frail and slight though she was. She was shaking a little but turned towards the door. 'Clare, I think it would be best if you left now. Please.' Every inch the headmistress.

Clare stood up to go, then thought better of it and sat down again. 'No, Ellen, I won't leave. We've got to sort this out. I'm really sorry I've been so clumsy. But I do care and I don't want to see you hurt.'

Ellen stood still very stiffly. 'I think it would be better for you to go. I would prefer to be on my own.'

'No, Ellen. Please come and sit down. I've never been in a situation like this before and I don't know what I'm doing. All I know is that I'm not trying to be unkind. I'm trying to talk to you about something important even if I'm not making a very good job of it.'

Ellen sat down again, slowly. She wouldn't look at Clare.

'Ellen. Please, look at me. I'm don't want us to fall out over this. I'm very fond of you. You're a lovely neighbour to have.'

Ellen was silent.

For a minute or maybe longer, Clare simply waited. Then, still looking at the floor, Ellen said, 'What you're saying is that I can't see to clean any more or keep my home properly. You're trying to tell me I am becoming a liability.'

'I want to see if there's anything we can do.'

'We? There isn't anybody. I'm on my own.'

'Could you really not contact your son . . .' Clare was silenced by another fierce look.

'We could do something, Ellen. I can take you to have another eye test. We could get you a cleaner. There are all sorts of things that could help.'

Ellen didn't reply immediately. She seemed to consider and then looked up at Clare. 'I do see what you're trying to do, Clare, and I can see that you're being honest. It's not easy to be honest. That took courage.' At this point, her voice cracked and tears sprang into her eyes. Clare reached out her hand and touched Ellen's wrist but Ellen withdrew it instantly.

'No, I'm all right. Please, *please*, leave me be. I really do want to be on my own for a bit now to think over what you've said.'

Clare realised she had to go and got up. 'Ellen, listen to me. I'll go now. But I'm intending to come back later. I've give you a ring in a while to see how you are. I'm not going to disappear.' She walked back through the mess on the floor to the front door. 'And don't clean this lot up,' she shouted in the direction of the kitchen. 'I'll do it later. OK?'

No answer.

'Is that all right, Ellen? Will you let me help with that?'

'We'll see,' she heard in response.

'I'll see you later,' said Clare and went out, quietly closing the door behind her. What a mess I made of that, she thought to herself. She felt mortified. What a dreadful, dreadful mess.

97

Once back in her own flat, Clare continued to fret. She didn't know what to do with herself, she felt so upset. She sat down, stood up, sat down again, stood up again, made some tea and didn't drink it, tried to read but couldn't take anything in; she even phoned Angie at work, just on the off chance that she might be sitting at her desk, but she wasn't available.

Why hadn't she minded her own business? she asked herself over and over again. She should have thought through everything much more clearly before encroaching on such delicate territory. She didn't even know the woman that well, for heaven's sake. The phone rang. She wondered if it might be Ellen, but it was Sophie.

'Hello, Mum. Are you in this evening? I was thinking of coming round and cooking you dinner.'

'Goodness, that sounds . . . wonderful. I'm in, yes, love . . .' her voice trailed off.

'Is anything wrong?'

'In a way, yes. I went to see Ellen and it all went wrong. She was terribly upset and asked me to leave.'

'Dear. Sounds awful.'

'It was. It still is because I have to do something about it.'

'Look, don't do anything until I get there.'

'You mean you're going to come and sort it all out, I suppose?' said Clare.

'We'll talk about it all while I get supper ready. How about that?'

'I don't know. It will be good to see you anyway. I'm driving myself mad here, thinking about it all.'

'I'll see you in about half an hour.'

'Fine. See you soon.'

She replaced the receiver and then sat down. What was she going to do? She couldn't leave it as it was, despite Ellen's independence and pride. She didn't want to make things worse than they were already but she couldn't walk away now. She couldn't just sit and wait either.

She decided to go and try to put things right, so went out and rang Ellen's bell. A voice said, 'Who is it?'

'It's me, Clare.'

The door opened. Ellen stood there looking very tired and older than Clare had ever seen her. Her heart sank.

'I've come to clear up the earth.' Ellen didn't say anything but opened the door further to let Clare in. Everything was still as it was when she'd left.

'Where's your dustpan and broom?' asked Clare.

'In the cupboard there,' Ellen replied slowly with no life in her voice at all. Had she taken a tranquilliser? Clare wondered.

She found what she needed and swept up everything carefully. The pot wasn't damaged and the plant was still intact. She tidied up and put everything back in order. When she'd finished, she found Ellen sitting in her living room at the table, with some photo albums spread out before her, two of them open, revealing some family pictures.

Clare sat down at the table. She watched in silence as Ellen turned the pages and looked at the photographs. Clare found herself rehearsing some cheerful phrases in her head to open a conversation about Ellen's family but then stopped when she realised it would be entirely false. She decided to wait until something that felt genuine came into her head or heart.

She sat there for well over five minutes. Then Ellen looked up and pointed to a photo of a stern, rather handsome man. 'That was my husband, Gordon,' she said. 'We were married thirty-four years when he died. And that,' she said, pointing to a different album, at a photo of a grinning schoolboy, Clare guessed in his teens, 'is my son William.'

Still Clare found she could think of nothing to say that came from a true place, so she kept quiet. Ellen turned over a few more pages and contemplated the photographs.

'Were you happy with your husband, Clare?' she asked out of the blue.

'Yes, I was,' replied Clare. 'We were good companions and he was a good father.'

'Did he love you?'

'Yes, I think he did. Yes, he did.'

Ellen nodded slowly. 'Gordon didn't love me, you know. I don't think he liked women at all really. He wasn't nasty to me or anything, but was never kind, never affectionate. I don't think he knew how to be. So we weren't close. I was so grateful for my work, you know, that I could bury myself in it and find my fulfilment there. Especially after . . .' She stopped. 'We had a daughter, Belinda, who died when she was only four. Whooping cough. There wasn't any cure then. She took ill and coughed agonisingly for two weeks and there was nothing we could do but watch her die. That was when I went back to school to work. I couldn't bear being at home any more.'

'Do you have a photo of Belinda?' asked Clare, nervous now after being so clumsy earlier on.

'Yes.' Ellen reached for the album furthest away from her that was still closed. She opened it and found a page where there were two sepia photographs of a sweet little girl with curly hair, dressed in a smocked dress. She was standing in a garden among some lupins, the happiest of smiles on her face.

'She *was* lovely,' said Clare, struck by the sweetness and light in the little girl's face.

'Yes, she was indeed.'

There was a pause.

'William was older by four years,' continued Ellen. 'Gordon insisted on sending him away to school, too early in my opinion, but Gordon insisted it would help make a man of him so off he went. I was alone in the house with the memories of Belinda. So I buried myself in work. I was lucky to have a job I was good at. William didn't seem to need me or his father. He came home for the holidays but we hardly knew each other any more.'

Ellen hesitated. 'Are you close to your son? I know you are to Sophie.'

'Yes, I am close to him,' replied Clare. ' Well, I think I am. He lives six thousand miles away which may say something about his needing to be away from me, but when we speak, he's affectionate.

I've never had any problems with Daniel. It's always been an easier relationship somehow than with Soph.'

'But you seem to get on well with Sophie.'

'That's only recently. Until three months ago' (my goodness, is it only that long, thought Clare) 'we would probably both have said we had a very distant relationship, you know, polite but cool.'

'Really? I am surprised. To see you together now, it's hard to believe.' Ellen looked back at the photo. 'William . . . I don't know why he is as he is. I remember when he came to his father's funeral: he had been abroad, but obviously came back to help me clear things up and sort out all the legal paperwork and that kind of thing. But while he was staying here, I remember thinking it extraordinary that I felt so distant. He just called me "Mother" and spoke to me with alarming condescension. He wouldn't give me a kiss or show any affection, just like Gordon really. I often wonder what I did wrong.'

'Why do you think you did something wrong?'

'Because other sons love their mothers, usually a lot, don't they?'

'I don't think you can blame yourself, Ellen. There are too many factors involved. You weren't cruel to him, or unloving. He's just who he is.' She hesitated. 'Is that why you were so cross with me for suggesting you get in touch with him earlier?'

'I got cross because you were meddling in something you didn't understand. Well, it felt as if you were meddling anyway.'

'I think that's fair comment,' admitted Clare. 'I was trying to help but it was intrusive.'

'I know you were trying to help, now that I've had time to think about it. In fact, you were being very kind, actually, to do what you did. It showed that you cared about an old woman for whom you had no responsibility whatsoever.'

'Oh Ellen, I do want to find some solution.'

'Do you? Why?'

'Because something needs to be done.'

'But why do you care?' asked Ellen, looking levelly at Clare.

'I don't know,' said Clare. 'I just do. You're a sweet woman, you've done a lot of good work, you're vulnerable. You've been messed around by the Allinsons and I can't simply close my eyes because I'm not related to you or because you're not my official responsibility.'

Ellen smiled a tired, sad smile. 'Well, I don't know what to do. I can get a cleaner, I'm sure, to come in a couple of times a week. But I don't know after that. I suppose I should go and see the optician again after what you said.'

'I'll come with you.'

'You don't have to.'

'I know, but I have a car and I have the time so I'd like to. We can easily make an appointment on one of the days I'm not working.' She waited for Ellen to respond.

'I'm frightened, Clare,' Ellen said suddenly. Clare felt her insides contract sharply.

'I know you are,' said Clare gently. She couldn't find any other words because all the clichés seemed trite. She didn't at that moment feel sorry for Ellen. She felt moved that this woman trusted her enough to be so honest. It wasn't easy for people of Ellen's generation, or for any of us, to say these things.

They sat together, the two women, without speaking, letting the energies of vulnerability and honesty and trust and fear float around them.

Eventually, Ellen sighed.

'Ellen, I can't make you unafraid,' said Clare, finding her words again, 'but as long as I'm here, I'm quite willing to help in any way I can. I tell you what, would you come and have supper with us, this evening? Sophie rang and is coming round soon to cook. She's going to stay over. She'd love to see you too, I know she would.'

'I don't think so, I'm very tired,' said Ellen.

'It won't be for a while yet. Why don't you lie down for a couple of hours and then we'll come and tell you when we're nearly ready? It won't be till about seven.'

'Are you sure?'

'Positive. Tonight is definitely not the night for spending on your own,' said Clare firmly. 'I'll see you later,' she went on, getting up to leave. 'Have a good rest.'

98

Keepers of a Different Way

The power of gentle keeps both eyes open. It helps you to see the truth of the whole picture and will not allow either eye to close in fear.

Consider the possibility of a different energy, a different light. A world of shadow and the underside of things, of the spaces in between the obvious, the emptiness between the occupied and the silence in between the words. Just as music still plays through its silent beats, so life still exists through the empty spaces.

This is the mystical space of moonlight, existing at the interface of the animal, the human and the divine. It is an energy conveyed through an unfamiliar language, represented by different tools, through forgotten signs and symbols.

Perhaps we can again be keepers of this different way, guardians of the power of gentle. Perhaps we can unearth the tools, relearn its language and get back in touch with the interconnectedness of the earth.

Instead of shoring up a system that makes us powerless and blind, perhaps we can rekindle the fires of cleansing and change.

99

The kitchen was in complete chaos. Every available surface was covered with debris or peelings or used pans, even the floor. The focus to which all this energy and chaos had been directed was a vegetable concoction, now out of sight in the oven. Sophie was red-faced with all the effort and slightly anxious about the outcome.

'Do you want to go and tell Ellen we'll be ready in about half an hour?' she asked.

It was already 7.30 so Ellen would have had plenty of time to rest. She might even have assumed that there had been a change of plan. Clare decided to phone.

A few minutes later Clare returned. 'That's fine. She woke up a little while ago and was just beginning to wonder what was happening. I'll leave the front door open.' Clare looked at the clock. 'Are you *sure* it's going to be ready at eight?' she asked.

'I'm sure it will,' replied Sophie, with that slight edge of uncertainty in her voice that made Clare feel almost weak with hunger at the prospect of a very late meal.

'I think I'll just go and have a cold shower, Mum. Is that OK?'

'Yes. Go ahead.' Clare decided to clear up, resigned to the shambles that invariably occurred when Sophie took over the kitchen. The end result would be good but the preparations were always a nightmare. Clare had to restrain herself from taking over and doing everything in her own (more efficient) way.

She had almost finished when Ellen arrived. 'Let's go and sit in the living room,' said Clare, 'I need to get out of the kitchen.'

Ellen said yes to a sherry and Clare poured herself a glass of wine.

'This is very kind of you,' said Ellen.

'Not at all. Sophie's done all the cooking, not me.'

'While I remember, Clare, if you're really quite sure about coming with me to the optician's, will you tell me which days are convenient?'

'Any Monday or Wednesday would be fine. I'd be delighted to come.'

'Hi, Ellen.' Sophie appeared in the doorway, her head swathed in a towel, the rest of her wrapped in Clare's dressing gown. 'I'm really pleased you could come. Sorry it's all so late.'

'Doesn't matter at all, dear. I haven't got a deadline, you know.'

Sophie smiled and disappeared out of the room again.

Ellen took a sip of her sherry. 'That's nice,' she said. 'Very fortifying.' Looking at Clare with a smile, she said, 'You're quite right. I would have hated being on my own this evening.'

100

Mending

Putting competition and comparison aside, you appreciate the commonality of women's experience in this world. You reach out across the invisible distances between us with compassion and a regard of mutual pride.

One thing's for sure. We can't achieve much alone. It would help if we fostered more love between women. Not sexual love (a separate choice) but love and regard for each other. This would entail real closeness, a closeness nourished by a love that challenges, pushes and listens, a love that inspires honesty and truth. A love that will not let other women be less than they can be. A love that is loyal and seeks to withstand the vicissitudes of our relations with men.

We are often fearful of other women, afraid to get close enough to experience rejection again. There are invisible distances between mother and daughter that stay long in the memory and in the heart. We have been many times let down, exploited, criticised and hurt by other women in our lives; these experiences and our unacknowledged feelings reduce our capacity for emotional intimacy with one another.

Taking the concept of womanhood out of the closet and dusting it off means looking at its meanings: what we have absorbed from our mothers, through their mothers and grandmothers, and what we, ourselves, pass on to the next generation.

Our mothers will have borne the brunt of the bonbon effect all their lives as well. Without much concrete learning, daughters are often put off womanhood through an abstract sense of 'absence' in the culture. Mothers sometimes pass on to their daughters a sense of disappointment, tangible, even if unspoken. Many women gain their sense of completeness through having sons: a son after all will separate from his mother and take his rightful (higher) place among men. In this aspect he is more secure than his sister.

A daughter, who has no external power, has a different experience and her sense of personal power will be deeply affected by the example of her mother. What does she learn through imitation and example?

Reflections of a daughter on her mother

What does a daughter see?

Does your mother have personal power? Does she celebrate being a woman? Does she take care of her body, rejoicing in its chaos and rhythms and uncertainties? Does she teach her daughter its wisdom? Does your mother respect herself? Does she remain true to her own language, her own wisdom, her emotions or does she deny them?

Does she (overtly or covertly) see men as higher up? Does she accommodate their needs through love or fear? Is she afraid for good reason or chronically fearful? Is your mother direct and clear in her communication or does she pretend?

Does she acknowledge your separateness? Is she positive or critical about your body? Does she feel good enough about herself to let you be who you are? Does she say no firmly when she means it? Can you trust her to hold firm?

Does she share her grief with you? Her rage? Does she teach you ambivalence: that you are inferior but should pretend to be superior? Does she equip you for the monocular world with courage or with shame? Does she tell you to hide your truth? Does she teach you that vulnerable means weak, but that dependence is inevitable.

Does your mother let you share her joy in being a woman? Does she initiate you into the ways of gentleness? Does she teach you about the mysteries of being a woman? Does she instruct you in the sacredness of integrity? Does she train you to use your instinct?

If your mother shares her beauty with you, inspires you, teaches you that love and anger go together, and loves the woman you are, you are indeed a fortunate daughter. However, if she fails in any of these tasks or encourages you to compete in a world of competitive objects, there can be no blame. The hurt goes too deep and the loss between mothers and daughters is profound. A sense of betrayal – woman to woman – is permanent in its effect.

A legacy of hurt and anger, envy and blame easily undermines the possibility of closeness between women. The roots of our first woman-woman relationship affect our bonds (or lack of them) to sisters, friends, colleagues and beyond. This can only be addressed by looking at each other with compassion, by intentionally building a spirit of enquiry, honesty and trust. To attain a meaningful closeness we need to experience both the rigour and the gentleness of a woman-shaped heart.

101

The vegetable concoction turned out to be delicious. They sat at the table, each of them tired after their individual days but none of them quite ready to move, still held together there by an invisible thread.

Clare had managed to tell Sophie a little about what had transpired earlier with Ellen – about William and Belinda and the photos – but wasn't sure how much Sophie had taken in as she had been preoccupied with cooking. She was surprised therefore by the direction in which the conversation between the three of them now proceeded.

'It's all so silly, really, that we should all be alone so much, isn't it?' said Sophie out of the blue.

'What do you mean?' asked Clare.

'Well, you're on your own, without Dad, and Ellen is. And I know I'm living with Phil, but there are different kinds of aloneness, aren't there? You remember all those years at school when I was crippled with loneliness because I was different.'

'How were you different?' asked Ellen.

'I couldn't read or write as quickly as the other kids.'

'But teachers are supposed to help you with those sorts of problems,' said Ellen, frowning.

'I'm sure they are. I think they tried their best but rather gave up on me,' replied Sophie. 'Anyway, all I mean is that we are all lonely in our own ways. I still feel different today, although I don't have the school thing any more. Don't you ever feel like that?'

'I don't think I feel that different underneath,' said Clare.

'But it's never about underneath, is it? That is what I mean.'

'I don't understand,' said Clare.

'Do you mean that we're only different on the surface but the same underneath?' asked Ellen.

'Something like that. I mean it's only when you find out about someone that you find that you're not alone after all.' Sophie hesitated. 'I don't know if I should say this, but Mum told me, Ellen, that you lost your little girl. Her name was Belinda, wasn't it?'

Ellen looked wide-eyed at Sophie and just nodded.

'Well, you don't know this but I lost a daughter too. Six years ago. It wasn't the same because she was much younger than Belinda. In fact, she wasn't even born but it still makes us alike in that we've both lost a little girl.'

Ellen was too surprised to reply. Clare opened her mouth in astonishment but, unable to find any words, shut it again.

'I'm sorry.' It suddenly struck Sophie. 'Do you mind me mentioning it, Ellen?'

'No. Not really. It's a subject I never ever talk about so it's strange to be speaking of Belinda twice in one day.'

'You don't have to say anything. I felt a kind of link with you, when Mum told me. I also felt a link when she said you were lonely. Because I think it's really awful in this world when you don't fit in for some reason.

'You know,' she continued, 'I've given myself such a hard time for not thinking like other people, not wanting the same things, not having the same goals, just not *seeing* in the same way other people see. Sometimes I feel as if I have different eyes and different ears, even a different nose because I experience a different reality. It's not like someone liking dots and the other person stripes; I'm not talking about taste here or approach to things, even, like Mum and me in the kitchen,' she said, grinning at Clare. 'It's something much deeper than that.'

Sophie paused and then remembered something. 'Helen said the first time I met her – Helen's the woman Mum works for and I've been seeing her a few times,' she told Ellen – 'that she thought it likely I would feel as if I were from another planet. She recognised me though.'

'Is she from the same planet as you?' asked Ellen.

'I don't know. I'd never thought. She could be. What do you think, Mum?'

'I've never thought about it,' replied Clare. 'I wouldn't say you were really similar as people.'

'I don't know,' said Sophie. 'All I know is that she recognised in me something that was different. And that made a huge difference to me.'

Clare privately felt a huge glow of happiness, seeing her daughter like this. There was a joyfulness in her, something quite irrepressible that she had hardly ever seen before. Certainly not for a long time, not since she had been a very small child. But now, she was no longer a child. This inner something was strongly settled within an adult frame. It was as if Sophie possessed a clearer outline than before, not harsh or rigid, but somehow more pronounced around the edges.

At around eleven, Ellen went back home. Sophie kissed her on the cheek and Clare followed suit. Ellen was surprised but touched. It somehow seemed quite appropriate.

While they were in the kitchen clearing up together, Sophie said suddenly: 'Mum, did you mind about me mentioning Belinda?'

'I did at the time, but it seemed all right afterwards.'

'Look, I didn't want to say anything before talking to you, but I was wondering what you thought about asking Ellen to the ritual.'

'Heavens! I really don't see Ellen being comfortable with that sort of thing.'

'You don't know what sort of thing it's going to be.'

'Do you?'

'Not yet.'

'Well then. People can feel very awkward. It's the kind of thing that makes people very self-conscious. I don't think she'd like it at all.'

'At her age, you mean?' said Sophie, teasing her mother.

'At her age, perhaps, but not only that. It's not just her age.'

Clare was aware of moving towards a thought on the edge of her mind when Sophie put words to it first: 'I wonder, Mum, if you aren't talking about yourself. Are *you* worried about being awkward and self-conscious?'

'Possibly.' The more accurate answer would have been definitely, but Clare felt too defensive at that moment to admit it.

'It's OK,' said Sophie gently. 'We won't talk about it now. I'll ask you again in the morning,' and she kissed her mother goodnight.

102

Helen sat looking at the picture she held in front of her, entitled *Kali, Goddess of Death*. It was an exquisite watercolour, painted in black on a white background, framed in simple black wood. The movement and form were powerful and Kali's expression quite awesome. Sophie had inscribed it in the bottom right-hand corner: *To Helen, with many, many thanks, love Sophie.* She had presented Helen with it a few minutes ago.

'It's beautiful,' said Helen.

'I found it while I was looking for something else at home. It had been hidden away but I knew, as soon as I saw it, that this was what I could give you. I am really proud of it — I did it for A level art — and I think it is one of the best things I did before I stopped. Not just technically, I mean, but there's a lot of me in it. It means a great deal to me.'

'It's a perfect gift. I'll find a special place to hang it.'

'Do you really like it?' asked Sophie shyly.

'I'm absolutely delighted with it, I really am.'

'You were right. You said I'd know what to give you when I saw it.'

Helen smiled at her and nodded, then placed the picture carefully on the floor beside her chair. 'Now, we need to think about your ritual. Have you given it much thought?'

'No, not a lot. I've asked Mum and I was also thinking of asking Ellen who is an elderly neighbour of Mum's.'

Helen looked at Sophie without saying anything.

'It's because she lost a daughter, too, when the little girl was only four. A long time ago, I know, but I wondered what you'd think about me asking her. Mum thinks Ellen would be too uncomfortable but I decided I'd ask you.'

'First, I think that you need to be clear about what you want from the ritual. Then we need to have some design in mind, which can be open to spontaneity as well. Then you can think about who you want to be there. So let's start with what you want.'

Sophie thought for a moment. 'I don't know. You were the one to suggest it in the first place.'

Helen smiled. 'I know I did but you must have some picture in your mind by now of what you mean when you say ritual, especially if you've invited others to attend.'

'I imagine a kind of ceremony and some words ... that's all really.'

'All right. It would probably be a little easier if I explained what I mean by ritual. It's a ceremony, as you said, which can be elaborate or very simple. Whatever it is, there is a symbolism attached and this is what is important. You attach to the symbol, or symbols, different elements of the whole. You give them power to represent people, thoughts, feelings, entities, anything in your life. And you order them in such a way to give them meaning.

'The meaning is important because it affects every aspect of you, so ritual is very powerful. This is why funerals and wedding ceremonies can be very emotive occasions. We get caught up with the ritual and the meaning and lose ourselves in it temporarily. It comes to mean something beyond ourselves. It's pure left-eye vision – do you remember we've talked about that a bit?'

Sophie nodded.

'Rituals can be empty and meaningless when you don't feel part of them. You know, they become mechanical in some way?'

'Yes,' said Sophie.

'Well, this can't happen when you design your own. You tailor-make a ritual to suit you. It doesn't have to be original or complicated. It's better to borrow ideas from other rituals and then invent new parts. You can design them for when a beloved pet dies, or someone needs to heal a wound of any kind or when someone moves into a new home or two people decide to celebrate their relationship.

'It can be any event, really, that you want to ritualise. You give it a framework and, by committing your imagination to reality, you invest the occasion with a power that makes it significant for you. Unlike conventional ritual, there is emotion involved because you are being yourself in it, not playing a part. That's an important distinction.'

Helen stopped. 'So what do you want to do with yours?'

'Say goodbye to Melanie.'

'What else?'

'Nothing else,' said Sophie, frowning and puzzled.

'Tell me what you feel about her.'

'I'm sad she's gone.'

'What else?'

'I don't know what you mean.'

'Well, you might want to celebrate something about her. Or say something to her.'

'I'm sad I never saw her grow up: I didn't even see her born.'

'I know. It was a short time together but isn't there anything she taught you in that time? Is there anything you learned?'

'Learned?' Sophie thought hard. 'I remember that when I knew she was a girl, I felt so much sadder. I don't know why but it made me feel much worse to think I'd lost a little girl.'

'Can you think of any reason?'

'It would be a part of me, I suppose, that's the obvious thing, but in the time since, I've clung to the thought that we could have been friends. She would have been such a special little soul.'

'Do you think her death triggered something in you, an awareness of being female perhaps?'

'Do you know, that's odd. I used to look at women's bodies more, not sexually, you know, but I did start noticing female forms and skin and their shape more. I'd never thought so much about the difference before. I actually started drawing, sketching women's bodies for a while. I'd never connected that with Melanie.' Sophie shook her head slowly in amazement.

'I also felt, after the miscarriage,' she went on, 'that my body was a place of death. I found that very hard. That something in my body had killed Melanie, had taken away her life. That's not what the doctors said, of course, but that's how my body felt – a vehicle of death. I remembered that recently when I was crying about something. I felt I was crying about that whole thing. I don't feel morbid about it now but I did for a long time. Now I feel more comfortable because I'm sure I'll get pregnant again one day. I certainly want to.'

'So,' said Helen, gathering some of Sophie's thoughts, 'there's an awareness of the specialness of being a woman, in a woman's body; there's also an awareness of the power of our bodies and our closeness to death as well as birth.'

'Yes.'

'They're two mighty things that Melanie taught you during her short existence here.'

'I suppose so,' said Sophie quietly. 'I hadn't seen it like that before.'

'That's why we're talking about it now. And you want to say goodbye and possibly hello to a new experience?' Helen continued.

'Yes.'

'This is so important, Sophie. Ritual helps us to connect past to future, you know, to move through and on. Sometimes when women suffer losses like this, they are offered medication or sometimes counselling. These help in the short term but until you can close one chapter completely, you cannot fully go on to the next. You go on, of course, but there is always a part of you locked away in the past, often interfering with your capacity to be open to the new.'

'That makes sense,' said Sophie.

'Now before we look at how you want to structure your ritual, tell me why you're keen to invite your mother and maybe someone else.'

'Well, I've not felt close to Mum until I started coming here. No, there was a time not long before that when she came round and really surprised me. I suddenly saw a new side to her. It made me begin to see her as a person, not just my mother, I think. Anyway, it felt an obvious link her being there because I kept her out at the time. I just didn't want her around.'

'And Ellen?'

'That's because when I heard she'd lost a little girl, I wondered if she felt like me. In fact, now you've helped me see what Melanie taught me, imagine what Ellen's daughter may have taught her in four years!'

'The difference is that Ellen hasn't chosen to look at her loss in this way.'

'She doesn't know how to, does she? Nobody's ever told her.'

Helen gave a very deep sigh. 'This is very tricky, Sophie. I understand your wish to connect with other women in the same position and we can reflect that in your ritual: connection in ritual is essential.'

'What do you mean?' asked Sophie.

'I mean this isn't only an enactment for you, Sophie. At the same time as it will be for you, personally, this ritual, it also enables you to participate in a bigger picture: part of being human, part of being everywoman. Learning from a daughter, learning about your body, experiencing the power of death: these issues are relevant to all women, so connection is important to any ritual if it is to have any life.

'You see, it's quite different from the conventional marriage ritual, for example. Think how often a couple are encouraged to think only of themselves, like stars of a show. Sometimes, it's a lavish show designed more to make an impression of wealth and grandeur than any celebration of connection with humanity, or with past and future.'

Am I becoming cynical? Helen wondered briefly to herself.

'Anyway,' she continued, 'I think it's great that you want to include other women as part of sharing this experience. However, I'm not comfortable with Ellen being asked to participate when she hasn't made a choice. That's the difference. An observer, yes, a witness, yes, but I'm not sure you can push her into it.'

'I don't want to push her,' objected Sophie. 'I only wanted her to have a chance to do something she might welcome at this stage of her life.'

'I'll leave it to you to decide. What I'm going to do is put together a rough format that you can pull to pieces and amend in any way you want. Would that help?'

'That would be great.'

'So back to the nuts and bolts. Where do you want this to take place?'

'I was wondering about that. Everywhere I think of has the disadvantage of being public. I don't really want other people around looking curious.'

'Do you know of anywhere private, like part of a park or part of the forest?' asked Helen.

'Yes, but it's the same thing. You can't tell if anyone's going to appear at any time,' said Sophie with a sigh.

'So what had you thought then?'

'Well, I was wondering,' Sophie gave a little cough, 'if you would consider us using your house or rather your garden here?'

'Here?' Helen replied, in total astonishment.

'It was just a thought. You've a lovely garden. I thought that when I was working in it the other day.'

'Oh you did, did you?'

'Well, what do you think?'

Helen thought. 'I think I'd prefer it to be somewhere neutral. Except that this is neutral for all of you, isn't it?' A few seconds passed while Helen considered. 'I guess we can do it here but you'll have to help with setting it all up.'

'Of course. I'll do everything. That's brilliant.' Sophie beamed at Helen. 'Thanks so much.'

103

Counting the Cost

You are willing to take due responsibility for the harm you have done to others through intent or neglect; you do not need to hide behind the sterility of guilt but can feel the sorrow that comes with true acknowledgement.

Reaching out to other women beyond divisions means we cannot hide from our complicity, direct and indirect. Through generation after generation, women have stood by while those who were powerless to help themselves have suffered from the violence of a monocular system. We still do.

As long as children of any colour and nationality continue to be deprived, raped, tortured, allowed to starve to death or be killed in the name of profit or war, we continue to be part of the violence. We don't need the indulgence of breast-beating or guilt, both of which keep at bay more painful and authentic feelings. Experiencing our part in it, even for a few moments at a time, shifts our perception.

Whenever we enjoy the fruits of our aggression closer to home, we make our particular contribution to the general force of violence. Whenever we too despise the vulnerable, the weak, the fragile in ourselves and others, we give that force more power. We cannot escape our part in the blind cruelty of a system ruled by fear.

It is clear to see that the rulers of the world today, regardless of colour, race or creed, continue the same practices of racism, genocide and oppression of the poor through denial, greed, egocentrism and corruption. The same old story. And our part continues.

How hard we strive to look good, to be good, to please, to carry others, to make a success of things: we make such efforts to do the right thing and make the right impression. But the world is not balanced. This means we will experience moments of madness. This is the power of crazy. It is mad, this whole situation, and it is dangerous.

Taking one small step of responsibility for our own small part, together, creates the space for another energy to come alongside.

104

Dear Sophie,

Some first ideas for your ritual:

Preparation
On a small table, which can be decorated in any way you choose, you need to place the following items. Start with a memento of Melanie: draw a picture or choose an object, something that can represent her for you. It could be more than one thing, but keep it simple. Include candles to represent the element of fire, containers of water and earth and something to represent air. I usually use an incense stick but if you prefer to use something else, do so. It might also be useful to determine where north is so you know which way you're facing for later on.

This table then becomes the focal point for your ritual.

Think where you want people to stand or sit, whether you would like them to participate or not.

For simplicity, I have divided the ritual into beginning, middle and end.

Opening

Sophie: 'We are gathered together today to celebrate the short life and death of Melanie. I want, with you as witnesses, to honour her, give thanks for her, and say goodbye.'

You may here want to say what happened, the factual history, that sort of thing, addressing those present, with as little or as much as you choose.

Turn to your table and to what represents Melanie.

State what you want to thank her for, as we talked about.

Middle

Take each of your 'symbolic elements' in turn and move to the four corners of the garden (let's hope it's fine) and say what you want to say in celebration of Melanie. For example, 'May the powers of the air (facing East) take your soul safely and gently. Thank you Melanie. I am now able to bid you goodbye.'

Closure

You could invite your mother to join in part of this. Turn to the table and say 'Melanie, as mother I bid you goodbye now.' Then turn to your mother and say, 'As a daughter, I'd like to welcome you into my life. If I have failed to cherish you, it was because I was unable to see your strength or beauty. I now want to make amends and share my pride in being women together.'

(I'm still unsure about Ellen's actual participation. Have you asked her yet? We can talk about this later.)

End with a circle of everyone present, best in silence, to reflect on everything shared together. Holding hands perhaps.

Then you can ask them to have cake and tea or something. It's good to have something after all that!

Remember, Sophie, that this is only a guide to get you started. Words on paper sound stilted and off-putting but once they are being said, in situ, with meaning, they offer a completely different and powerful experience. That's when it comes to life.

You may want to include some music as well.

Have a think and call me next week. Have you thought about a date?

Best wishes,

Helen

105

Living the Paradox

Remember there are three life energies of creativity, challenge and curiosity, rooted in our primary emotional impulses. Each of these has a paradoxical element. As humans, we are presented with an impulse forwards and *at the same time* faced with a barrier.

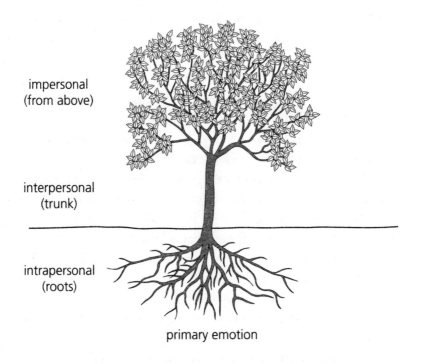

impersonal
(from above)

interpersonal
(trunk)

intrapersonal
(roots)

primary emotion

The paradox of creativity

The creative impulse concerns all life activities that enable us to generate, to make new shapes, to initiate, to spark something into life and to nurture it into growth. As we develop this capacity for giving life in all its forms, we are presented, at some point, with the challenge of the opposite: as we open to the experience of beginnings, we cannot avoid the experience of endings. Birth is the first beginning/ending and we encounter this in continuing cycles through life.

Beginnings and fruitfulness are balanced by endings and decay. The optimism of beginning is balanced by the sadness of ending: the passing of youth, the lapsing of friendship, the death of a beloved, our own imminent death. We are faced with endings of all kinds: the end of an illusion, of summer, of life as it was, the loss of identity, a cherished conviction, the ending of a class or completion of a project, the end of a relationship.

Through openness to endings, to deaths of all kinds, we are challenged to experience that tension between life and death. This tension will, in itself, elicit *sadness* and *grief.*

We don't have to plan this: it occurs naturally.

The paradox of challenge

Challenge describes our impulse to develop and change. The inherent paradox is that we have an urge to impose our will at the same time as having to acknowledge the limitation of that will. Through trying to exert control and break through obstacles, we will experience our power and, at some point, our lack of it.

We discover powerlessness collectively. We have to acknowledge the intractability of nature: earthquakes, hurricanes, drought, floods, volcanic activity and disease are all phenomena that defy human attempts to control the ultimately uncontrollable.

We also encounter powerlessness on a personal scale. Sometimes the odds are simply too great: we can do nothing to help someone however much we love them; we cannot prevent suffering or injustice; we fail to make a difference. When we discover the limits of our will, the tension between the energy of challenge and the reality of helplessness naturally elicits *frustration* and *anger*.

The paradox of curiosity

The life-energy of curiosity gives us the impulse to find out. It makes us want to understand, to explore, to uncover the truth, to solve the puzzle and explain the reasons why. Once again, at the same time as we seek knowledge, we come face to face with our limitation: we encounter the unknowable.

Our search for meaning brings us up short against meaninglessness: illness or death with no known cause, the baffling question of why some people suffer so much in this life, the occurrence of the unpredictable, the elusive, the inexplicable. We can guess, suppose, hypothesise, research and claim to prove, but ultimately we have to live with unanswerable questions. The same impulse that urges us to find out confronts us with our ignorance. However much we move in search of security, the unknown is always there and this tension between knowing and not knowing naturally elicits *anxiety* and *fear*.

The experience of contradiction

Each time we experience these inherent contradictions, we will feel the pull in both directions. This pull will inevitably cause tension. If we allow this to happen, and allow the release, the physical release (through the body) of this tension, the tension gives. Something shifts inside and our emotional level is altered, irrevocably moved onwards. The energy can flow freely again.

If, on the other hand, we seize up and there is no release of emotion, the tension increases. The natural process required to restore balance gets stuck. We resist. Bipolar becomes 'monopolar'. Instead of accepting death and ending, we label what we don't want as negative. We deny its importance or sometimes its very existence. We pretend that it won't happen, regarding it as undesirable.

Similarly, we deny being powerless. We pretend we are insuperable and end up not knowing when to *stop* going against nature. We refuse to take 'no' for an answer: we defy death with cryogenics, infertility with *in vitro* fertilisation, the limitations of natural biology with genetic engineering, the process of ageing with HRT. We 'play God' because acknowledging powerlessness implies failure and defeat.

We deny fear by becoming rigidly fixed on certain beliefs. We use dogma and prejudice to avoid doubt. We settle for the diet of half-truths fed to us by the media because the alternative risks stimulate too much uncertainty. We take refuge in hierarchies where we feel safe and everybody knows their rightful place.

Binocular vision and understanding emotion differently makes it possible to hold both realities at the same time. We can create and generate with the acceptance that there will also be a time for everything to cease. We can still commit ourselves wholeheartedly to change, accepting that we will face times of helplessness. We can be eager to discover and commit ourselves to research while at the same time accepting the unknown.

But we can't do this with our intellect alone. We have to accept that we will *feel* emotions naturally in response to this paradoxical predicament. Each impulse demands a full and brave commitment: to move in one direction while keeping an awareness of the tug of its opposite force.

We will probably be preoccupied with going in one direction or the other but accepting the need to be flexible reminds us to shift direction when necessary. It helps us to recognise when to let go, when to withdraw, when to recede, when to accept limitation and also when to go full steam ahead. Responding to the rhythm and moving back and forth requires us to stay alert. It requires a vigilance that comes with internal power.

106

Clare stopped reading, lay back and closed her eyes.

She had booked her flight earlier that day. Danny had insisted on paying for her ticket as he'd promised. He said he could afford it so she accepted graciously.

Ruth had phoned a few days ago. Not a long conversation but enough to tell her that things were still undecided between her and David. She'd told him she wanted to stop waiting around and had spoken to the children about the state of play. Of course, they'd known something was wrong. They didn't seem unduly alarmed, she said, in fact, they were a lot more pragmatic than she was, maybe because they were used to this happening with their peers. She reported that she'd managed to stay out of the 'failure' trap, which she was delighted about, even though David had apparently been a little surprised by her nonchalance (as he called it).

She was looking into the possibility of seeing a counsellor there but she had opened up to a friend who lived nearby, who'd turned out to be very supportive. So, uncertain as everything was, she'd been really keen to have Clare come and visit for a few days on her way back from California. It hadn't made a huge difference financially so Clare had agreed.

All that was ten weeks away. She'd arranged to take Ellen to the optician's next week and Ellen herself had got hold of a cleaner through a recommendation of a friend. Clare didn't know what the future would hold but then, who did?

She went back to her reading.

107

Psychosomatic Wisdom

As women, we often feel we're pulled into two (or more) different directions at once, so the prospect of experiencing another emotional pull may seem like more hard work. But this is different.

It is more to do with something we *allow* than something we have to hold on tight to at all costs. These experiences are difficult to put into words in our own, monocular, culture, but are fundamental to cultures very different from our own. By living the paradox, and not fighting it or avoiding it, we can transcend the tensions inherent in being human. To transcend means that we are moved to another level. And this is what happens. Something shifts deep down in our awareness.

When we allow ourselves, for example, even for a short while, to experience the full meaning of endings *and* beginnings, it moves our ideas about love to another level. Our vision and understanding expand not only to embrace love experienced with individuals who are close to us but also allow us to touch the presence of *communion* with others, in life or death. This sense of communion with fellow creatures and humans is made possible through the link of the body: through love and grief we share.

An acceptance of power and powerlessness – holding the two together – allows us to move to a place of *surrender*. This is not the shame or dejection of defeat and failure but the joy of surrendering, of yielding to a greater power than one's own. Allowing and releasing our personal anger enables us to transcend the tension of that particular paradox.

Allowing and releasing our personal fear, aroused by the tension between the known and the unknown, enables us to experience a universal fear and to embrace the quality of *mystery*. By accepting the presence of mystery in human life, we are enabled to accept the unknown in and beyond ourselves.

As individuals, we can touch a universality: a grief beyond our own personal grief, an anger at violation beyond our own immediate experience and a fear beyond our own individual concerns. Seeing images relayed round the world on the news is one thing: we respond with mild or intense feelings. Through the physical experience of feeling, we find a connection at the most profound level. We discover an awareness that goes beyond the human to touch the edges of the divine.

In this way, through release and acceptance, the energy of our emotions is transformed. This is what is possible. Emotions are not concrete entities but energies: strong, mild, intense, explosive, gentle energies. Like all energies they can be channelled, suppressed or transformed.

Through emotional transformation, we are open to a glimpse of experience beyond our own finite being and this connects us to the possibility of the divine. Not the Divine up on high, but the divine on the edges and in the midst of humanity, rooted in our biological, animal origins.

All of us can engage in this learning. All of us can learn to touch these moments. It doesn't take an extraordinarily rare or rarified mortal to do so but it does involve a radical shift in attitude to emotion as a bridge between body and mind and its integration into our concept of spirituality.

108

Clare put the pages down, got up and went into the kitchen. She filled and switched on the kettle.

She remembered that Sophie's ritual was next week. Apparently it was going to be at Helen's house. She was surprised Helen had agreed but could see why Sophie liked the location. Sophie had decided to ask Ellen, who had said she'd love to come, although Clare wasn't at all convinced that Ellen had any idea what she was letting herself in for. Anyway, she didn't want to interfere so she said no more. Something about her train of thought made her think of Angie so she thought she'd phone and see how she was. Angie had been a bit down, Clare remembered, when she'd come to supper.

'I was wondering how you were,' said Clare when Angie answered the phone.

'Oh, not bad. How are you?'

'I'm well. Lots of things have been happening.' Clare told her about talking to Ruth and booking her trip to America.

'I'm glad her optimism has paid off,' said Angie. 'I enjoyed meeting her. It was a good evening. Did you get my card?'

'Yes, I did.'

'How is that dear lady with the burn?'

'Ellen?' Clare then recounted the saga of her first disastrous visit and then how she went back and sat and looked at Ellen's photos. She was in the middle of telling Angie about Ellen's daughter, Belinda, when she stopped. She'd completely forgotten, when she'd started, about Angie's own miscarriages.

'I'm sorry,' she said. 'I wasn't thinking.'

'It doesn't matter, Clare,' said Angie. 'These things happen and it was a long time ago now. It's quite a common experience, you know.'

'I know, but I'm cross that I didn't see that one coming. I'd forgotten until just this moment.'

'It's fine, Clare, really. I'm not that sensitive. Carry on with your story about Ellen, for heaven's sake.'

'Well, Sophie phoned out of the blue, saying she wanted to come round so she cooked for us all. I'm taking Ellen to the optician's next week. Honestly, Angie, I don't know what's going to happen in the long term. Her son apparently is not close to her and she insists he won't want to know.'

'All you can do is a little at a time. The practical things.'

'Yes. I'm really happy to do that. She's got a cleaner now, or will have one soon.'

'She must trust you, Clare, to talk to you.'

'Yes, I think she does . . . a bit.'

'That's the important thing, isn't it. If she trusts you, as a friend, in some way, then you can keep the channels of communication open about the future. I think that's the hardest bit.' Angie paused.

'You get to a certain age,' she continued, 'and you're so used to being self-contained that you don't believe anyone could give a toss about your concerns. In fact, they don't, most of the time. But there's a rigidity that sets in around the whole situation. You know, you don't speak about personal things anyway, let alone your panic that you're peeing in your knickers or can't see well or forget where you're going . . .'

'We haven't got to that stage yet,' Clare laughed.

'You know what I mean. It's a real trap, all that, because you decide nobody is interested and that perpetuates itself. You feel more and more alone with it and the more isolated you are, of course, the worse it gets. All of us are actually healthier for some contact with other human beings and it only makes us more and more vulnerable to keep everything shut in.'

'She did admit to me she was frightened.'

'Well, that's a real breakthrough, Clare. Honestly. There's a chance then that she might talk to you again if she's worried about something. I think you've done really well. Better than a lot of bloody professionals, I can tell you.'

'Don't be daft, Angie.'

'I'm serious. If you've got her trust, you can really help her manage her own life without taking over.'

Angie paused a moment and then asked, 'What will happen while you're away? Would you like me to come round? I could visit a couple of times each week, if she'd like that.'

'Heavens, I hadn't thought that far ahead. I'm sure she'd love it, Angie. Shall I ask her?'

'Do. It will probably be evenings or at the weekend but I'm really happy to come round. I'd enjoy it.'

'OK. I'll ask her tomorrow.'

'You haven't really said how you are yet, Angie. Are you still with Geoff?'

'Yes, just.' She laughed. 'I don't know, I give up on the idea of finding any real heart-to-heart stuff any more. He's good to me and I think he genuinely cares about me but the problem is in me. I must be having a delayed or post-mid-life crisis.'

'How's everything going at work? I forgot to ask,' Clare enquired, suddenly remembering.

'Well, I did manage to say something to Brian a couple of weeks ago. I told him I'd been surprised that he'd ended up giving a lecture to *my* students but I found it hard to pinpoint exactly what I was objecting to. I seemed to be up against something so much bigger. It was like walking into a dense fog where you're groping to find your way. There were other things, you see, Clare, connected to that one event. Remember he is being groomed for promotion – over me – so there is always the contrast between his assurance about his future and my uncertainty but I couldn't talk about those things to him. I tried to explain what it had felt like but what stopped me was his total lack of awareness.

'He couldn't understand what I had a problem with. He had no concept of my experience and wasn't that bothered about finding out. So how could he take any responsibility for what he'd done? It was like talking to someone from a different planet.'

'It was good that you said something anyway.'

'I don't know. It all feels too big an issue and I'm left feeling confused and ... a bit helpless, really. The wind's certainly gone out of my sails.'

'Are you going to stay there?'

'I'm not sure. I feel very uneasy now about my future. I'll have to make a decision sometime.' Angie sighed. 'Anyway, how are things with you and Sophie?'

'Much better. Something's changed in a way that I can't describe. But I'm really pleased at what's happening. She's having a ritual soon and she actually asked me to be there. I was stunned. Partly because I'd no idea what a ritual was and then that she should invite me.'

'A ritual for what?'

'A ritual to . . .' For the second time in one phone call, Clare hit something face on, without seeing it coming. 'God, Angie, I don't believe it. I've done it again.'

'What are you talking about?'

Clare took a deep breath. 'It's a ritual for the baby she lost, you know, the little girl, six years ago.'

Angie was quiet for a while.

'Are you still there?' asked Clare.

'Yes. I didn't know it was a daughter.'

'I didn't know either until Sophie asked me to come.'

'Why is she doing a ritual?' Angie asked quietly.

'You remember she's been going to see Helen? This is one of the things that Helen suggested would help Sophie to move on, because she thought Sophie hadn't really said goodbye. Or that's what I've gathered. I haven't asked her everything, obviously, but that's what Sophie said: it's a ritual to say goodbye properly to Melanie.'

'Melanie?'

'Yes, that's the name Sophie gave her, years ago apparently, but she didn't tell me until recently.' There was a silence. 'Oh, Angie, what's going on?'

'I don't know. Nothing really. It's strange thinking about the sex of an unborn child. It makes it a more definite life, doesn't it, than just being labelled a miscarriage?'

'Did you know about your miscarriages?'

'No. Only nameless, genderless, bloody accidents. No life, no mourning. In a way I envy Sophie her opportunity. To genuinely make peace with something like that in your life and move on from it.'

'Well, maybe you could do one too!'

'Oh yes,' said Angie sarcastically. 'Sounds just my style!'

'No, seriously,' Clare insisted.

'I couldn't do anything of the sort,' said Angie. 'I'm not a believer.'

'Well, I don't know that I'm a believer either but I want to be there for Sophie.'

'Of course you do.'

It was on the tip of Clare's tongue to ask Angie if she wanted to come too, but she dared not. It was Sophie's show, this, entirely.

There was a moment of awkwardness. Clare didn't know

whether to change the subject. She then decided the only thing to do was to be truthful.

'Angie, I'd love to ask you to come but I can't, it's Sophie's thing, you know.'

'I know it is. I wouldn't dream of coming anyway. I'd be far too embarrassed.'

Clare couldn't say anything about Ellen.

'I could mention it to Sophie.'

'Don't you *dare*, Clare. Don't you say anything. Now, promise.'

'Well,' said Clare, wriggling, 'I would like to give Sophie the option and then she could give you the option.'

'No, Clare, do you hear me? *No.*'

'I hear you, Angie, but I care for you too. I'll have a think.'

'You're not to ask Sophie.'

'We'll see.'

'Clare, you're impossible.'

'I know, I'm getting that way,' retorted Clare with a chuckle. 'Listen, Angie, changing the subject, when are we going to see each other? Maybe we can meet up, the two of us, and have some fun.'

'Sounds good. There's a possibility I may have to go and give a talk in Brighton in a few weeks' time. If you like, we could travel down and you could amuse yourself while I do my thing and then we could enjoy the weekend together.'

'That sounds a great idea. It should be just before I go away, which will be perfect.'

'OK I'll let you know.' Angie paused. 'Listen, Clare, I don't want you to say anything to Sophie, please.'

'I'm not sure. Trust me.'

'You really are getting impossible.'

'I'll talk to you soon.'

''Bye. Thanks for ringing.'

109

'What on earth's NETBANG?' asked Clare, seeing the title of a folder on the desk.

'It's what we're going to do today. It stands for Not Enough To Be A Nice Guy!'

'So you do think there are some around then?' asked Clare as a deliberate tease.

'Stop it, Clare,' said Helen with slight impatience. 'You know perfectly well what I think.'

'Have you written it for men?'

Helen shook her head. 'I doubt many men would be interested in my ideas. I've put this chapter in because all women live in relationship with men – in some way, at some level – in their lives. Even if there's no intimate relationship, women don't function in a vacuum – we have fathers, colleagues, friends and so on – and there are things that we see and are aware of but simply don't know how to talk about. My hope is that by articulating some of the issues, women can start their own dialogue with the men who matter to them.'

'You make it all sound so serious.'

'I'm sorry,' Helen replied, looking quite crestfallen. Clare immediately regretted her flippancy.

'I didn't mean . . . '

'It doesn't matter. I know I can be too serious at times.' Helen gave Clare one of her looks. 'But it *is* serious, you know, Clare, there's a lot at stake. Now, shall we get started?'

110

It's Not Enough To Be A Nice Guy

Men also must open their eyes.

There are, of course, men whose eyes are open from birth, sensitised and alienated individuals who find the process of this life very tortuous and difficult. Then there are men who become vulnerable after some circumstance interrupts normal linear progress: a serious physical injury, the death of a child, witnessing extreme suffering, imprisonment. As a consequence, their eyes open and they learn compassion.

There are many men who perpetuate the system, living resolutely focused through the right eye, and who have no interest in any other way, preferring to retain monocular power. There's no reason that they can see for change.

There are men who hate the relentlessness and the heartlessness of the system in which they labour every day. They come home and find an antidote through the innocent wonder of a small child, or being Dad and playing with their children. Sometimes the accumulated tension is defused through sport activities and alcohol, sometimes through extramarital excitement. Even though men on the lower rungs may find fault with monocular vision, their disgruntlement usually emanates from a personal sense of grievance or disadvantage. They rarely confront the system as a whole, preferring to opt out or hide behind an irresolute, indeterminate stance.

Whether up or down, change will only occur if those individuals with the bonbons – however chauvinist, macho or 'new' and nice they are – acknowledge a system in place: the reality that hierarchical power is overwhelmingly unevenly distributed. Then they will become aware of something they hadn't understood before: living with bonbons in the culture is a different and unequal experience from living without them.

This reality has to be felt. Token intellectual acknowledgement is insufficient, being one of the very devices used in monocular culture to defuse any criticism. Another such device is distraction: undermining an argument with an irrelevance or a diverting statistic.

Distraction describes the way we bring into someone's line of vision anything that will cause a temporary loss of their focus and direction. It is extremely effective: taking advantage of the speaker's momentary confusion, the other person 'wins' the argument and probably a lot more in maintaining the status quo.

There is a particular distraction used so frequently in relation to gender issues that real listening and discourse is inevitably and cleverly obstructed. Whenever there is a suggestion that there is a fundamental difference in how women and men are seen and treated by the culture, the automatic response, from women and men alike, is 'yes, but men suffer too'.

'Yes, but men suffer too ...'

Point out to anyone that 90 per cent of depressive patients are women, 90 per cent of patients who are prescribed tranquillisers are women, that in every single country of the world, domestic violence towards women is an evident and growing problem and out come the 'Yes, but-ers' in chorus. We hear: 'men get depressed too'; 'I know a man on tranquillisers'; 'women hit men sometimes'.

Mention that 90 per cent of anorexics are young women, that young women are overly concerned about slimness and obsessed with their appearance and the immediate retort is: 'but some men are anorexic too'; 'men are really concerned about their appearance too'.

Women who have been raped, beaten or abused as children rarely mention the involvement of a woman. Why? Because it is men who are perpetrators of rape. State this and we hear 'Yes, but it's only because women can't physically rape' or 'women allow it to happen and participate sometimes'; 'boys are abused as well as girls'; 'women are violent too'.

Yes, women can be violent too. But whereas skin colour and social disadvantage are cited by more sympathetic observers as crucial contributing factors to the incidence of crime among young black men, for example, nobody points out that women themselves are disadvantaged because they are women.

Even though we are all aware of changes in gender and social roles, women prefer to keep their heads down. We keep quiet, as we have seen, not daring to ask too many questions: embarrassed and uneasy at any whiff of feminism or solidarity, our bonds of dependence on men tighten and silence us. As long as we keep quiet, it is unlikely that men are going to bother to point out any inequity.

For any of us to participate voluntarily in a process of change, we have to believe we have something to gain. Once men see the system in place, they can understand how they, too, are oppressed by it. They can then take responsibility for their part in the system and, most importantly, collaborate in its subversion.

111

Clare still felt a little uncomfortable when they stopped for a break.

'Helen, I didn't mean to make fun of all this. Of course, I realise it's serious. I suppose I find it hard to identify with it all sometimes. I had a husband who was never threatening and my son, too, is a gentle kind of young man. So it's difficult for me understand the kind of chauvinistic men you have in mind.'

'Clare, you're missing the point!' said Helen. 'Come on. I'll explain downstairs.'

A few minutes later, they sat at the kitchen table.

'Right,' said Helen. She thought for a moment and then said, 'You see, Clare, that by dividing men into the good guys and the bad guys, you make the same mistake as most men make. The point is that even without the extreme behaviour of the minority, there is always the oppressive maintenance by the majority. It's about more than individual behaviour because even the nicest of nice guys is responsible for neglecting to challenge or confront a system in which they all, willingly or unwillingly, participate.

'So what are they supposed to do about it?'

'*Open their eyes!*' said Helen, staring at Clare in such a comical way that Clare laughed. Helen drank some of her coffee and then continued.

'It doesn't involve an epiphany, necessarily: it can happen very simply. I'll give you an example. A young sales rep, Andy, attended a series of talks I gave, not long ago, to promote one of my books. Andy was the kind of nice ordinary regular guy we're talking about, not at all macho. He sat in the audience and listened to the general discussion as women spontaneously gave examples of their problems at work. He was there at the first talk, not out of interest, but because it was part of his job.

'The second evening, he came because he was intrigued. On this occasion, one of the women in the audience asked to practise a role-play in which she wanted to ask her new boss to stop standing directly behind her, watching the screen while she typed. She felt very intimidated by him. I asked Andy to take the part of the boss and he agreed. We went through the role-play a couple of times and the woman was satisfied with what she learned.

'After everyone had gone, Andy came to me in a state of mild shock. The anxiety on the woman's face had disturbed him. Nobody, he said, had ever looked at him with fear in their eyes like that before. I told him that she wasn't really looking at him personally, and explained that in a role-play situation we project the real 'other' on to someone else, deliberately, to evoke the feelings which we can then learn to deal with in a safe context. I reassured him that, for those few minutes, she had seen him as the boss who intimidated her, not as Andy. He understood my explanation but still felt disturbed.

'After the third and final evening, we had a long talk. He told me that the whole experience had opened his eyes. Apparently, his wife, a lawyer, had been terribly upset for months because of being bullied by male colleagues at work. Andy had cared, obviously, and wanted to be supportive, but hadn't known what to do to help. Now, he realised that this was because he'd had no idea of what his wife was going through.

'The woman who shared his bed and sat opposite him at breakfast wasn't at all timid or self-conscious. She had absolutely no qualms about saying what she wanted or being cross with him if she felt like it. What Andy hadn't seen before was that a woman reacts differently in a context in which she does not belong, where she is marginalised and bullied. From that moment of seeing, he could better understand the reality of his wife's harassment at work. She wasn't a timid, unassertive woman with a 'problem': her difficulty arose precisely because she was a competent woman doing her job within a monocular culture. Andy hadn't seen or understood before how the system rendered his wife so powerless and afraid. It was a major catalyst for him.'

'But what could he do about it?'

'He could be a lot more supportive. And then it would give him an awareness of his own behaviour. That's when it becomes possible to take responsibility, you see, for your own attitudes and your own choice as to whether you continue to collude with or challenge the system.'

Clare suddenly found Angie's words going through her mind '*up against something much bigger ... no concept of my experience ... how could he take any responsibility for what he'd done? ... like talking to someone from a different planet*'. Caught somewhere in between Helen and Angie, she said slowly 'It's hard though sometimes to get this across to men, isn't it?'

'It certainly is. Andy was able to open his eyes because he wasn't directly to blame. None of us can listen when we're being blamed for something. And it wasn't the same as witnessing his own wife's fear, either, because he would have been instantly protective and probably aggressive to the other man. The fear of a complete stranger, on the other hand, directed towards him, had opened his eyes to the connection between the experience of two very different women. This connection was possible because he had witnessed and felt the impact of a woman's fear. It was real and he had seen that.'

'What a pity that kind of insight doesn't happen more often,' murmured Clare.

'Indeed it is. And it won't, until men first open their eyes and see the connections for themselves.'

112

Every man has a partner, daughter, girlfriend, friend, sister, mother, aunt, grandmother or colleague who lives with the bonbon effect every day of her life. Men don't see it because they don't experience it: even if they do sense there is some inequality somewhere, personal discomfort, helplessness and cowardice are obstacles to genuine understanding.

Seeing the system in place goes way beyond personal indignation at the behaviour of another man towards my wife or my daughter or my whoever, which is too closely linked with position on a higher rung. It is much more personally confronting to see that women are lower down the scale and more powerless because they are women. This means *all* women − women who men consider attractive, gorgeous, ugly, miserable, mean, charming, boring, cute, neurotic, sexy, tiresome, interesting, demanding, the beauty and the bitch alike. The implications of this are considerable and generate understandable anxiety.

In a monocular system, a man cannot be raised without being subject to the perceptions of sexism, any more than white men and women can avoid attitudes of racism. None of us is impervious. All we can do is acknowledge and take responsibility and make amends. It is not even enough to opt out of the system and declare an alternative unless we make sure it's coherent.

Beware of wolves in new men's clothing

The new man is spending more time with his children but what values is he demonstrating? Is he teaching them to be image-conscious, to win, to scorn vulnerability, ugliness and powerlessness? Is he persuading them to be sexual before their time? Is he promoting objectism, suppression of fear and weakness, teaching the virtues of aggression? Or is he encouraging them to be open and honest with their feelings? Does he do the shit work in the home or does he leave this for his co-(female) parent?

What does the new father teach his sons? Is there coherence between the official line and the informal behaviour? Or does he claim equality while constantly rebuking the children's mother for her stupidity and incompetence? What happens in the home is crucial in forming attitudes to gender and children will certainly pick up any ambiguity, even if they don't have a word for it.

Very often, men who publicly profess to want to explore the softer sides of masculinity still end up ruling the roost. Just as the penchant for pretty young girlfriends can persist, so can the assumption of their authority. They (and women) take it for granted that they will head their own organisational ladders. They play the same political games and are no less likely to take over with their ideas, their language, their personalities and their egos. If there are changes, new men still want to be on top.

It is simple to make the assumption that sexism is somehow easily transcended. Similar to the generalisation that all gay men are sensitive sweeties and understand women like no straight man can, many women fondly assume that men who enter the counselling and caring professions, for example, will somehow see women differently. They are genuinely dismayed to find that hidden attitudes endure.

Facing up to fear

Fear of loss of power has been embedded in the foundation of masculine identity for thousands of years. Men don't like taking second place because competition is so ingrained. Recent American men's movements like Iron John groups or the Kingdom of God are keen to redress the lack of male support and friendship and the loss of masculinity while reasserting real male identity. They seek to bond man to man because they are often envious of the solidarity of women's groups and afraid at what they perceive as the increasing autonomy of the women in their lives. If only. The myopia of monocular vision is quite staggering at times.

As long as the spirit of redefining masculinity is based on 'it's our turn: women have had their chance to feel good about themselves, now it's time for the boys' or 'we can exclude women now because they excluded us', little will change as aggression still runs the show. There is no room at all for the vision of the left eye, no room for humanity.

Many new men remain stuck within the old system. Without the balance of the left eye, men who want to reinvent themselves will aim only to recoup perceived losses or protect themselves from the 'ravages' of feminism. Agreeing to drop the excesses of chauvinism, as long as they can maintain their position in the monocular system, is not taking responsibility but a response to fear.

This fear is reinforced by women themselves renouncing their softer (feminine) qualities. While we aim up the ladder, it fuels the competition to retain or regain perpendicular power. It is no wonder some men feel so often aggrieved and ousted by women and afraid of what will happen. It's exactly what many of us appear to have done: switched from power under to power over in one linear movement.

Maleness in transition

Fear is fanned at a less conscious level. Exposure to reports of genetic irrelevance and the apparent decline in the male species, while, we are told, the female is in the ascendant, is guaranteed to disturb men. These issues stifle any concern about becoming more human.

Many young and not so young men are uncertain now about their maleness. They are not sure what it means: a desire not to oppress women, where this is genuine, risks developing a reduced traditional masculine identity rather than anything actually new. Some men end up not being able to be fully themselves because they don't want to offend: even sexual activity is affected.

Many men lose touch with their lust because of this confusion. Having a good fuck, enjoying his penis and lust and sexual vigour is part of being a man. As is the unbeatable thrill, for many men a higher rated thrill even than the win of a favourite football team, of having their potency confirmed when they make a woman pregnant! It is easy to confuse this with unacceptable chauvinism.

The symbolism of the penis and the whole phallocratic emphasis of the past have been heavily criticised, not without cause, but where is the alternative? Isn't it possible to celebrate male procreativity without the relentless linear emphasis? Men could learn a new relationship with their own bodies, including their genitals. Through a binocular vision of masculinity, lust can exist alongside love: the heart is connected to the penis, the body is whole and not fragmented and emotion is valued alongside intellect, vulnerability alongside power.

The first hurdle for men is to accept that monocular power is not the only power that matters. Imagine the difference it would make, for example, if the left eye opened and men were able to see connections. They would understand the continuum of the violence of objectism connecting men who rape, who batter, who masturbate to pornography, who pay for underage sex, who intimidate and bully women at work.

The deeply entrenched attitudes of sexism cannot simply be removed by changing a mindset. Gender transition unsettles us all. Breaking new ground entails travelling through emotional minefields because both 'sides' have accumulated a great deal of anger that easily translates into a need to apportion blame and fight for the superior position.

Monocular culture always seeks to blame. A decade ago, women's new sexual assertiveness was openly held to be responsible for the increase in incidence of erectile dysfunctional problems. The effect of a strategy like this is to increase resentment of the injured party and further entrench the offenders into their deferential and rightful position! Nobody wins.

Men need to help and guide each other through change but change will only be effective if emotion is included. Monocular power is addictive and plays games with the mind: it is only emotion that can effect the transition from monocular to binocular. Emotion can be a bridge because emotional understanding and experience work more deeply and effectively than anything else. Men fear *fear* but surely deeper down are feelings of grief and rage at their own oppression within a monocular system.

Few men are willing to risk an alternative because they have more external power to lose and are afraid of being toppled. What they stand to gain, however, is increased humanity. Gentleness, coherence and compassion will never be part of monocular vision.

Women cannot make this transition for men. Men will have to risk the drop to second place before they can understand that first or second place are only the temporary imposition of the right eye. It will take a genuine humility and a commitment to be open – to actually experience the fear of transition – until we can envision, together, the true consequences of equality and collaboration. This means going beyond the seesaw and shivering for a while in our own uncertainty before we discover and create something new.

113

A few days later, after Clare had dropped her at Harwell House with three huge cardboard boxes, Sophie announced to Helen that there were to be five witnesses, six, with herself.

Helen was astonished. 'It's going to be quite a party, then,' she said.

'I know. It's just grown. Angie's a friend of Mum's from ages ago. Mum told me they'd been talking and asked what I thought about Angie coming. It was fine. Angie was very good to us when we were kids and I really like her. She's had miscarriages too so that's why she's coming. And then there's Abbie, the friend I told you about who was really sweet to me at the time. It took me ages to track her down. She said she'd come but I'm not sure she'll make it.'

They went into the garden and both looked up at the sky.

'It looks a bit uncertain,' said Helen.

'Do you think it's going to rain?'

'I don't know, but it is quite windy and a bit chilly.'

'I know, but I'd like to have it out here if we can. People can wear warm things.'

'Whatever you want,' said Helen. 'Now where are you going to place your main table, your focal point?'

Sophie surveyed the scene and chose a spot in a clearing among four old apple trees towards the end of the garden. It was sheltered but wide enough for everyone not to be cramped.

'Let's move the table,' said Helen. They carried the round wooden table to the chosen spot.

'You've brought your things to decorate it, have you?'

'Yes. More than I need, I'm sure.'

'If you want to use any foliage or flowers, help yourself.'

'Thanks.'

'Did you think about music?'

'Yes, I brought a CD player.'

'And food?'

'For afterwards?'

'Yes.'

'Well, there's a cake. I made it specially.'

'Good. I'll sort out some cups and saucers in the kitchen for you. Look, Sophie, I'm going to leave you for a bit to settle in. I'll be upstairs if you need me but I'll let you get on with your arrangements, and if you want, we can talk about the procedure when you're ready to. How would that be?'

'That's great. Thanks.'

Helen went back inside. Sophie started unpacking. She felt excited and scared in just about equal measure.

114

At the Core

You may surprise others with your forthrightness because you are not afraid to speak out. This power is clear in the way you respond honestly and emotionally to a situation but, like meeting a wave, allow yourself to move through it to the other side.

When you look at the world through both eyes, you get a very different picture of power. The power of gentle comprises integrity, equality, compassion, honesty, emotional attunement, lack of blame or vengeance, responsibility, and connection: a far cry from the familiar. But it does exist and it's there for the claiming if we have the courage.

At its heart, its core, is courage. The word for courage in many languages stems from the word for heart. We need courage to make a commitment, to speak out, to withstand loneliness sometimes and to take a stand for our convictions. From this place, we need not play power games or give our power over to others in submissive postures. Nor do we need to wield it over others.

Courage helps us deal with inevitable times of darkness. We

are likely to be misunderstood because we're different. We are open to attack if our integrity makes others feel uncomfortable. We may have to face resentment from those who abide by an either/or approach as our power will be seen as a threat to their own.

It's possible that you will be criticised, marginalised, stereotyped and frustrated because your stance and your integrity mean that the higher echelons of external power remain closed to you. You may be seen as competitive even when you're not; your behaviour may be labelled authoritarian even when it isn't. The power of gentleness is often attacked because it is not understood. It is different.

As a woman, you will find others may well be afraid of you and unable to see the paradox of vulnerable and strong, preferring the narrow focus on one or the other but never both. They may not be able to understand the paradox of you. Not being seen and embraced in your totality, however much you yearn for this, may be painful.

We need courage to step into the unknown. But for any truly dynamic shift in consciousness to occur, a limited intellectual approach to emotion has to be discarded to make room for unfolding to take place. This means nothing less than making an ongoing commitment to be fully human. It is the wisdom of the body that will lead women to a different experience of their souls.

115

They all sat in silence in the car as Clare drove to Harwell House. Ellen was in front; Abbie and Angie in the back. They were running late because Abbie had phoned to say she'd missed her train and they had to go to the station to meet the next one. Clare had only met Abbie once before; she had wild curly black hair, a silver nose stud and every single item of her clothing was black.

Clare was thinking of the last pages she'd read. Helen had said they were drawing to an end now. Clare had sensed a slowing down. She'd asked Helen what happened next; she'd said she would try and get it published. Clare asked whether she could do anything else and had been surprised by Helen's eagerness. Apparently she wanted to write a children's book next, something she'd never done but had long wanted to. She asked if Clare would like to continue and she'd said that of course she would.

What she hadn't said was how relieved she was to be asked. She'd been sad at the prospect of leaving Helen because she hadn't wanted to lose touch with her now, after so much had happened: Helen seemed to have impinged on her life in so many ways. She'd learned so much through working with her but, in a way, she felt she'd only just begun.

Three miles to go.

116

Sophie was adjusting some roses on the table. 'What do you think?' she asked Helen, who was carrying out two more chairs, with some papers under her arm.

'It all looks fine. How are you feeling?'

'Exhausted. I'm glad they're late.'

'Are you clear what you're doing?'

'More or less.'

'Just remember, there is always room for mistakes and starting again. This ritual is yours, so enjoy it. Here, I've printed off some sheets for everyone.'

'That's brilliant,' said Sophie, looking at them, each printed on a different coloured paper. 'They look great.'

'Do you want me to do the music?'

'Yes, if you wouldn't mind. Helen, do you think people will want a cup of tea when they arrive?'

'It's not a good idea. Everybody tends to feel awkward and

anxious about these things so it's better to get straight in and then you can have the tea while you're relaxing when it's all over.'

They heard the car drawing up.

'I'll go and let them in,' said Helen. 'You stay and gather yourself.'

Helen disappeared round the side of the house; there was a sound of voices and then Clare, Ellen, Angie and Abbie appeared.

'Abbie!' Sophie squealed. 'You made it!' She rushed up to Abbie and hugged her. She turned to Angie. 'Angie, thank you for coming,' she said, giving Angie a hug as well.

'My pleasure,' said Angie, looking round the garden a little warily.

'Ellen, it's lovely to have you here.'

'It's lovely to be here, my dear,' replied Ellen.

Sophie looked at Clare. 'Hello, Mum.'

'Hello, love.' They hugged too. Helen appeared through the kitchen doors.

'Do you want to keep your coats on? It will probably be chilly without them.'

'I'll keep mine on,' said Ellen. They all stood there for a moment.

Helen looked at Sophie. Sophie looked at Helen. 'Go on then,' mouthed Helen.

Sophie took a breath. 'OK. Hello everybody. We'd better start. I'm going to ... hang on a minute. Here's a copy of the programme.' She handed everyone a sheet.

They all stood looking at them uncertainly.

'As you'll see,' said Sophie, 'it's divided into three parts. We're going to stand by the apple trees up there.'

The six women and one dog went across the grass towards the trees. Sophie stood with her back to the table, the others in a semi-circle, Helen at one end and Clare at the other.

'I'm extremely nervous,' said Sophie. She smiled at everyone and the heart of every woman there reached out to her and held her in an invisible curl of care.

She cleared her throat and began. 'I've asked you here today because I want to say goodbye to Melanie. Melanie was my child, my daughter for a very brief time. She was conceived and came to life and died within the space of my body, all in only five months.

'On this table here, I've made a little presentation to her. There is a clay form I made while thinking of Melanie the other day.' She indicated three deep apricot roses in a glass vase. 'I chose these because of their scent and colour. There is also a daisy chain that I made today because it's what I think she would have done as a little girl.

'There's some earth from Helen's garden,' said Sophie, indicating a small terracotta bowl, 'some water in a porcelain jug I've had since I was a child myself – it belonged to my grandmother – and a candle that Mum gave me last year. It's inside a glass holder so it won't blow out. Two incense sticks . . . that's it. Oh, and this lovely cloth,' she added as she stroked the red shot silk cloth that she'd draped over the table to reach the ground, 'was something I was given by Narita, a friend from college ages ago. She gave it to me for my birthday once. It's Indian silk and I've always loved it.'

Sophie turned to look at her sheet and then up at the group; she swallowed and then smiled. 'I must remember to breathe.'

She did so.

'One of the things I found hardest about losing Melanie was that I couldn't find an explanation for it. It was all so futile. I know there were medical reasons but I couldn't make sense of them. So preparing this ritual has given me the chance to think about what I've learned from her, so I can celebrate her part in my life, even for such a short time.'

Sophie half turned to the table so she didn't have her back to the group. 'Melanie,' she said, raising her voice a little, 'even though we were together a short while, you opened my eyes. You helped me to see the beauty of women, and my own beauty. Inside and out. Your death made me understand the power of my woman's body and the capacity for both birth and death. This is a power I want to honour for the rest of my life.'

Sophie walked to the table and picked up the earth. Then she walked towards a small circle of stones that she had placed near one of the trees. She stood inside the circle, which was just big enough for her feet. She spoke quietly but everyone could hear her.

'Powers of the North, guardians of the earth and everything that is born and dies, grows and withers, waxes and wanes, the whole cycle of life and death, take Melanie's spirit and let her rest in peace.' She threw some of the earth in front of her as she spoke and it fell on to the grass.

She stood there a moment and then went back to the centre. She put the pot back on the table and picked up the incense sticks. She walked at right angles to her first path and stood facing the back of the garden. She spoke again.

'Powers of the East, guardians of air, of inspiration, of wind and breeze, take Melanie's spirit and let her rest in peace.' The wind made the tips of the sticks glow and the smell of incense wafted over to where the others stood.

Sophie came back to the table. Putting back the sticks, she picked up the candle. She walked this time towards the group and faced them, without looking directly at them.

She held out the candle in front of her and said, 'Powers of the South, guardians of warmth and fire, flame and sun, spark and blaze, take Melanie's spirit and let her rest in peace.'

As Sophie spoke her words this time, Clare found herself in tears. She'd never seen her daughter look so . . . regal, almost. She looked as though she'd been doing this for years.

Sophie replaced the candle. She picked up the porcelain jug and walked in the final direction.

'Powers of the West,' she said, 'guardians of mist and water, river and lake, raindrop and ocean, take Melanie's spirit and let her rest in peace.'

She walked solemnly back to the table and replaced the jug.

Then she turned to face the others. 'Right.' She sighed and smiled, feeling more relaxed now.

She looks so lovely, thought Ellen. A young woman, beautiful and strong.

'I wanted to include you a bit more here.' Sophie paused with ceremonial solemnity.

'Abbie, you first. I'm really pleased you came. I am so grateful to you for all your care at the time I lost Melanie. You were the only brightness then for me and I want to thank you.'

Clare felt her guts go into spasm. She didn't know why but she found herself in turmoil.

Sophie held out her arms to Abbie, who smiled sheepishly and walked forward. She took Sophie's hands and returned her gaze. 'Come and stand next to me,' Sophie said. Abbie took her place by Sophie's side.

'Now,' Sophie continued, 'I want to invite Angie and Ellen. I know you have lost children too. It was important to have you here because I know what happened to me wasn't unusual, but it felt necessary to feel something shared.'

She picked up the three roses from the table and handed two to Angie and one to Ellen. They both looked surprised but smiled. By now they were too wrapped up in Sophie's open and inclusive welcome to let self-consciousness take over completely.

'What I thought we'd do is to play some music and then you can both place your roses back on the table.'

She looked at Helen, who turned on the player. The garden filled with the strains of *Pavane for a Dead Infanta*. Soft, sorrowful, tender. There won't be a dry eye in the house, thought Helen wryly. And then remembered, more gently, her own loss, long ago.

The music and the occasion touched everyone now. Clare still felt wretched. By now, she'd identified a large amount of envy that Sophie should thank Abbie for being there when she herself had wanted to be there so much. She struggled hard to keep a hold on herself.

Angie and Ellen both looked at their roses, faces open and lost in their own thoughts.

The music came to an end. Sophie looked at Angie and Ellen. 'Would you like to place your roses on the table now?'

Ellen went first. Slowly, and a little unsteadily, she stepped towards the table, holding her rose. She put it down carefully, saying quite audibly, 'Goodbye, Belinda dear. I love you always.'

Nobody there could remain untouched by Ellen's gesture. How

lovely she looks, thought Sophie. An old woman, beautiful and strong.

Angie went up next, tears streaming down her cheeks by now, and placed her two roses on the table. 'For my two unborn children, no names, but you lived in me once and were loved . . . still are loved by me. I won't forget you.'

Angie took Ellen's arm and they walked slowly back to join Clare and Helen. Abbie followed them back to the semi-circle.

Then Sophie turned to Clare. 'Mum. Your turn now.'

Clare was paralysed with confusion. 'Come here, will you,' said her daughter firmly. 'I'd like you with me for this bit.' Clare moved forward awkwardly to stand in front of her.

Sophie turned towards the table and said, 'Melanie, as mother I bid you goodbye now.' She then turned back towards Clare. 'As a daughter I'd like to welcome you into my life. I know I've failed to cherish you, in the past, because I was unable to see your strength or your beauty. I now want to make amends and share my pride in being women together.'

She held out her arms and Clare almost fell into them. They both stood and wept together. The others looked on; six women and a dog, caught in a moment of woman-shaped love.

Closure

After a few moments Helen took the initiative and turned on Sophie's second choice of music. As the strains of 'Your Song' filled the garden, she took Angie's hand and led them all towards Sophie and Clare. Sophie caught Angie's eye.

'My God, it's stirring stuff,' muttered Angie. Everyone laughed.

'Can we hold hands?' asked Helen. Everyone did so and stood there listening to the music, separate in their individual memories, thoughts and feelings, and at the same time connected with each other.

As the music finished, Helen looked at Sophie. 'OK?' she asked.

Sophie nodded.

Helen gestured with her hand towards the kitchen.

'Oh, yes,' said Sophie, remembering. 'Thank you all for being here. We're going to have tea and cake now.' Helen disappeared quickly into the kitchen while Sophie walked the others back and settled everyone in chairs.

'Are we going to be warm enough?'

'Yes,' said a chorus of voices.

'I wouldn't mind something more round my shoulders,' said Ellen. Abbie took off her jacket and put it around Ellen. Angie wandered off to a safe distance from the others so she could have a cigarette.

'That was lovely, Sophie,' said Ellen. 'It was a real privilege to be invited. Thank you, dear.'

'It was my pleasure,' beamed Sophie.

'I've been thinking, you know, I might take Belinda's photo out and get a frame for it. Put it up so I can see it.'

'That's a great idea,' said Sophie.

'Can we keep the programmes?' said Abbie.

'Course you can,' Sophie replied.

'Did you think this all up yourself?' asked Ellen.

'I was going to ask that,' said Angie, from her corner of the garden. 'You did it very well. Terrific poise, I thought.'

'Well, Helen gave me a framework and made some suggestions and then I put in what I wanted and chose the music and things. She asked me questions so that I could work out what I wanted. It was really helpful having a structure to follow. At first, I just wanted to be spontaneous but Helen said these things were so powerful that if there were only spontaneity, it wouldn't feel safe enough. She said we had to have structure and simplicity, and then you could do whatever you wanted to do.'

At that moment, Helen came through the doors with a loaded tray.

Clare stood up to help. 'Can I do something, Helen?'

'Just put these out, will you, and I'll get the rest. Does everyone want ordinary tea? There's herbal tea if anyone would prefer.'

'I'd like a herbal tea please,' said Abbie. 'Whatever kind you have will do.'

'Me too,' said Sophie.

Helen put down a tray full of different unmatching cups and saucers and jugs and plates. Clare smiled, remembering when she'd first noticed this . . . how long ago was it now?

Angie walked over to rejoin the group. 'That was an extraordinary experience,' she said. 'I don't know what I'd expected but it wasn't what I'd imagined. I thought it was going to be a bit twee, a bit precious, you know. I thought I'd be squirming with embarrassment half the time.'

Clare smiled, but said nothing. She was too full. Of everything. Too much love inside her.

Helen reappeared with a huge pot of tea and a smaller pot of tea for Abbie and Sophie. 'There you are – verbena and mint for you two. I hope that's all right.' She went back inside again.

Clare started to pour. Helen brought out a round iced white cake, which everyone looked at.

'Look at that,' said Ellen. 'What kind of cake is it?'

'Sophie made it,' said Helen.

'It's lemon sponge with lemon icing,' Sophie explained. On the cake were six candles. 'I put one for each of us,' she added.

'I've got matches,' offered Angie, 'but I don't know if it will be too windy.'

Sophie managed, after a couple of false starts, to get all the candles alight. 'Thank you for coming, everybody,' she announced. 'It's been a really important day, so although it's not my birthday, I'm going to make a wish anyway, before the wind takes them.' She took a big breath, blew and wished. As the candles sputtered, there was a small round of applause.

117

They sat for a while, in silence, immersed in private thoughts in between tastes of tea and cake. Then a murmur of conversation began.

Helen sat at the end of the table listening and not listening. She felt very peaceful. Humility, truth, courage and gentleness, she said to herself, all around and in us here, today. She loved these precious moments of communion: wordless, transparent moments which transcended our usual reality but were held by it at the same time. In some recess of her being, it felt an affirmation of everything she believed, of everything she saw.

'What's your new book about?' She was startled by Angie's question.

Helen smiled. 'It's difficult to say exactly. It's about all this, in a way, you know, what we've shared this afternoon. It's about a different way of seeing and being together that stems from a very different concept of power.'

Seeing Angie's puzzlement, Helen looked at Clare. 'What do you think it's all about, Clare? You're the only person who's read it. Can you explain it to Angie?'

Clare sighed. 'I'm not sure I can. Because it's something that for me, anyway, has had an effect on the inside. Little by little, I have let something in, I suppose, and whatever it is has helped me to be more myself, to be more in my own body. It's very powerful, I know that, and it's helped me not to be so afraid to be myself.'

'Sounds intriguing,' said Angie.

'Is it for women?' asked Ellen.

'Yes, it is,' replied Helen.

'Why?' asked Sophie.

'Well, it's hard to explain. It seems to me that when any movement emerges to challenge a dominant power, it only keeps its radicalism and idealism on the way up. As soon as the challengers become those in charge, the idealism evaporates and they end up repeating the same kind of system that they once fought so hard to bring down. It's an addiction to up/down power – you know – having power over others. I have never yet met a man who was willing ultimately to forego that kind of power for the sake of *real* change.'

'Lots of women like that power as well,' said Angie.

'They do,' agreed Helen. 'We've spent a long time running in a race towards the same goal. Why I've written this book is because I believe that there are some women who are really tired of running and are wondering whether this is, in fact, a race they want to be competing in anyway.'

'I can identify with that, certainly,' said Angie, nodding thoughtfully. 'But what makes you think women can change anything?'

'Because we're different?' asked Sophie.

'Because, I think, we could *make* an extraordinary difference if we wanted to. Look, Sophie, this is your day. I don't think we should talk any more about this.'

'But that's what it's about, isn't it?' Sophie persisted. 'It's about everything you and I've talked about, it's about women seeing their beauty and about being clear and coming to terms with the power that we do have – or could have . . . if we saw ourselves differently.'

'Yes,' said Helen with a smile. 'You're absolutely right.'

'It's like today,' added Sophie, 'I felt it so strongly with every-one. More than anything, it's to do with love, isn't it, it's the actual power of love.'

118

After everyone had gone, Helen cleared away the tea things. When she went back into the garden, she saw that someone had kindly put back the table into its usual place. The early evening air was wonderful. The sky was beginning to turn pink.

She walked over to the softer grass and lay down. It was a bit damp but not enough to mind. She looked up. Watching. Thinking nothing. Empty and full. In a gap between the trees, she spotted the crescent of the new moon.

Rusper came snuffling up. He was always delighted to find her on his level so gave her forehead a lick and then barked. As he barked, she watched the sound travel up the entire length of his body, from tail to nose. A bark of glee. He rolled over on the grass. He looked at her again and did another perfect roll, as if awaiting her applause. She smiled and imitated his roll, feeling very cumbersome in comparison. He turned neatly once more and came to sit beside her.

She looked at her watch and reckoned they had another hour of daylight. 'How about a walk, my friend?' she asked him. 'Maybe we'll go and find some ivy.'

Afterword

The power of gentle demands a revolution of being. It also requires a revolution of action. From a central core of being, there are endless possibilities of translating this power into action.

Have the courage to say, 'This is what I see; I don't like what I see. I care enough to speak out loud.'

Practise forgiveness. Forgiveness allows you to name the truth and then allow the slings and arrows of others' demons to fall into the water and pass by. You can then move on.

Put competition and comparison aside and appreciate the commonality of women's experience in this world.

Stop joining in with something that would compromise your integrity: dare to disagree.

Remember that you are not the clothes you wear, even if you enjoy wearing them.

Honour those you have known or currently know in your life who are gentle people. They may be your children, your friends, your partners, colleagues – men or women, young boys or girls – who are 'different' because oversensitive, difficult or fragile, who cannot quite manage the tough aggressive demands of 'normal' life. Perhaps their hearts and souls belong to a different vision. Maybe they are still in your life, maybe not. Name them. Talk to them. Express your feelings.

Turn off the television more often. Passive watching is as dangerous for the imagination as passive smoking is for the body.

Be aware of those you've competed with or oppressed in order to get higher up the ladder. Don't give yourself a hard time. Write down the names of those you've knowingly oppressed or helped to oppress. Once you've acknowledged your complicity, burn the paper.

Think twice before you treat your body as an object, by unwanted sex or cosmetic surgery or overeating. Then think again. Acknowledge the real cost.

Reconsider the meaning of shopping. Do you really want that article or is it part of an addiction?

Apologise only when you are genuinely regretful.

Learn to express a minority opinion, gently: you can avoid compromising your own integrity without having to win the argument.

Recognise envy between women. Don't be afraid of it in others but acknowledge your own. Choose to reach out in spite of differences.

Whenever you have an opportunity, try fostering mutual pride and regard between women instead of competition.

Reconsider the word 'family'. Extend it to include others you do not call your own. Practise thinking laterally along the paths of connection instead of the narrowness of individual units.

Familiarise yourself with solitude and engage with any of your personal demons that may await you there.

Go public more often. Stand by a woman who makes a mess of things or whom others call a bitch instead of using the opportunity to boost your own popularity ratings. Go public about the bonbon effect, gently.

Free a tree.

Now, as never before in history, millions of women – in the richer parts of the world – have unprecedented economic power. Consider how you use this power. Do you simply prop up the monocular system? Could you use your wealth to be more coherent with your integrity? If financial independence allows you the privilege and power of change, how do you use it?

Learn about your emotional landscape and take responsibility. It can be dangerous to allow yourself the indulgence of confusing emotion with sentiment.

Reflect once a day on the word 'interiority' as a balance to all those tendencies to make others the reference points outside yourself.

Keep a clear boundary between yourself and others – not so far that they become objects and not so close that they become objects.

Reconsider your relationships and close emotional ties. Re-evaluate them: ask yourself what quality of relationship you want in your life.

Learn to laugh when a situation becomes impossible, to avoid self-blame setting in. Let yourself off the hook and learn the value of crazy. Live with knowing others won't always understand you.

Use some of your energy regularly for being genuinely creative. In any way that challenges you.

Name your feelings, to yourself and then to others if you choose. Avoid blame, however tempting.

Say 'ouch' when you realise someone is regarding you as an object – because of your gender, your race, your appearance, your age, or simply because they're using you as an 'extra' in their own personal scenario. A simple 'ouch' will suffice to break the cycle of collusion; communicate further if the situation is appropriate.

Learn how to handle perpendicular power without oppression. Allow someone to express their feelings in response to your decisions without being defensive or backing down. Remember equality and compassion are key.

Question instead of jumping to (what you believe are) certain conclusions. Not everyone operates in the same way so you can easily put two and two together and come up with five. Acquire the humility to ask what is going on: ask what someone is feeling or ask the reason for someone's action *before* launching in with your own assumptions.

Learn about rituals. They are wonderful and simple ways to give meaning to the mundane as well as to special life events. You can do these on your own but you could dare to invite others and survive the self-consciousness together.

Define what spiritual means for you and look for the ingredients that meet your needs. Look for coherence: compassion, an affirmation of women as equal, a connection with others and the relevance of emotion and our bodies. If you can't find anything that is right, create something that works for you.

Learn to live with silences without jumping in to fill them.

When you have tears in your eyes, learn to distinguish whether they are tears of anger and frustration or self-pity; are you trying for effect, genuinely sad or just slicing onions?

Find yourself a positive metaphor for life and live into it.

Upright is a good image to create: neither convex (too far out and aggressive) nor concave (too bent in and unable to be true). Somewhere in the middle is the upright position: your feet firmly on the ground allowing you to be both flexible and grounded at the same time.

Find your voice and use it. The full range of it. Play with it. Make sounds of all kinds. Find your voice within a crowd to disagree. To sing. To make a noise. To say no.

Stop lying to yourself about *anything*.

Reconsider woman-shaped reality. Try and look at the roundness of things with new eyes.

Walk away from winning.

The next time you want to snigger at the old man's wig that has slipped, or at the elderly woman's lipstick covering the thinness of her lips, stop and ask yourself why. Are you scornful? Terrified of being like that when you get older? See if you can move to a more generous place within your heart, for your own sake, not theirs.

Reconsider the meaning and effort of love in your life.

Kick the habit of saying you don't mind or you don't care when you do.

Keep your eyes on a future that includes us all, as equals, where your voice will be heard as a valued voice … speaking of another way.

Further Reading

Any newspaper, any day, any country.

Index